AWAKE IN
A NIGHTMARE

AWAKE
IN A
NIGHTMARE

Jonestown: The Only Eyewitness Account

———

Ethan Feinsod

W·W·NORTON & COMPANY

NEW YORK   LONDON

Copyright © *1981 by Ethan Feinsod*
Published simultaneously in Canada by
George J. McLeod Limited, Toronto.
PRINTED IN THE UNITED STATES OF AMERICA
ALL RIGHTS RESERVED
FIRST EDITION

Library of Congress Cataloging in Publication Data
Feinsod, Ethan.
    Awake in a nightmare.
    Based on interviews with Odell Rhodes.
    1. Peoples Temple. 2. Jones, Jim, 1931–1978.
3. Rhodes, Odell. I. Rhodes, Odell. II. Title.
BP605.P46F44 1981   289.9   80–20229
ISBN 0–393–01431–2

W. W. Norton & Company, Inc. 500 Fifth Avenue, New York, N.Y. 10110
W. W. Norton & Company Ltd. 25 New Street Square, London EC4A 3NT

1 2 3 4 5 6 7 8 9 0

Contents

Acknowledgments

Anyone who writes a book about a tragic subject must be affected by the experience. One consequence of the way I have been affected is that I find myself troubled and conflicted about what should be the satisfying duty of expressing gratitude to those who have helped in the preparation of the book.

So many of those to whom I owe my debts—the Jonestown survivors—have suffered so enormously that thanking them for reliving their tragedy seems to border on moral callousness. Nonetheless, the debt is owed, and I do acknowledge it; but, at the same time, more than gratitude, I would much rather express the respect and affection I have come to have for the members of the Jonestown community I have met. Virtually without exception they are truly remarkable people, and knowing them has led me to the inescapable conclusion that those who did not survive the tragedy must have been remarkable people as well.

I owe a special debt to two of the survivors in particular: Stanley Clayton, who *is* "grace under pressure," and Odell Rhodes, whose honesty and intelligence I admire more than I can say.

I owe one other very special debt. It is to Hardat Sukhdeo. If there is a hero in this story, he is it; and I have borrowed shamelessly from his wisdom.

I should also thank many of my friends—they know who they are—for help of many kinds: listening to me, talking to me, reading what I have written, and helping me cope with the manuscript.

To my family I owe a debt I would not know how to explain, especially F. T. D., who has seen it all. Finally, there is another debt beyond words, but this is not the place.

E. F.

AWAKE IN
A NIGHTMARE

1

A Church Wedding

Despite its picture-postcard name, Redwood Valley, California, is not really a picture-postcard place. A small farming community about two hours' drive north of San Francisco, the town itself boasts nothing more scenic than a few gas stations, hardware stores, and farm-machinery dealerships; but a few miles outside of town the countryside rises into a line of pleasant—if unspectacular—rolling hills, some of them covered with stands of redwood trees, many of the others planted with vineyards. In 1967, on the top of one of these hills, an energetic young minister, the Reverend James Warren Jones, built himself a church: a big, red, tin-roofed hulk of a building that would have looked more like a barn were it not for the cross over the door and the sign that announced the People's Temple Christian Church. Rustic, secluded, and so manifestly unchurchlike it could only have been intentional, the Reverend Jones's church was, nonetheless, a beautiful and romantic setting for a wedding.

When Grace Lucy Grech married Timothy Oliver Stoen in the big red church on the hill in 1969, everyone agreed she was a perfect bride, sweet and innocent, just the way a bride is supposed to be. In 1969, sweet and innocent were easy for Grace Grech. She was only nineteen, barely a year out of high school—and twelve years younger than the man she was marrying. At thirty-one, Tim Stoen was a well-regarded young attorney in Ukiah, the Mendocino County seat, a few miles south of Redwood Valley. But even at thirty-one, Tim was still boyish looking; he wore his hair fashionably long, drove a sporty Porsche convertible, and, despite the difference in their ages,

Tim and Grace's romance had been serious from the day they first met at an Earth Day demonstration in San Francisco.

"Serious" was a word people often used to describe Tim Stoen. He was a very serious young man, not somber or humorless, but the sort of person who gave others the impression that he knew exactly where his life was taking him—and was so sure of the road ahead and so well-organized for the journey that he could afford to take time out occasionally to laugh and have fun; he could even afford to marry a girl like Grace, so young and innocent and full of potential—and so eager to learn from a man like Tim, an older man who knew where he was going. And there was no question in anybody's mind that Tim was going places. He was bright, hard-working, and far more than merely competent in his profession; furthermore, in addition to talent, energy, and skill—as if those qualities were not enough—he also happened to possess the very best credentials, credentials without which even a young lawyer of the most exceptional abilities may never be able to open the doors that lead to real success. Tim was a Stanford Law School graduate and could have used that prestigious degree to enter any top-quality law firm in San Francisco, or virtually anywhere else where the very best credentials can be sold to the highest bidder.

But a career as a high-priced corporate lawyer was not what Tim Stoen had in mind. Nobody who knew him would have claimed he was without ambition; but, as with many of his generation, Tim Stoen's ambitions ran in a slightly different direction. He had what probably seemed at the time to be the great good fortune to come to adulthood—to graduate from college and choose a career—during the brief thousand-day presidency of John F. Kennedy. For many of his generation, especially the brightest and most serious, those thousand days of the Kennedy presidency were an enormously exciting time; and, when the idealistic young president issued the challenge, "Ask not what your country can do for you, but what you can do for your country," they became the generation that flocked to the Peace Corps and VISTA. Armed chiefly with only their idealism—often without any great understanding of issues, policies, or the realities of political life, but always bristling with the determination to build a better world—many of them rushed down any road that led to the great adventure that had been promised on the New Frontier. And, convinced as they all were that most of society's ills were caused by a preoccupation with material success, even many of the most ambitious among them crowded into graduate and professional schools to prepare themselves for careers that offered the opportunity to acquire not wealth but power—the power to change the world.

When Tim Stoen graduated from Stanford Law School, he went to work for a federal antipoverty program in sleepy, rural Mendocino County, where, at the same time he served his country, he would also have the opportunity to dip his toes in the sort of small political pond in which a talented and aggressive young lawyer might someday grow up into a big fish—and really serve his country.

In 1969, the year of his marriage, Stoen's career was, to all appearances, right on schedule: his legal reputation had long since begun to precede him, and—perhaps more importantly—he was now beginning to assemble the kinds of contacts which a talented young lawyer with an itch to take a plunge into politics can not afford to do without. Taking it all together—his career and the beautiful young woman waiting to marry him—Tim Stoen's cup was very close to running over.

If there was anything wrong in Stoen's well-planned life, it was only background noise: the news from the outside world that filtered over the mountains into peaceful Mendocino County. In 1968 and 1969 the news was anything but pleasant: assassinations, riots, an endlessly frustrating war, and mounting protest against the war, much of it increasingly violent. There were those who were saying that the level of tensions between Americans had not been so high since the Civil War. Although very little of it—either the events or the violent spasms in the body politic—touched anyone in Mendocino County directly, the issues involved—civil rights, the war, student protest—were as much discussed, as controversial, and as divisive as they were anywhere else in the country. For Tim Stoen in particular, because his education and career made him far more attuned to the distant rumblings of events and issues than most of his neighbors, the background noise of 1968 and 1969 was suddenly becoming a disquieting presence that was difficult to ignore.

So much seemed to be happening so rapidly—and so much of it seemed ominous: conflict everywhere; black against white, young against old. For someone like Stoen who had only a few years before—or was it eons?—marched off to the New Frontier it was almost inconceivable (even if it was indisputably true) that the generation now protesting the war on college campuses, the angry middle-class students who spoke of love and threw bricks at policemen, would consider a thirty-year-old lawyer who dressed in business suits and worked for the government their enemy, a member of the hated "establishment." For someone like Stoen it must have seemed as if the breezy, upbeat music which had played in the background through that "brief shining moment which was Camelot" had now suddenly turned into a chorus of moans, cries, and angry shouts; and he had to be wondering if the idealistic commitment he had made to the beat of the Kennedy years had not left him out of step with a vastly changed world.

Whatever thoughts Stoen was having about the state of the world, Mendocino County was a lonely place to have them. It was not a place that often attracted people of his age and his education. But Tim Stoen was lucky. Late in 1968 he happened to meet a remarkable man, a local minister who was completing a busy and successful term as foreman of the county Grand Jury. The minister's name was the Reverend Jim Jones.

Reverend Jones was someone Stoen already knew by reputation; everybody in Mendocino County knew about Jim Jones. Although he had settled in the county only a few years before, he was already an important local figure, the minister of a large and ever-growing congregation—and a man to be reckoned with. With his pale white skin, jet-black hair, the dark glasses he wore day and night, and a restless energy that seemed to ooze from his pores, Jones was a man people noticed—and the kind of man people in a small town like Ukiah liked to talk about. He was said to be a spellbinding preacher who could charm the very devil if he felt like it, or scare an entire congregation with word-pictures of fire-and-brimstone if he was in the mood. He also had a reputation as a healer, and there were those who claimed to have witnessed with their own eyes the miracle of the Reverend Jones coaxing a deadly cancer from the body of a poor soul given up for dead.

There was another side to Jones's reputation as well. In the county courthouse he was known as a public-spirited citizen who involved himself in youth programs, programs to help the elderly, and almost anything else that served the disadvantaged. Among the politicians he had a reputation as a good man to know at election time, someone who could mobilize a small army to stuff envelopes or ring doorbells at a moment's notice.

Although the thought of an army of willing precinct workers might have titillated Stoen, what impressed him most about Jim Jones was something else. It took the two men no time at all to discover that they could talk to each other in a way neither could talk to anyone else. Despite having come from vastly different backgrounds, and having had vastly different educations, they shared so many ideas, values, beliefs, and attitudes about politics, social issues, and the state of the world that even when they disagreed each could follow the other's train of thought. They began to have frequent conversations, which sometimes lasted into the early morning; and they quickly became close friends.

Although Stoen had next to no interest in fire-and-brimstone or miracles of faith healing, what he saw at the big red church up the road in Redwood Valley impressed him nonetheless. In the People's Temple there was none of the conflict that filled the morning newspaper and echoed in the back of a serious young man's mind; blacks and whites, young and old communicated with each other and respected each other's point of view. If Tim Stoen had been wondering what had happened to the dream of building a better world, what he saw in the People's Temple might have softened his skepticism about miracles after all. Wherever idealism was hiding in the rest of the country, in Jim Jones's church it was alive and well and hard at work.

For Jim Jones the road to Redwood Valley began in Lynn, Indiana, a small farming and manufacturing center southeast of Indianapolis, where he was born in 1931. The man who was to become "Dad" to a church family which would eventually number in the thousands grew up himself in a mostly fatherless home. His own father, James Thurman Jones, was a sometime farmer and sometime factory worker with a limited education and a provincial outlook on life. The elder Jones had been gassed fighting in France during the First World War, had never regained his health, and had died when his son was still a boy. James Thurman Jones was not a man his young son grew up to admire. In fact, later in life Jim Jones was to talk about his father as a "mean old redneck racist," an opinion he formed less from personal experience than from discovering some years after his death that the senior Jones had been a pillar of the local Ku Klux Klan. Although there was nothing unusual about membership in the Klan in rural Indiana in the thirties, the discovery shocked Jones, and his mean old redneck father became a cross Jones carried for the rest of his life.

Lynetta Jones, his mother, was an entirely different story. She was a mother a boy could love, a strong, selfless woman who worked long hours in a factory supporting herself and her son and devoted her spare time to church and charity. Lynetta Jones's neighbors remember her as a local character, a forceful, enthusiastic woman with strong convictions about just about everything. She loved children, tramps, old people, and animals, and, although she was a regular Sunday churchgoer, she believed that religion was more a matter of helping the poor and the weak than of listening to sermons.

Unlike her husband, Lynetta Jones did not believe the world began and ended in central Indiana. Although she had not actually seen much of the world beyond Indiana with her own eyes, she kept a subscription to the *National Geographic* and liked to read—and fantasize—about faraway places. She was a firm believer in the transmigration of souls, and allowed herself to believe the polite fiction that she actually had traveled the world in some previous incarnation. She filled her son's bedtime stories with "memories" of her past-life voyages—long, vivid first-person accounts of voyages up the Amazon and life among the headhunters. The supernatural fascinated her—signs, spells, spirits, omens, and—most of all—dreams. Dreams, she believed, were visions of the future, and she dreamt often about her son. They were dreams which foretold greatness. James Warren Jones, she told the boy, was destined to grow up into a man who would dedicate his life to helping the poor and the weak, a man who would leave his mark on the world.

When Jim Jones graduated from high school, the only question about his future that remained unanswered was whether he would study medicine and devote his life to healing the flesh or prepare for the ministry and a life of saving souls. In 1949 Jones entered the University of Indiana in Bloomington still undecided, but a few months later the decision was made. During those few months Jones met—and immediately fell in love with—a serious, pretty young student nurse, Marceline Baldwin. Marcie Baldwin came from a family of missionaries; her commitment to God and good works ran easily as deep as Jones's own, and she encouraged Jones to choose the ministry. Jones and Marcie Baldwin were married within the year and shortly afterward Jones transferred to Butler University in Indianapolis to begin his formal studies for the ministry.

In 1953, at the age of twenty-two, unfinanced and unordained, Jones launched his ministry by founding a small church in a poor neighborhood in Indianapolis. Although the name he chose for the church, the Community National Church, made it sound as solvent as a bank, the Community National was very much a shoestring operation that Jones supported largely from his own pocket, mostly by selling live monkeys he raised at home—twenty-nine dollars the monkey.

Those who knew Jones during the early days of his ministry in Indianapolis remember two things about him: the irresistible force of his personality, and his sensitivity to the problems of his mostly poor, largely black, congregation. The poorer, the weaker, the more helpless his followers were, the more attention Jones lavished on them. "He had a lot of them," one early member recalls. "The kind of people most folks don't want to have nothing to do with. Fat, ugly old ladies who didn't have nobody in the world. He'd pass around hugs and kisses like he really did love them, and you could see it on their faces what he meant to them."

Love, Jones told his congregation, was the real message of the gospel, the only true message. According to Jones's theology, the real Jesus Christ was the Christ of the books of Luke and Acts, the suffering servant who walked among the poor, washed the feet of lepers, and instructed his disciples to throw the money-changers out of the Temple and distribute the wealth of the earth among the poor.

Late in the fifties, Jones made the first of what were to be several pilgrimages to the most successful ministry to the urban poor in the country, the Peace Mission of Father Divine, in Philadelphia. Never too proud to learn, Jones studied Father Divine carefully. He discovered that the success of the Peace Mission was built on two premises: an absolute insistence on Father Divine's divinity and frequent, visible demonstrations of the power of faith, particularly through feats of healing. When he returned to Indiana, Jones began experimenting with his own versions of Father Divine's miracles. Blessed with a flair for the dramatic that rivaled the master's own, Jones's versions were an immediate success, and his reputation as a healer gave a new impetus to his struggling church.

As it grew, the Community National Church began to create a minor scandal in Indianapolis, not because of the faith-healing, which was standard procedure in Midwestern fundamentalist churches, but because Indianapolis had never seen a truly interracial church before. The spectacle of blacks and whites enthusiastically praying together raised eyebrows—and occasionally tempers—in certain circles in the community. The church building was vandalized on several occasions and Jones's name became an epithet among neighbors with racial sentiments like those of his own mean old redneck father's. Opposition, however, was something Jones thrived upon. Every attack convinced him he must be doing something right and spurred him to redouble his efforts. He moved the church several times, renamed it several other times, and, by 1960, had built what he now called the People's Temple Full Gospel Church, on North Delaware Street, into a busy and prosperous enterprise.

Although he was, by all accounts, an excellent administrator with a special talent for fund-raising, by far the greatest part of his success stemmed from his talents in the pulpit. At the time, central Indiana had a special reputation in the Bible Belt for the quality of its preachers, but Jones was regarded as something extra-special, a spellbinding sermonizer with a gift for healing bodies and spirits which was second to none. His fame spread rapidly through the state and beyond.

Dale Parks, who was later to become Jones's personal secretary in California, was a boy of eight in 1960 growing up in a devoutly religious family in a small town in Ohio. Dale's grandfather was himself a lay minister who liked to quote scripture as proof for his unshakable belief that the world was flat. Dale remembers his grandfather packing the entire Parks clan into the family jalopy for the two-hundred-odd-mile roundtrip to listen to Jim Jones on Sunday mornings, and he remembers the services themselves as riveting drama, with a congregation, about half-white and half-black, held spellbound by Jones's powerful sermonizing and his superhuman gift for curing the ills of his flock.

By 1961 Jones was a substantial enough figure in Indianapolis to be appointed chairman of a newly created City Human Rights Commission, an advisory body that reported directly to the mayor on civil rights issues. At the tender age of thirty he was well on the way to fulfilling his mother's prophecy of his future. However, despite his success, Jones remained restless, less than satisfied with his accomplishments. He had always been eager to explore the world, the world beyond Indiana that had so fascinated his mother, and late in 1961 he decided to leave his church in Indiana for a year of missionary work in South America. He moved his wife and their young son, Stephan, to a *favela* in Belo Horizonte, Brazil, and spent the next two years preaching the gospel of social change through Christian love to the urban poor.

The Jones family finally returned to Indianapolis in 1963, after stopping on the way back for a brief sightseeing visit to British Guinea on the South American coast of the western Caribbean. Finally, back home in Indianapolis, Jim Jones discovered that during his two years in Brazil his own country had changed. A hundred years after the war to free the slaves the question of what America would do about its black minority had suddenly become a national priority, and the young minister of Indianapolis's first interracial church had returned just in time for the busiest summer of civil rights activity in the history of the republic, a summer of boycotts, demonstrations, debate about new legislation, and the climactic, historic March on Washington which brought a quarter of a million blacks and whites together to hear Martin Luther King, Jr., describe his dream of an America free of racism.

Jim Jones listened to Martin Luther King, Jr. and the other leaders of the movement with a deep and genuine sense of excitement. At last the country had finally caught up with Jim Jones. He began to make plans to join the March on Washington; and then, suddenly, a new voice exploded onto the national scene with a message that shattered Jones's enthusiasm and initiated the chain of events that would eventually bring him to Redwood Valley.

The voice belonged to Malcolm Little, a streetwise ex-drug addict who had converted from Christianity to Islam and taken the Muslim name Malcolm X. Malcolm X not only denounced racism with a clear, cold passion that made other black leaders seem pale and tame by comparison, he also singled out Christianity and America's churches for an especially bitter denunciation. What had Christianity done for the black man? According to Malcolm X, it had helped to make him a slave. Drawing upon both the history of black people in America and his own eventful life, with a moral sense that allowed no compromise, Malcolm X argued that Christianity had helped to enslave blacks by convincing them that their suffering in this world would be rewarded in the next world. It had taught them to forgive their oppressors, to be humble, to be meek, to turn the other cheek. It was no accident that, at the same time whites had made slaves of blacks, they had also made them Christians. Christianity was a religion that condoned slavery, and the love and peace it promised were nothing but cruel, clever hoaxes, which served chiefly to prevent blacks from demanding justice. There would be no justice, Malcolm X concluded, as long as blacks remained Christians, and he dismissed the civil rights movement as one more futile exercise in meekly expecting Christian charity from a country of slave-masters.

Malcolm X's angry logic galvanized Jim Jones. As Jones saw it, he had dedicated his life to the pursuit of social justice through Christian love; now Malcolm X was telling blacks they should trust no white man, least of all one who claimed to act in the name of Jesus Christ. Jones had hoped to be part of the solution; and now he was being told he was part of the problem.

Early in 1964, shortly after the assassination of John F. Kennedy and about the same time Jones himself was finally ordained a minister in the Church of the Disciples of Christ (a mostly white, moderate, Protestant denomination), Jones began confiding to those closest to him that he no longer believed in the Christian God, in Christian justice, or in his own ministry. Following his ordination, Jones spent the better part of 1964 in crisis with his faith, questioning his convictions and reassessing the meaning of his calling. Malcolm X—and the uncomfortable facts he had called attention to—had turned Jones's world upside down. If Christianity was a hoax, an instrument of oppression, then he, Jim Jones, had been a party to oppressing those he had wanted most to serve.

In Brazil Jones had been exposed to Marxism—or at least to Marxists. He was not well read in political philosophy, but it did not escape him that virtually everyone who worked in the *favelas* for social justice talked about capitalism and workers and revolutionary struggles. He had rubbed shoulders with Marxist students, Marxist labor organizers, and Marxist priests, and something had rubbed off

on him—enough to start him thinking that all the time he had believed he was a Christian perhaps what he had really been was a
socialist. If American blacks were in no better position than Brazilian
peasants, perhaps he could, like the worker-priests in Brazil, use his
church as a way to educate them to the real social causes of their
misery. He began to talk about infiltrating the religious establishment as an *agent provocateur* of the revolution. As an end in itself
the church might be morally bankrupt, but as a *means* to a greater
end—social justice—perhaps it could still be useful. He immersed
himself in what he could find of the literature of Third World revolution; but, just at the point of resolving his crisis and setting out to
become a secret-agent-behind-the-pulpit, he hesitated. He was still
not convinced that, even with the best of intentions and the firmest
of commitments, any white man could ever, in good conscience,
lead a congregation of blacks anywhere.

The question of the color of his skin and his role in what he was
now convinced would be a bloody revolution continued to trouble
Jones deeply, and in the middle of 1965, now confronted with what
he viewed as a desperate antirevolutionary war in Viet Nam as well
as by racism and injustice at home, Jones fell into despair. He confided to a few close friends that he felt he had wasted his life; and as
he looked around at riots in Watts, police brutality in Selma, and
genocide in Viet Nam, the causes he believed in seemed as hopeless
as his own life. Jones was not alone; 1965 was a vintage year for
despair about America, and putting it all together, Jones concluded
that the country was coming apart at the seams. A country so evil—
that even a good man like Jim Jones had unknowingly oppressed the
people he loved, so evil that even a good man was powerless to do
good—was surely not above destroying itself.

The more Jones brooded about the state of the world, the more
convinced he was that America was a terminal case, and he began
to fear that the leaders who had brought the country to the precipice
might very well take the rest of the world along in one final, terrible
leap into the nuclear abyss. If, as he had read, revolution was inevitable, how would the smug, evil men who ruled the country react to
their own defeat? The answer terrified him.

Even if, by now, Jones professed to believe nothing in the Bible,
he still retained a vivid, enduring fear of the Apocalypse—an image
of an evil world reaping the destruction it had sown. The Apoca-

lypse—that was the answer, and from his pulpit Jones began to speak of nothing else. Then, with his own beliefs in turmoil, with the country in chaos, and with nuclear destruction just beyond the horizon, Jones made the decision to abandon his ministry in Indianapolis. What good would it do to infiltrate the church or educate the masses when the world was about to end?

Having read in a magazine that for reasons of climate and geography the coastal valleys of northern California were among the safest places in the world to weather a nuclear war, he decided to set off for California and prepare for the worst. Late in 1965, with about thirty of his most devoted followers, Jones arrived in Redwood Valley fully expecting that 1966 would be a year of cataclysmic social collapse and nuclear war.

2

Plans, Dreams, and a Baby Boy

During the next three years many of Jim Jones's fears about the state of the world were vindicated. The war in Viet Nam widened and worsened; and as the war escalated, a spiraling cycle of protest and reaction at home threatened to divide the country into angry factions of those who supported the war and those who opposed it. At the same time an increasingly militant civil rights struggle added an additional strain to the suddenly fragile fabric of the body politic, and the epidemic of riots and civil disorders in black ghettos throughout the country during the long hot summers of 1966, 1967, and 1968 seemed to confirm everything Jones had said about the inevitability of black revolution. Only about the Apocalypse was he wrong. Despite everything, the world had somehow survived. And in the meanwhile the little church in Redwood Valley had grown and prospered. By 1968, the year in which Tim Stoen joined, the new People's Temple had grown to a congregation of several hundred members, including a substantial percentage of blacks. In lightly populated Mendocino County—the entire population of the Redwood City– Ukiah area was less than fifteen thousand, and only about 10 percent black—the new church was a more than modest achievement. By 1968, too, Jones's reputation had begun to spread beyond the local area, and as they had once done in Indiana, scores of visitors from as far away as San Francisco flocked to Sunday services in Redwood Valley.

Typical of the growing congregation were a recently married couple, Elmer and Deanna Mertle. The Mertles were from Hayward, a suburb in the urban sprawl between Oakland and San Jose on the southeast shore of San Francisco Bay. Elmer Mertle was forty; Deanna twenty-nine. Both had been married before and between them they brought five small children to the marriage. Both were white. Elmer Mertle was a college graduate who had worked at a variety of low-level white-collar jobs; Deanna had one year of college and worked sporadically as a secretary. Elmer Mertle had liberal political views and had marched in Selma in 1963. Deanna had no politics at all but she did have a strict Seventh Day Adventist religious background. Both were lonely people who had difficulty making friends. As did many Temple members, both came from fatherless homes; Elmer's father had died when he was young; Deanna's father had abandoned his family.

In 1968, after their honeymoon, the newlywed Mertles began to discover a host of problems in their marriage, problems with their children and problems between themselves. For help Deanna Mertle turned to the minister of her church. After diagnosing one of the Mertles' problems as acute loneliness, the minister invited the Mertles to join him the following Sunday for a trip to an unusual church he had heard about in Redwood Valley. Desperate for company and grateful for the invitation, Elmer and Deanna accepted immediately.

After a long, hot drive up Highway 101 the Mertles arrived at the People's Temple and found themselves in another world. As Deanna Mertle wrote later: [1]

"I'd never heard of a church where black and white people intermingled freely. I had never seen a minister sit at the pulpit. The choir was singing popular songs of the day instead of traditional hymns. Instead of organ music we were listening to a band that should have been playing at a dance. Instead of children sitting restlessly beside their parents, these children were sitting quietly and respectfully together." [2]

They sat bewildered as Jones began to speak about the "logical contradictions" in the Bible. When he began to speak about the King

James Bible as "slave religion" that forced blacks to give up "their own beautiful beliefs," Deanna Mertle blanched. "The man believed the exact opposite of everything I had ever been taught." [3]

The Mertles sat stunned as Jones ran through the usual themes of his sermons:

"The only people practicing real religion outside of our church are the Black Panthers."

"I have seen by divine revelation the total annihilation of this country."

"We have gathered in Redwood Valley for protection, and after the war is over we will be the only survivors."

"This church family is an example of what society will eventually be like all over the world." [4]

After the sermon there was an hour of testimonials to Jones, a display of prophetic mind-reading, an hour of faith healing, and then Sunday dinner.

Unsettled as she was by what Jones said, Deanna Mertle was impressed by the congregation, the cheerful camaraderie between the members, and, especially, the behavior of the children. Elmer Mertle was even more impressed; he was not a religious man, but Jones's politics had struck a responsive chord.

The Mertles returned to Hayward and for the next few weeks found their mailbox stuffed every day with letters from People's Temple members, gifts and handwritten messages from Jones himself. Deanna Mertle began rereading her King James Bible and discovered Jones was right; it was full of "logical contradictions." One night she had a dream about Jones, a dream in which he saved Elmer and her and them from a terrible monster. A few weeks later they returned to Redwood Valley, this time with their children. They were welcomed by name, fussed over and made to feel as if they had been expected all along. The children were taken away by other children and Jones himself personally came over to welcome them.

For a month the Mertles commuted to Redwood Valley every Sunday. Then they made their decision. They sold their house in Hayward, joined the Temple, and moved to a farm a few miles away from the Temple, a farm Jim Jones had found for them. Within a few weeks they were both working at jobs Jones had also arranged.

"Happiness flooded our lives," Deanna Mertle wrote. "From time to time we would ask one another, 'What did we do with our lives before we joined this group?' "[5]

Tim Stoen's conversion was of an entirely different kind. Far more sophisticated than the Mertles, Tim Stoen was not impressed by the logical contradictions of the King James Bible, the miracles of faith, or the security of belonging to a warm, supportive church family. When Tim Stoen looked at the People's Temple he saw a community in which people treated each other as he had been taught to believe people should treat each other—and he also saw the nucleus for a new kind of force in American politics, perhaps, someday, a force that might even operate on a national scale. If the other members of the People's Temple thought they had found Christ risen in the person of Jim Jones, Tim Stoen knew better. What they had, in fact, found was something perhaps even better: a unique political personality—a second coming, if not of the Lord, then at least of a William Jennings Bryan or a Huey Long, that rare born politician who effortlessly speaks the real language of the people.

It could not have been difficult for Stoen to appreciate the value of Jones's touch for the common people. Stoen himself had been born in a well-to-do family and brought up in comfortable circumstances in Wisconsin and Colorado. He had traveled in Europe, studied in England, and most of what he knew about the masses came from books. For theory and analysis his education could hardly have been any better; Stanford, where he had taken his law degree, had been, in the early sixties, one of the great centers of progressive, left-of-center political thought. In fact, the Stanford faculty at the time included several of the just-emerging New Left's most important theoreticians, including Robert McAfee Brown and Allard Lowenstein. Although the law school was considerably more conservative than most of the rest of the campus, anyone in Palo Alto interested in politics had been exposed to an unusually wide range of rigorous and creative thought about social issues.

When, during the late sixties, Stoen watched the coalition of New Left antiwar and civil rights movements stall, stumble and then turn violent and self-destructive out of frustration, he had the analytical tools to understand that the movement had failed because it had never been able to reach out beyond the intellectual community to significant numbers of ordinary people. As he began to know Jim Jones, it could hardly have escaped Stoen's notice that where some of the best academic minds of the time had failed, this unevenly educated minister had suceeded. By luck or genius—whichever—Jones's blend of gospel, toadskins, and politics amounted to a magic potion capable of rousing the sleeping masses and transforming them into a political force.

Impressed as he must have been with what he saw of the new community Jones was building in Redwood Valley, for the first several months he visited the church compound Stoen's contact with the people of the Temple was limited; he spent most of his visits alone with Jones or with a few of Jones's closest aides. In fact, at the time of his wedding, very few members of the church knew either of the Stoens at all well. Grace was hardly more than a stranger, and, although Tim was a familiar face, he rarely attended Sunday services or any of the other activities around which most of the congregation built their daily routines. To most of the congregation, he was actually something of a mystery. They were ordinary people: farmers, workers, housewives and their families. With his city manners, his educated way of speaking, and his busy, confident lawyerly air, Tim was different. Obviously different. He stood out from the others as unmistakably as his imported sports car stood out from their pickup trucks and jalopies in the church parking lot. Still, as out of place as the young lawyer seemed to the rest of the congregation, and, although there were more than a few who resented the way he marched briskly from his car to Jim Jones's office with little more than a quick nod of feigned recognition for anyone he happened to pass on the way, it was enough for most of them that Jim Jones had obviously taken a liking to Stoen. They welcomed him as one of their own, and the general opinion was that he was probably a cold fish on the outside with a warm heart underneath—or why else would the Reverend Jones give him so much of his precious time? After the wedding, when Grace began to spend more of her time at the church, the general opinion was confirmed, with satisfied nods all around. Not only was Grace so warm and caring that it was simply unthinkable to image her with a cold, arrogant man, but even Tim himself seemed to change. Not that he spent a great deal more time with the members of the congregation—but no one minded that; he was obviously a busy, important man. What was important to most people was that, as Grace began to make friends, Tim suddenly seemed more accessible, more relaxed, more willing to take a few minutes to pass the time of day. It was almost as if he were too shy to strike up a conversation, at least with ordinary, working people, and he needed Grace to break the ice. That was one opinion; but there was another, especially among the men, which not only seemed as much to the point, but carried the added weight of reputedly having come originally from Jones himself. It was expressed with various snorts, sighs, and leers, and—depending on the company—with various degrees of explicitness. The general idea was that, if Tim had seemed preoccupied, any man who had time to think about anything except the subject which makes the world go around while he courts a girl like Grace is not much of a man at all.

It would never have occurred to most of those who offered the opinion to count the endless hours Jones and Stoen spent together as time stolen from Grace. Time spent with Jim Jones was obviously in a special category. It was clearly special to Jones and Stoen; whatever it is that makes the world go around, the relationship between the two men was unusually intense, even for Jones who never shied from intensity in his relationships with anyone.

From Jim Jones's point of view a Tim Stoen could hardly have arrived at a better time. No one understood Jim Jones's appeal better than Jim Jones himself, but in 1968 Jones was not thoroughly convinced that he wanted to devote himself to building a political movement. Jones had moved to Redwood Valley four years before to find a refuge. He genuinely, sincerely believed the world was about to destroy itself—and if the world was poised on the brink of self-destruction, why bother to build anything, least of all a political movement? In Jones's view, America was too corrupt to save anyway, and nothing in America was more corrupt than politics.

But if Jones was thinking more about inheriting the world than reforming it when he moved to California, he was not too far gone four years later to entertain the possibility that he might have been wrong. The world had not, in fact, ended with a bang. The Redwood Valley project had been an enormous success; people in California seemed far more receptive than they had been in Indiana. And as for politics, Jones had discovered that the more he tried it, the more he liked it—especially the power.

Now here was this smart young lawyer who had been to all the best schools telling him he was the greatest thing to hit the political scene since the stuffed ballot box. The world was not about to end, and, even if it were, the thing for a man like Jim Jones to do was not to sit and wait for the fireball, but to save it. And what Jim Jones did not know about building a movement capable of saving the world, Tim Stoen did. Jones made a quick calculation and decided that if there was one Tim Stoen, there were many Tim Stoens, and if he still had any lingering doubts, Stoen's enthusiasm quickly put them to rest. Gradually, the conversations between the two men moved from theoretical discussions of current events, socialism, communal living, and free love to more practical matters: how to translate Jones's appeal to the masses into real political power.

One major policy decision concerned Stoen's role. Although members were normally expected to make an open and visible commitment to the Temple, there were obviously compelling reasons to relax normal procedure in Stoen's case. His connection to the Temple would not be a secret, but, at the same time, the importance of his role would be downplayed whenever possible. Stoen was clearly most useful to the cause pursuing his career—a career which might take him inside the local corridors of power. To do that he needed no help from Jones or anyone else, and any close identification with any special-interest group could only harm his prospects. Furthermore, as he made his way up the local political ladder, his ability to protect the Temple's interests, if the need arose, might well depend upon a public perception of his independence. Jones therefore did not press him to act as a spokesman for the Temple or represent the Temple in an official capacity. For the time being at least, Stoen's career and his involvement with the Temple would be kept as separate as possible. With Jones's blessing Stoen applied for and secured an appointment as an assistant district attorney for Mendocino County, the traditional first rung for a young lawyer climbing the political ladder.

It was also clear that in the long run Mendocino County was far too small a pond for the movement to grow in. Jones's strongest appeal was to blacks—of which there were few in Mendocino County—and his natural constituency was in the ghettos of San Francisco and Los Angeles. Once he had attracted a large black following, the white liberals, like Tim Stoen, would follow in droves.

If any of his scruples about a white man leading a movement of blacks still remained, it was only as a public relations problem, and, for that he already devised the harmless fiction that he was actually part Cherokee Indian.

The projected urban version of the People's Temple would be an operation on an entirely grander scale than the Redwood Valley Temple. What Jones and Stoen envisaged was something very like a state within a state, a self-contained interracial community that provided for the real material needs of the urban poor. With his combination of pyrotechnical Christianity and radical politics Jones would attract a congregation of poor blacks and idealistic middle-class whites. He would then, in effect, tithe the richer members, collect welfare payments from the poor, and redistribute the church's resources by providing food, lodging, medical care, and a wide range of other social services for the entire community.

During 1970 and 1971, Tim Stoen commuted between the old Mendocino County Courthouse and the People's Temple compound in Redwood Valley, leading a busy double-life; by day, a hard-headed, efficient assistant D.A.; and by night the right-hand man to America's new political messiah. Grace Stoen was also working for the Temple. She was called a "counselor," a sort of all-purpose ombudsman for Temple members. Although she had no formal, professional training in family or youth counseling, she had enough common sense and natural sympathy for the range of problems Temple members brought to her—problems concerned with children, family, housing, and jobs—to make a success of it. She was an immediate hit with the members, and by the middle of 1971 both Stoens were as close to indispensable presences as there were in the Temple. They were also, both of them, extremely close to Jones personally, as close as anyone in the Temple, including Jones's wife, Marceline.

Jim and Marceline Jones had grown apart over the years. Marceline remained a partner in her husband's work, managing the Temple's nursing home and its day-care center, and the people of the Temple loved her. She was the community's mother in the same way as Jones was the father, and Jones respected her contribution; but she was not any longer Jim Jones's lover, or even his confidante; and when Jim stayed up all night making plans with the Stoens, Marceline was not included.

As far as Marceline was concerned, it was just as well: plans, po-itics, and power did not interest her nearly as much as they did her husband. Marcie Jones was more interested in people.

The year 1971 was a crucial and difficult year for the People's Temple, a time of transition in which Jim Jones and Tim Stoen began to take the first nervous-making steps to expand the Temple's operations. During the year the two men made regular trips south to San Francisco and Los Angeles searching for property, and by the fall they had succeeded in buying two immense former synagogues in decaying neighborhoods in both cities. With an investment of several hundred thousand dollars in the two buildings, they were now committed to the undertaking.

Jones was working day and night, seven days a week, and before long he began to show signs of strain. Unlike a Father Divine, who compensated himself with Cadillacs and forty-room mansions, Jones had never appropriated his church's resources to buy luxuries for himself. Jim Jones had only one venal taste—for sex; and, as the pressures on him increased, his appetite seemed to increase also, at an exponential rate. He began making regular (and not especially discreet) sexual demands on several of the younger and more attrac-tive women members of the Temple. His sexual appetite was any-thing but a secret; in fact, Jones regularly boasted to the congregation about his sexual powers, claiming superhuman potency, technique, and endurance. For their part, many of the young women involved regarded sharing their leader's bed as a privilege, the least they could do for such a great man. One of Jones's secretaries kept a special appointments book for Jones's libido, and by the end of 1971 there was hardly a young attractive woman left in the Temple who had not done her part for the cause in bed. His sexual appetite astounded even Jones himself, and at one point he reportedly even sought ad-vice on the subject from a psychiatrist in San Francisco. Unless the advice offered was to indulge himself, Jones did not take it.

About a year later, on January 25, 1972, Grace Stoen gave birth to a baby boy. Although the boy's birth certificate listed his name as John Victor Stoen and his parents as Grace Lucy (Grech) Stoen and Timothy Oliver Stoen, John Victor Stoen's birth certificate was only the prologue to the story of his parentage. In a private affidavit (signed "under penalty of perjury" by Tim Stoen and witnessed by

Marceline Jones), Stoen acknowledged that the child's real father was none other than the Reverend James Warren Jones. According to the affidavit, Stoen had himself requested that "the most compassionate, honest, and courageous human being the world contains" sire a child by his wife "with the steadfast hope that said child will become a devoted follower of Jesus Christ and be instrumental in bringing God's kingdom here on earth, as has been his wonderful natural father."[6] The affidavit does not record Grace Stoen's feelings.

Whatever had taken place behind closed doors between the families Stoen and Jones, the birth of John Victor Stoen and the affidavit attesting to his parenthood sealed the alliance between Tim Stoen and Jim Jones, sealed it in something very close to blood. Somehow the relationship between the two men had generated its own powerful momentum. Eventually, it would generate even more—so much, in fact, no one would be able to stop it. Those who tried—and Grace would be one—would discover just how powerful its momentum was; and, ultimately, everyone connected to the People's Temple would be subjected to the same lesson.

3

Humanitarian
of the Year

Between 1972 and 1975 the People's Temple grew enormously, just
as Jim Jones and Tim Stoen had planned, from a small country
church into a powerful statewide organization with several thousand
members in its San Francisco and Los Angeles branches. The Temple was an immense, immediate, and highly visible success in both
cities, and, as its reputation grew, Jim Jones's reputation grew along
with it. In 1975 he was chosen one of "The 100 Outstanding Cler-
gymen in America" by the Foundation for Religion in American
Life; the following year he would also be named the *Los Angeles
Herald-Examiner's* "Humanitarian of the Year" at about the same
time San Francisco Mayor George Moscone appointed him chairman of the city's Housing Authority.

Although Jones traveled frequently to Los Angeles and Redwood
Valley, San Francisco was now the People's Temple's home base.
Jones and Tim Stoen (who was now an assistant district attorney for
San Francisco County) administered the Temple's affairs from a cav-
ernous, ungainly yellow brick former synagogue on Geary Boulevard
and Jones also lived in the building in an apartment on the third
floor. Situated in the city's Filmore District, a depressed, largely
black neighborhood which San Franciscans considered their inner-
city ghetto (to the surprise of visitors from large eastern cities who
would happily have traded their own inner cities for a dozen Fil-

mores), the Geary Street Temple had quickly become a center for community activities, a twenty-four-hour, seven-day-a-week beehive that offered free meals, free health clinics, free day-care services, and long list of other community services. Money was no object. Without even tapping the federal and state grants available for many of the services it provided, the Temple was an extremely solvent institution. Members who worked outside the Temple were routinely assessed a substantial percentage of their incomes, sometimes 25 percent, or even more. In addition, more affluent members were expected—often under considerable pressure—to sign property over to the Temple. Poorer members who received pension or welfare payments routinely signed their monthly checks directly to the Temple treasury. As attorney for the Temple—as well as chairman of its Board of Trustees—Tim Stoen drew up property agreements, assignments of leases and deeds, and a variety of other documents protecting the Temple's financial arrangements with its members.

Money also poured in from donations. Every meeting was a fundraiser, and a good weekend sometimes netted as much as thirty or forty thousand dollars in donations from members and visitors. In addition, as a nonprofit, tax-exempt religious organization the Temple was licensed to solicit funds publicly, and members who contributed neither a percentage of their income nor a pension or welfare check often donated their time to canvassing downtown streets and shopping centers with little tin coin boxes.

In return the Temple provided virtually complete support, not only food, shelter, and clothing, but medical care, entertainment, tuition for college students, a bus service for senior citizens, and day and night care for both the very young and the very old. Some members—those with the most to give—obviously lost in the bargain, but the vast majority, the poor, did not. For them the Temple's redistribution of its members' incomes was an unmitigated blessing.

Of the poorer members a large percentage fell into one of three categories: single parents and their dependent children; senior citizens; and undereducated, unemployed young adults. For an unmarried mother of three young children trying to support her family on welfare payments the Temple represented security and freedom. Marie Lawrence, a strapping black woman from Los Angeles who joined the Temple in 1971, for example, was a high-school dropout who had drifted into drugs and prostitution while in her teens. When she first met Jim Jones, she lived alone with her three young children in a dreary one-room apartment in a Los Angeles slum. As soon as she joined the Temple she agreed to sign over her monthly welfare payments, and she then moved into a Temple-owned apartment with two other fragmented families. Her children were fed breakfast, lunch, and dinner in a Temple dining hall, driven to school and picked up in a Temple bus, and cared for by the Temple's child-care service after school and on weekends. Marie Lawrence found herself free to return to school. She quickly finished high school, took a trade-school course in refrigeration mechanics, found a job, and began attending college at night. Eventually, she rose in the Temple hierarchy, became one of Grace Stoen's family counselors, and married another Temple member, Bob Rankin.

Like many other older members, Grover Davis, a retired railroad worker in his late seventies, was attracted to the Temple by Jones's faith-healing services. He joined in 1975 after Jones cured his wife's emphysema. "He just took her by the hand," Davis remembers, "when she couldn't hardly breathe at all, and he told God, he said, 'God, You take over,' and right away she was feeling just fine." Although his wife died a few months later, Davis attributed her death to an overfondness for barbecue. "It poisoned her blood so there wasn't anything he could do for her, but I'd seen he had the power, so I stayed with him."

Davis also turned over his monthly Social Security check to the Temple and in return was lodged with a Temple family, fed in the Temple dining hall, and given odd jobs to do around the Geary Street building. He enjoyed feeling useful and being around people of his own age; his most serious complaint about the Temple, despite the fact that he was partially deaf, was "all that rock and roll music those young'uns poison their minds with."

Typical of the young, portable-radio set who were the bane of Grover Davis's ears was Stanley Clayton, a young man in his early twenties from a poor neighborhood across the Bay Bridge in Berkeley. Clayton had been born into a "family" which included eight children, one mother and several different fathers. Each of the children had grown up on a circuit of foster homes and the homes of various relatives, occasionally spending a few weeks or months with their mother or their respective fathers "I grew up wild," Clayton admits, adding that in his boyhood travels he rarely ever lived in a household headed by a male—"someone to whip me". Although he readily acknowledges that he might have benefited from some judicious discipline, he does not blame any of his mothers, real or foster, for not providing it. "There was always too many babies around to whip all of us all the time."

When his natural mother joined the Temple in 1972, Clayton, who had already, at the age of fourteen, seen the inside of several juvenile courts, was sent to live with a Temple family in Ukiah. There, to the astonishment of those who knew him in Berkeley, he finished high school and even began making plans to go to college. A summer back on the streets of Berkeley, however, led in a different direction—to the Santa Rita Correctional Institution for Juvenile Offenders—after he was arrested drunk on the street one night and convicted for carrying a concealed weapon, a switchblade knife.

When Clayton's mother reported to one of Jones's aides what had happened to her son, Jones dispatched a Temple lawyer to the State Parole Board and Clayton was promptly released in Jones's personal custody after serving half of his six-month sentence. Back in San Francisco, Jim Jones himself read Clayton the riot act. This, Jones told him, was his last opportunity to make something of himself. If he stumbled this time, he could rot in prison. Clayton was then installed in a dormitory for young people, registered in a trade-school welding course, and closely monitored by Temple counselors.

Although Stanley Clayton's family history was more lurid than most, family pathology was a persistent feature of the lives of Temple members, especially, but not exclusively, the poorer, black members. In 1970 the decadal national census showed that a quarter of all black households were headed by women and that a third of all non-white children were growing up in fatherless homes. Jones, who was well aware of these statistics—and well aware that broken families were the rule within the Temple—openly advertised the Temple as a surrogate family. In fact, he even liked to claim that the breakdown of the American family was a blessing in disguise. In Jones's view, old-fashioned nuclear families were a species of social dinosaur, outmoded relics of a dying society which oppressed poor people by isolating them from those with whom they had common cause. The wave of the future, according to Jones, was for poor people to join together in an entirely new kind of family, a broad extended network of associations not based upon the narrow, accidental bonds of biology, but upon the utopian ideal of the brotherhood of mankind.

To an unmarried mother like Marie Lawrence, an elderly widower like Grover Davis, and a neglected adolescent like Stanley Clayton, it was a powerful argument. In the new extended family everyone would be everyone else's brother and sister; and, most importantly, in this particular version of the extended family there was a strong, present, caring father for everyone. Although religious leaders who claimed the role of a father were hardly anything new, in Jones's case the term was far more than an honorific one or a metaphor, and to a considerable extent his authority over the lives of his followers stemmed from his protean ability to function successfully *in loco parentis* for an enormous number of members.

In addition to the poor and the black, Jones also attracted a sizable contingent of more affluent middle-class members; and, if the Temple was one gigantic extended family, the better educated, white middle-class members tended to form a family within that family. Many of them belonged to the Temple's Planning Commission, a large group of over a hundred members, which, in name at least, was charged with setting Temple policies. Although, in fact, important policy was almost always set by Jones himself, in consultation with a very few advisers like Tim Stoen, the Planning Commission did function by a different set of rules than the rest of the organization.

The members of the Planning Commision were overwhelmingly white, ranging from people like the Mertles at one end of the socioeconomic spectrum to the Stoens at the other end, and Jones made no bones about demanding more from this inner family than he did from the rank and file. Since many of them had first been attracted to the Temple in the first place by its social ideology, Jones's challenge to donate their energies (and their pocketbooks) to the cause was nothing more than what many of them bargained for.

For Planning Commission members there were no Bible lessons, no faith healings, and no miracles. They were the vanguard, the insiders, and for them the People's Temple was serious business—a steady diet of hard work, responsibility, and sacrifice. Especially sacrifice. In pursuit of the revolution, Planning Commission members were expected to sacrifice their time, their money, their undivided energies—even their private lives. Contact with family and friends outside the Temple was seriously frowned upon, and within the Temple Planning Commission members were expected to live their lives in glass houses—and to be prepared for Jim Jones to cast stones at the sight of anything less than total commitment to the cause.

Planning Commission meetings were frequent and intense, often all-night psychodramas on the theme of struggle: the collective struggle against the oppressive capitalist system and, even more importantly, the struggle within to replace bourgeois egocentrism with an unwavering commitment to the cause of building a perfectly egalitarian society. Even the most minor backsliding might subject a member to a marathon of merciless criticism with Jones himself leading the attack.

"How can you complain about the sacrifices I ask you to make," Jones might ask a member accused of spending money on luxuries or taking an unauthorized day off, "when you know what we're fighting against? When you know the poor go to bed hungry at night all over the world? When you know the conditions in which poor people live right here in this city? When you know that even as we're sitting here there are children dying because they don't have enough to eat?"

It was preaching to the already converted. Many of the younger members, especially, were already veterans of similar meetings on college campuses. For others, the very intensity of the meetings, aside from their content, was a powerful intoxicant; and when a Planning Commission meeting broke up in the early-morning hours a hundred inspired revolutionaries would drag themselves back to work full of the excitement of a just cause.

Because of its size, its cohesiveness, and the energy of its leadership, the Temple was an unusually efficient organization, and its combination of resources allowed it to wield a good deal of power in a smallish city like San Francisco. With several thousand members who could be mobilized not only to vote in a bloc but to stuff envelopes and ring doorbells as well, the People's Temple had a way of catching politicians' eyes. A persistent piece of mythology both within the Temple and among its critics—with different emphasis— maintained that during the elections of 1974 and 1976 several local officeholders owed their offices to Jim Jones. Among those mentioned were the mayor of San Francisco, George Moscone (who appointed Jones to be chairman of the San Francisco Housing Authority); the sheriff of San Francisco, Richard Hongisto; and the district attorney, Joseph Freitas (who hired Tim Stoen to be one of his assistants).

Whether or not Jones deserved his reputation as a kingmaker, he was certainly treated with the deference politicians like to pay to a man who can deliver votes. An invitation to address the congregation's public Sunday meeting was considered a plum by politicians, a plum enjoyed by virtually every liberal officeholder in San Francisco and Los Angeles, the lieutenant governor of the state of California, and a whole host of state legislators.

Although Jones carried no more political clout than any number of labor and business leaders in San Francisco, he enjoyed exercising the clout he did carry. During 1973, for example, Jones managed to embroil himself in a petty vendetta with the Los Angeles police department. The trouble grew out of one of Jones's more lurid faith healings at the Los Angeles Temple during which the police responded to a report of a critically injured accident victim outside the Temple building on Alvarado Street. The police could not have known it, of course, but the truth was that the supposed victim was not in such serious straits that he could not, as planned, be brought back to the pink of health by a few words from Jones, but ignorant of Jones's scenario, the police rushed in with sirens blaring and ambulances following. When Jones's security staff attempted to keep them from the victim a small melee ensued. Jones was furious, and the following day called in a few political debts for the purpose of pressuring the LAPD to reprimand the officers involved. The result of the pressure, however, was pure gaseous backfire; the department resolved to even the score. A few weeks later Jones was arrested for soliciting sex from an undercover officer in the men's room of a movie theater where Jones was taking in a matinee of *Jesus Christ— Superstar*.

At that point, Jones trotted out the heavy artillery, calling in political debts from several well-connected allies. Eventually he not only managed to have the charges dropped, but also to have the arrest record sealed by a Los Angeles judge.

Normally, however, Jones and Stoen made an attempt to use their influence within the normal rules of political commerce, generally for the benefit of their constituency. The net effect for the people of

the Temple was very largely positive. Jones's reputation and Tim
Stoen's position allowed the Temple to intercede regularly with local
and federal bureaucracies on behalf of members whose experiences
with bureaucracies often tended toward the inexplicable form, the
endless line, and the deaf ear. Anyone in the Temple who had ever
found dealing with a welfare agency, a housing authority, or a court
an exercise in frustration, now, suddenly, found that, with Jones and
Stoen to speak for them, they were magically transformed into citizens of substance and influence.

Jones himself was especially proud of saving several members, including Stanley Clayton, from youth shelters, reformatories, and
prisons; and he liked to boast—with cause—of the Temple's phe-
nomenal rehabilitation rates, especially with youthful offenders.

Political power and political alliances inevitably have their way of
generating political grudges and political enemies, and Jim Jones
made his share of both. He had an especially stormy relationship
with the press. Much like the no-holds-barred battler who inhabited
the White House at the time, Jones believed that politics was war
and unfriendly journalists were combatants. When it pleased him,
Jones was capable of courting friendly reporters with the zeal of a
Hollywood press agent; but the unfriendly ones he unhesitatingly
consigned to a thoroughly Nixonian hell complete with enemies
lists, anonymous telephone calls, letters, threats of lawsuits, lawsuits, and, occasionally, physical intimidation. In Jones's mind, he
was a public figure cut from the mold of Malcolm X, Martin Luther
King, Jr., Fred Hampton, the Chicago Seven, or any of the other
New Left Leaders who had discovered during the sixties that politics
can be a very rough game indeed. Jones cherished the homily which
reads, "Those who do not understand history are condemned to repeat it." He was not inclined to be one of them. He worried constantly that the F.B.I. or some other government agency had tapped
his telephones, and he kept a pair of binoculars in his office to check
the streets outside the Temple for lurking government agents.

There was another group of critics to whom Jones was especially
sensitive—critics who were former members. He considered leaving
the Temple, for whatever reasons, a betrayal of the cause, and virtually anyone who did leave, especially those who had served on the
Planning Commission, went immediately to the head of the enemies

list. Ex-members' houses were routinely watched to make sure they were not consorting with government agents or hostile journalists; and their private lives—sometimes including their garbage—was combed for the makings of blackmail ammunition. One could leave the Temple, but in one way or another one would pay for the privilege.

Early in 1975, Elmer and Deanna Mertle began to seriously consider leaving the Temple. The Mertles had been happy enough in Redwood Valley raising a large family that included not only their own six children but several foster children as well; they had both enjoyed their small farm and their work for the Temple, Elmer as Jones's personal photographer and Deanna as a secretary in the membership office. But when the Temple moved to San Francisco, both Mertles felt something had changed, something about the Temple, something about Jim Jones, and something about their own lives.

As the Temple's membership grew, both Mertles felt that discipline was replacing love as the first principle of life in the Temple. At Temple meetings, they watched in horror as children and adults were publicly paddled for such acts of misconduct as smoking a cigarette, eating a Big Mac, or the cardinal sin of returning a Temple vehicle with a parking ticket stuck to the windshield. Jones did not deny that Temple discipline was tightening, but he justified the paddlings on two grounds. Many of the new members who had grown up wild on the streets of the big city needed to be impressed forcibly with the rules they were expected to live by. In addition, Jones explained, as the Temple grew and began to exercise its power in the community, it was absolutely necessary that Temple members appear to outsiders as paragons of good behavior. "We cannot allow our enemies the opportunity to exploit our weaknesses," he told Deanna Mertle after Elmer Mertle's sixteen-year-old daughter was paddled for a minor infraction.

Up to a point the Mertles accepted Jones's explanations, but as Jones's perspective grew ever more militantly political, the Mertles grew ever more unsure of their commitment to the cause. Deanna Mertle especially had never wanted to be a soldier in a ceaseless struggle against the capitalist power structure and she had difficulty understanding the sacrifices she was supposed to be making for a cause she did not believe in. She was also frankly horrified by Jones's sexual conduct and his interference in the sexual lives of his congregation.

Both Mertle's were members of the Planning Commission, and during 1974 and 1975 Planning Commision meetings were becoming increasingly bizarre, especially with respect to Jones's sex life. It was not unusual for several hours of a meeting to be devoted to Jones's sex life, all to advertise the proposition that a night with Jim Jones was guaranteed to stimulate revolutionary zeal in revolutionaries of both sexes. He ranted about bourgeois sexual attitudes, insisting that members publicly confess their sexual fears and fantasies. At one point he demanded celibacy from the entire Planning Commission over a stretch of several months as a kind of libidinal hunger strike to demonstrate revolutionary discipline and the resolve to give up mere sensual pleasures.

On another occasion, in a different mood, Jones forced a white man to perform cunnilingus on a black woman during a Planning Commission meeting as a public demonstration of his lack of racial prejudice. Deanna Mertle could hardly believe her eyes. Another time, during an all-night meeting, Jones refused to allow anyone to leave the room until the issue under consideration was resolved. He ordered a tin can placed in a corner of the room for those whose bladders were unequal to the revolutionary struggle with nature.[7] While Jones contended that sexual frankness and communal urination were merely symbolic demonstrations of the community's openness, Deanna Mertle began to suspect that perhaps the real point was that the emperor had no clothes; and, what was worse, there was nothing this emperor seemed to like better than exhibiting himself to his subjects.

The Mertles began to make plans to leave the Temple. Leaving, however, was not an easy matter. Two of the Mertles children lived in the homes of other Temple members and had already begun to feel more commitment to Jones and their new extended family than they did to their natural parents. In addition, the Mertles had deeded their Redwood Valley farm and most of their other assets to the Temple; their paychecks also came from the Temple, and having supported themselves through the Temple for five years, they were afraid of setting out again on their own.

In the spring of 1975, however, Elmer Mertle's mother gave them the deed to a profitable rest home she owned in Berkeley and offered to advance the Mertles the down payment for a house in nearby Oakland. With their financial worries eased, Deanna Mertle picked up the telephone one afternoon and announced to one of Jones's aides that she and her husband had left the Temple. Immediately, all hell broke loose. A delegation from the Temple arrived from Geary Street to persuade them to change their minds. The Mertles stood fast. Other delegations arrived demanding to search the Mertles' house for stolen Temple documents. Deanna Mertle threatened to go to the press with lurid stories of Planning Commission meetings. The Temple responded by threatening to smear Elmer Mertle publicly as a child molester. Threats and counterthreats passed back and forth between Jones and the Mertles on the subject of the foster children living with the Mertles and the Mertles' own children living with other Temple families. Eventually, the Mertles placed documents they believed to be damaging to the Temple in a safe deposit vault in a Berkeley bank, swore out an affidavit charging Jones with a long list of perversions and malfeasances, changed their names, and resolved to devote their lives to fighting Jim Jones and the People's Temple.

The Mertles (now legally Al and Jeannie Mills) immediately entered the People's Temple mythology as arch-villains. From the pulpit Jones denounced them as moral cowards unwilling to sacrifice worldly pleasures for the sake of building a better world, traitors who had sold out their brothers and sisters "for a pocketful of credit cards and a fancy car."

4

Summer of '76

Despite the faint echo of rumblings from within, 1976 was a banner year for the People's Temple. Both the Los Angeles and San Francisco Temples were routinely filled to capacity; money continued to pour in at a rate that astounded even Jim Jones; and, best of all, from Jones's point of view, his reputation had grown to the point where it was impossible to talk about politics in San Francisco without mentioning the Reverend Jim Jones.

For the summer, the long-awaited bicentennial summer of '76, Jones decided to celebrate. The plan was for a month-long national tour by Jones and several hundred Temple members aboard the Temple's fleet of motor coaches. At major cities along the way the caravan would stop and hold services in rented local churches. New members would be recruited at the services and periodically sent back to San Francisco in one of the buses. The main body of the caravan would then proceed to the next city, returning to San Francisco on the eve of the Temple's own gala Fourth of July celebration.

After two weeks on the road the bus caravan had settled into a routine of driving through the night (to save on hotel bills) and stopping at local churches along the way during the day. In major cities—Denver, Kansas City, and Chicago—local churches were rented for major, pre-publicized meetings highlighted by Jim Jones's sermons and faith healings. The caravan reached Detroit early on a fine, bright summer morning. It rolled through the quiet early-morning streets and pulled up in front of the Central Methodist Church on East Adams Street.

The church, an enormous gray stone building which covers an entire city block, faces a small triangle of concrete and indifferent greenery called Grand Circus Park. From a bench in the park, where he had slept the night before, a thirty-three-year-old drug addict, street hustler, and occasional petty criminal named Odell Rhodes, Jr. looked up from his breakfast jug of wine and watched the buses begin to unload across the street. Odell Rhodes remembers the banner stretched along the side of the lead bus: The Reverend Jim Jones People's Temple.

Odell Rhodes had never heard of the Reverend Jim Jones or his People's Temple. He knew nothing about urban ministries, devoted followers, or Humanitarian of the Year Awards, and the truth was that Odell Rhodes could hardly have cared less about any of it: interracial churches, California politics, socialism, miracles, or ambitious young ministers. As Rhodes would have been the first to admit, his interests that morning, and every morning, were, for all practical purposes, limited to a single subject: heroin—most particularly the heroin he was right that moment thinking about buying, cooking, and injecting into a vein somewhere in his body not already too abused to accommodate a hypodermic needle.

For eight years virtually every dollar that passed through Odell Rhodes's hands—most of them the result of talking his way into somebody else's wallet—had gone directly into his veins. Most mornings, in fact, Rhodes would already have been on the streets panhandling or otherwise trying to promote himself a few dollars with which to buy the day's first heroin high. This particular morning, however, Rhodes's pockets happened to be unusually flush, and with the day's necessities already spoken for, he was feeling as much like a man of leisure as a man with a serious habit can feel, so he allowed himself the luxury of taking in the strange spectacle unfolding across East Adams Street.

For Rhodes, Grand Circus was a public park in name only. Inasmuch as he lived more or less exactly where he was sitting he considered the park and the streets around it to be something very much like his own private front yard, and being a man with a healthy streak of natural curiosity, he liked to keep track of what was happening on his doorstep. Rhodes was not alone in his curiosity. Although Grand Circus Park sits virtually in the heart of downtown Detroit, the area around the park is a classic victim of the peculiarly modern social alchemy by which a bustling downtown crossroads is transformed into a ghost town of vacant lots, boarded-up buildings, and a population of urban ghosts: junkies, winos, hookers, and pimps. Except for the few minutes twice each working day when commuters from downtown office buildings hurry through on their way to and from the suburbs, strangers rarely venture into the area around the park; and the caravan of People's Temple buses, a dozen strong with license plates from faraway California and a mixed cargo of old and young, black and white seemed to Rhodes only slightly less noteworthy than a squadron of flying saucers.

Together with the other regulars in the park that morning, Rhodes watched the crowd across the street and traded speculations with friends. "I guess there were three or four of us sitting there and we kicked it around for awhile—like, 'What the hell *is* a People's Temple?' Finally, a friend of mine named John Dine picked himself up and went over and asked somebody."

Rhodes and the others watched John Dine disappear inside the church but Rhodes, whose curiosity by now losing the unequal battle with his habit, did not wait for a report. While Dine was accepting an invitation to attend the Temple meeting that evening and find out firsthand from Jim Jones himself what a People's Temple was, Rhodes set off in the direction of his neighborhood heroin dealer.

Later in the afternoon, a delegation of Temple members fanned out through the park extending more invitations, including one to a now happily stoned Odell Rhodes. Rhodes declined, but was nonetheless impressed by the invitation. "We used to get church groups coming through the park now and then, but generally they just wanted to give you something to read and tell you to open up your heart to Christ or love your neighbor or something of the sort. It was a very rare thing when one of them actually wanted some dude with his eyelids down around his knees and a bottle in his pocket inside their precious church."

Rhodes's friend John Dine did attend the meeting, and the following morning a rumor spread through the park to the effect that John Dine had found God right there on the spot and was already on his way back to California. Odell Rhodes received the news with a who-would-have-thought-it shrug; but if eight years on the streets had taught him anything, it was never to be surprised at anything a junkie may do. "The part about John finding God didn't seem real likely, but, then again, the part about a free ride to California seemed just about right."

Dine was, in fact, on his way back to California, and, while he spent his bicentennial Fourth of July celebrating freedom with the People's Temple, Odell Rhodes remained in Grand Circus Park doing what came naturally. "I didn't give John too much thought after he left," Rhodes remembers. "I guess I was too busy. I wasn't doing anything much except scrounging dimes and getting high, but when you're living like that I guarantee you feel like you're pretty damn busy most of the time."

The Temple bus caravan returned to San Francisco a few days before the Fourth of July, but Jim Jones was no longer in any mood to celebrate. In New York, at the end of the trip cross-country, disaster had struck. Grace Stoen had defected from the Temple.

It was a move she had considered for more than a year. No longer nineteen—and long since past sweet and innocent—Grace took a good look around and did not like what she saw. Since the birth of her child Grace and her husband had grown apart. As far as Grace could tell, if Tim was married to anybody, it was to Jim Jones. In terms of time spent together, emotional closeness, and shared experience, Tim and Jones were far closer to each other than either was to Grace.

Grace had gradually drifted at least some distance away from the Temple. During the previous eighteen months she had taken some college courses, seen a little bit of life outside the Temple, and she was beginning to long for a more conventional life. But Grace Stoen still had many of the same problems the Mertles had had. For seven years, virtually her entire adult life, she had known nothing but the People's Temple. How did one leave the Temple? And where did one go when one left? Besides, Grace had an additional problem: her son.

John-John was growing up into an unusually gifted and likable child; and he had become the undisputed apple of Jim Jones's eye. He spent far more time with Jones than with his mother, and Grace knew Jones would never give him back to her if she left the Temple. The idea was so ludicrous there was no point in even entertaining it. She understood that she could fight for custody in the courts, but she had little taste for airing her private life in public, and she knew that if she fought Jones in court her husband would line up with Jones and she would wind up fighting both of them together. Hardly anything was more inconceivable than successfully contesting the combined wills of Jim Jones and Tim Stoen.

For a solid year Grace Stoen weighed her alternatives. Then, finally, a few days before the Fourth of July, she made her decision. Without a word to either Jones or her husband, she left the caravan, flew back to California, and disappeared. Vanished. Drove to Lake Tahoe and spent a week doing absolutely nothing for the revolution but tan herself.

Jones at first did not believe she had defected. Tim Stoen knew better. He was not surprised; he knew how depressed his wife had been. When he finally tracked her down and confirmed his suspicions, he went directly to Jones. Jones was furious. He could barely conceive of John-John's mother as a traitor. But, if she was, she was no different than any other traitor, except perhaps slightly more dangerous. Jones had two serious nightmares about Grace's defection. One was that she might go to the press with what she knew about the embarrassing details of Jones's personal life and the potentially even more embarrassing details of the Temple's financial affairs. Jones and Stoen had, for some time, been transferring large sums of Temple money to hidden bank accounts in Europe and the Caribbean, and, although the motive appears to have been political principle (to keep the money away from the claws of American capitalism) rather than embezzlement, disclosure of the practice would still have invited unpleasant speculation.

The other (and far more disturbing) prospect was that Grace might try to regain custody of John-John through the courts. As far as Jones was concerned, however distasteful the thought of Grace washing the Temple's dirty laundry in the press might be, the thought of a court procedure was even worse. Bad publicity was bad enough, but it was only publicity—and, compared to the possibility of losing John-John, the worst press in the world was nothing more than an inconvenience.

A court action would be something else again. It did not require a lawyer of Tim Stoen's skills to understand the legal situation in a custody suit. The situation was simple: were Grace to ask a court to award her legal custody of the child, the court would almost certainly follow precedent and custom and award custody to the child's mother. Even were Tim to beat Grace to the punch and sue for divorce himself, the court would in all likelihood still award custody to Grace.

At all costs then the primary objective was to keep Grace out of court. For as long as possible Tim would use what powers of persuasion he could summon to convince Grace, for John-John's sake, to keep the quarrel within the family. But whatever Jones thought of Stoen's persuasive powers, entreaties with an angry woman were not his idea of a sufficient guarantee against the calamity of losing John-John. Was there nothing else to be done?

There was, Stoen explained to Jones, nothing which would be likely to affect the court's decision. But there was one obvious way to make whatever a court decided irrelevant. Should Grace actually file a custody action, John-John could be physically removed from the court's jurisdiction. He could simply be taken out of the country. That way, no matter what the decision, it would be impossible for the court to enforce the decision, and the legal procedures necessary to return the child to California could probably be strung out for years, or perhaps forever.

Stoen immediately began researching the extradition treaty between the United States and Guyana, where the Temple was beginning to build a small experimental farm. When he discovered that the treaty did not cover custody cases, he drew up legal authorization, as John-John's legal father, for two aides, Maria Katsaris and Joyce Touchette, to travel with John-John to Guyana.

Jones then ordered Maria Katsaris to be ready to leave at a moments notice. But, even with the authorization in his pocket and Maria Katsaris's suitcase in his closet, Jones could not relax. The slimmest chance of losing John-John—even the very thought of it— infuriated Jones and depressed him at the same time. It was simply not fair.

While Jones brooded about Grace's defection and hounded Tim Stoen about extradition treaties and strategies to use against Grace, Tim Stoen spent hours on the telephone relaying messages back and forth between Jones and Grace, trying to reassure both of them of the purity of each other's motives. Jones, in particular, was not easily reassured. The more he thought about Grace, the more he suspected her of motives that went far beyond John-John. He began to believe that she had joined with the Mills in a conspiracy to discredit him and destroy the Temple. In Jones's mind it all added up: first the Mills, then Grace, now government spies lurking about the Temple.

They were all out to destroy him. They had done away with the Kennedys, Martin Luther King, Malcolm X, Fred Hampton, George Jackson—and now it was Jim Jones's turn.

Between worrying about John-John and checking for government agents behind parked cars, Jones had little time to do anything else. Although most of those close to Jones were convinced of the deadly seriousness of the threat posed by the embryonic conspiracy as Jones was, others, including Tim Stoen, were beginning to have their doubts. Although Stoen continued to help Jones work out strategies for keeping John-John and defending himself against his enemies, it occurred to Stoen that fighting a rearguard defensive action against what was probably a grossly exaggerated threat was no way to build a grass-roots political movement.

Nonetheless, virtually all of the Temple's programs in both San Francisco and Los Angeles continued to function smoothly, and from outside the inner circle there was nothing to suggest to anyone that anything at all was wrong inside the People's Temple. Publicly, both Jones and the Temple continued to ride the crest, and, by the end of the summer, Jones himself was again feeling expansive enough to plan a working vacation. His ultimate destination was Cuba, but he decided to kick off his journey with an encore mini-performance of the summer's national tour. He would take a bus caravan with him as far as Detroit, then cross over into Canada for the flight to Cuba. On October 1 an advance party, which was to arrange food and lodging and publicize Jones's appearances, left San Francisco, and a few days later the main body of the caravan followed.

Because the climactic meeting of the tour would be in Detroit, where the members of the caravan planned to give their vacationing leader a rousing send-off, John Dine, the new recruit from Detroit, was assigned to the advance party and charged with the responsibility of drumming up a full house for Jones's appearance at the Central Methodist Church. After tacking up posters on walls throughout the city, Dine spent the afternoon before the caravans scheduled arrival wandering through his old neighborhood looking up old friends. Walking through Grand Circus Park late that afternoon he bumped into his old friend Odell Rhodes, who had hardly given a thought to John Dine or the People's Temple since the night in June when Dine had joined the Temple and left for San Francisco. This time, the sight of his old friend made an enormous impression on Rhodes.

"When I saw him," Rhodes remembers, "you could have knocked me over with a feather. I mean, when John left, he was so dirty you couldn't even say what color his clothes were. Now there he was dressed up in a suit and I'd never seen anybody change like that. Like one day you see him, and the next time, you have to look real close to see who the hell you're talking to. The only way I can describe it is that he looked like a businessman—like he was 100 percent business—and he conducted himself altogether different than the John Dine I knew. I guess I figured if they could do it for him, they could do it for me."

Dine put Rhodes in touch with Marie Lawrence, the ex–drug addict from Los Angeles who had been assigned to interview prospective converts. Marie Lawrence took Rhodes to a quiet spot on the curb in front of the Central Methodist Church and struck up a conversation. Rhodes does not recall the details of the conversation; what he does remember is how it ended—with Rhodes taking a knife out of his pocket and telling the woman to move away from him.

The night before, Rhodes and an acquaintance he remembers only as Lester had stolen a fur coat from a parked car. Following the theft, Lester took off with the coat leaving Rhodes with Lester's hammer which the two of them had used to smash the car's vent window. When Lester broke into a run, Rhodes, whose right leg had been shattered by a bullet that ended a street-corner argument in 1971, made a quick check for a police car, then hollered for Lester to slow down. Lester did not look back; and Rhodes, forced to conclude that the cause of Lester's haste could only be Rhodes's share of the coat, returned Lester's hammer air mail. "I hit him," Rhodes remembers sadly, "but I didn't slow him down."

Sitting on the curb with Marie Lawrence the following afternoon, Rhodes noticed Lester across the street in the park approaching with the air of a man who has fenced a fur coat and is now ready to discuss a hammer in the back of the head. Cautioning the woman to move away, Rhodes opened his knife under a piece of newspaper.

"You hit me in my fucking head, man!"

"That ain't half of what I'd done if I'd caught you."

"Well, what you gonna do about it now, mother-fucker!"

Rhodes stood up, intending an exercise in ghetto show-and-tell— show him the knife and tell him where you plan to stick it; but Marie Lawrence had not budged an inch from his side.

"All of a sudden I kind of looked around and I saw that there were five or six other people from the Temple standing right back of us— all of them males and all of them about twice as big as me and Lester put together." The confrontation—and Lester—evaporated.

"We're peaceful people," Marie Lawrence explained, "but when one of us is in trouble we're all in trouble." Rhodes was so shocked— and moved—he had to excuse himself to shoot a load of heroin. "There I was a perfect stranger and they were willing to get involved like that. I wasn't used to it—on the streets, the more trouble you're in, the more you're on your own."

With his mind about halfway made up to join, Rhodes continued on to his uncle's house on the west side of the city. "I guess I went to say goodbye. In fact, I *did* say goodbye, but by that time my family had heard so many plans out of me they really didn't pay much attention. You know, just Junior talking about tomorrow again."

He hurried back downtown, stopping only to buy and shoot yet another bag of heroin. "Guess I must have been trying to find out what they'd say if I showed up good and high." They said nothing. Marie Lawrence simply explained the rules: No drugs, no drinking, no smoking; a probationary period during which Rhodes and the Temple would decide if they were right for each other. Rhodes agreed, and, with the intention of loading up one more final good-bye time, announced he was going home to pack his suitcase. Marie Lawrence shook her head. "You don't need anything but the clothes on your back," she told him in a voice that said she understood it wasn't clothes he had on his mind.

That night, Rhodes caught his first glimpse of Jim Jones. Given his condition, it was not much more than a glimpse, but that did not prevent Rhodes from forming a first impression: "I was pretty high so I didn't catch all that much of what he was talking about—but it didn't take but two minutes to figure out he was a con man. I guess it takes one to know one."

Rhodes admits he felt some mild surprise that the People's Temple leader was a man with a readily identifiable streak of the street hustler in him; but the realization deterred him not at all. "The thing was, what the hell difference did it make? So, he was a con artist, so what? What the hell was he going to con me out of? I didn't have shit. Besides, Jones didn't have anything to do with me joining up. What blew me away about the Temple was the people. I don't even think that I realized it at the time, but the worse thing about the streets is how lonely you are. In eight years, I basically never really had a friend. I might hustle with you, get stoned, drunk, but when it got right down to it, I couldn't afford to actually have any feelings about you. It's something everybody out there understands—you look out after your own ass first.

"Now all of a sudden here's this bunch of people who don't know me from Adam, and they're all over me, asking me what they can do for me, wanting me to join up with them. I'd just plain blew my mind—I'd forgotten that people like that existed.

"How did it make me feel? Like I'd been some kind of damned fool for not being with people like that all my life. I just figured, this is it. This is exactly what I been looking for—this is what I been looking for all my life."

5

The Life and Times of Odell Rhodes

Whatever Odell Rhodes had been looking for all his life, the fact was, he could hardly have been a more perfect candidate for the People's Temple. Through no particular talent—or fault—of his own Rhodes had managed in a busy thirty-three years to experience just about everything Jim Jones despised about America.

Born in 1942, in Greenville, South Carolina, to poor, black teen-age parents, Rhodes never spent a minute of his life in a household in which both of his parents were present. By the time Rhodes was born, his father was already overseas, at war, and although the senior Rhodes survived three years of combat in Europe, the marriage did not. When the war ended in 1945, Odell Rhodes, Sr., decided to make a career of the army, and as part of his separation agreement with his wife, arranged for his son to be sent to Detroit to be raised by his sister and brother-in-law.

The Aikens, Rhodes's aunt and uncle, were hard-working church-going people who raised Rhodes the same way they raised their own four children—with a firm hand. "My uncle is a man of very few words," Rhodes says admiringly, "but you damn well better listen to all of them."

Jay Aiken held a steady job with the National Tool Company and moonlighted summers cutting lawns and planting gardens. The family lived comfortably enough in what was, at the time, an integrated working-class neighborhood on the east side of Detroit, and Rhodes remembers his childhood as happy and, above all, uneventful. He went to school, sang in the Baptist Church choir, delivered newspapers, washed cars, and spent most of his free time earning Boy Scout Merit badges.

Although the Aikens treated him well, Rhodes was acutely conscious of missing his parents. "With my uncle, when I was on his good side, he'd call me his son—and when I wasn't, I was only his nephew." But if Jay Aiken was a father only when Rhodes pleased him, his real father was much less—a distant presence represented by an occasional postcard, a yearly Christmas package, and a whirlwind visit every year or two.

From the age of eight or nine, when he was old enough to travel by himself, Rhodes lived for his summer vacation. With a basket full of sandwiches and soda pop, he climbed aboard a Greyhound bus in Detroit and, an adventurous day and night later, arrived in Greenville to a mother waiting to spoil him. In addition to his mother and younger brother, there were other relatives as well—his mother's family in Greenville and, especially, his father's large family who lived on a farm near a small town, Easley, about twenty miles from Greenville. "He didn't have much money," Rhodes says about his grandfather, "but I never saw him want for anything. They grew most of what they had, and they didn't have a tractor, just mules, so they worked hard. But, to me, every night seemed like a party. The house was always full of people—neighbors and cousins and aunts and uncles—and even though they didn't have a lot, whatever they had it always seemed like enough."

Years later Jonestown reminded Rhodes of his summers in South Carolina: "It was the same kind of life. Hard work, but work you felt good about doing—growing things for yourself and your family. Maybe it was just being around people who really cared about one another, but when I got to Jonestown I almost felt like I was finally going home."

Rhodes's summers in South Carolina ended abruptly in 1956, when he was fourteen. That spring, after years of begging his mother and the Aikens, he had finally won permission to move permanently to Greenville. He was already celebrating, bragging at school and saying goodbye to friends, when his mother died suddenly, a few weeks before he was scheduled to move. "It was," he remembers, "like somebody taking your dream and spitting on it."

His last trip to Greenville was to bury his mother. His father did not attend the funeral, and her death did not change his relationship with his father, except in Rhodes's imagination.

Largely because he saw him so rarely Rhodes developed an active fantasy life about his father, and Odell Rhodes, Sr., gradually became the dominant figure in his life. To Rhodes, he was a grand, romantic hero who roamed the globe in a smart uniform, snapping off crisp salutes with one hand and slaying dragons with the other.

"I had his name and I guess I was like any other kid—I wanted to be just like my father. My aunt had this box full of medals he'd won, and I'd take them out and look at them every chance I got. I never wanted to be a fireman or any of those other things kids want to be when they grow up. I always wanted to be a soldier, like my father was."

A high school ROTC course provided an opportunity for Rhodes to have his first taste of soldiering. Always an indifferent student, he blossomed during the course, and, when he turned seventeen, the summer before what would have been his senior year, he enlisted in the army.

"I was just a baby. I didn't know it then, but that's what I was. It's kind of hard for some people to believe that a black could grow up in a city like Detroit and get to seventeen without knowing anything about drugs or drinking or getting into trouble—or even sex—but that's how I was. A baby."

After basic training in Kentucky and an advanced artillery training course in Oklahoma, Rhodes was sent to Korea in the spring of 1960 as an artillery surveyor with the Seventh Infantry Division. He grew up quickly in Korea. Stationed near the Demilitarized Zone with an artillery battery whose 280mm canons were on constant alert guarding the Liberty Bridge connecting the two Koreas over the Han Estuary, Rhodes felt very important indeed, but the larger part of his education came during weekend passes when the entire company regularly invaded one of the nearby GI towns where rice whiskey and government-certified working girls combined to make the visiting soldier more than proud to defend a free Korea.

When his overseas tour ended late in 1961, Rhodes promptly reenlisted for a six-year hitch, even though there was still better than a year remaining in his original enlistment. He was sent to Fort Carson, Colorado, where a new secretary of defense, Robert McNamara, had organized a pet pilot project for modernizing and streamlining the armed forces. The goal was to train and equip an entire combat division from scratch in six months, and when the project succeeded a few weeks ahead of schedule, a very proud Odell Rhodes was selected to bear his company's colors as President John F. Kennedy personally reviewed and congratulated the men of Fort Carson.

Rhodes was now more than ever convinced that he had found a life in the army. About six weeks later, however, fate, or, at least, bad judgment, intervened. One afternoon, while, according to Rhodes, he was cheerfully minding his own business on the streets of downtown Fort Carson, another soldier stopped him and asked him for a favor. The favor was to pawn a suit of clothes; something, the soldier claimed, he could not do himself because he was not of legal age. For a small commission, Rhodes obliged. A few days later he was arrested, charged with grand larceny, and thrown into the post stockade. It turned out that the suit of clothes Rhodes had pawned had been stolen from another soldier in Rhodes's own company.

At his court-martial Rhodes offered no defense other than his story about a favor for an unknown, underage soldier—a story that impressed nobody, partly because Rhodes could not identify the soldier or even the company he belonged to, and partly because Rhodes himself was not of legal age either. "I guess," Rhodes shrugged, "he figured I looked older than he did." He was identified by the pawnbroker and promptly convicted.

"Maybe," he says, "I should have screamed and hollered and made somebody look for that other soldier, but at the time I was just a soldier doing what people told him to do. I didn't even really understand what the court-martial meant."

He was sentenced to loss of rank, forfeiture of pay, a year in prison, and a dishonorable discharge. "Even after the sentencing, the only thing that really bothered me was the double-D. I wanted to stay in the army, and then there was my father. I'd gone into the service because I wanted to be just like him. Well, he was a master sergeant with a chest full of ribbons, and there I was about to score a double-D. I didn't see how I was ever going to be able to face him again."

Rhodes spent the first few weeks of his sentence in the Fort Carson post stockade, a minimum security lockup known to its inmates as "The Motel," largely because of its commanding officer, a somnolent lieutenant who snored the other way when a prisoner took an occasional, unauthorized overnight leave. He was then transferred to the army's maximum security prison at Fort Leavenworth, Kansas. If the seriousness of his situation had not impressed Rhodes before, the sight of Leavenworth's bleak stone walls and live gun towers convinced him.

"Seeing Leavenworth was like getting kicked in the teeth by an elephant. I damn near broke down and cried when I saw the place."

At his first dinner in the Leavenworth mess hall, Rhodes sat with a group of other new inmates. The conversation turned to the offenses that had brought each of them to Leavenworth. Around the table it went: one had beat his commanding officer to death with his fists; another had taken a tire iron to a motorpool-sergeant's head. To Rhodes's innocent ears each crime was more unbelievably lurid than the last, and by the time it came to his own turn, stealing a suit of clothes he had not really stolen) seemed not nearly good enough. Rhodes stammered through the story purposely omitting his innocence, but the omission did not forestall the chorus of ridicule, and Rhodes went back to his cell determined to work up a more dramatic version of the crime he had not committed. "It wasn't like I really began to believe the things I was saying about myself, but even if you don't believe them, you start thinking about yourself a little differently anyway."

For a few weeks Rhodes did nothing but sit in a six-foot by eight-foot cell, furnished only with a cot, a sink, and a toilet, and wonder about whether it was preferable to be an innocent laughingstock or a make-believe hard case who was one of the boys. He never did decide.

"After you sit there for a week or so you stop thinking about anything except what you have to do to get out—even for five minutes. So then they start coming around and asking you if you want to work, and by that time you're happy to shovel shit or anything else they want you to do. So the first place they take you is straight to Death Row. They tell you you're gonna clean up the room with the electric chair. But, when you get there, you see that damn place don't need any cleaning. They just want you to have a good look at the furniture. And when you figure *that* out, it just makes it worse. You know they're fucking with your mind, but there ain't a damn thing you can do about it."

Because of his previous service record and the classification of his offense, Rhodes was eligible for a program under which first-time offenders were effectively paroled to active duty after serving one half of their sentences. Convinced by both the furniture in Death Row and by a tough, paternal long-timer that Leavenworth was not the place to be one of the boys, Rhodes applied to the Bureau of Military Personnel for Retraining and Reassignment.

The selection process involved a review of his service and prison records and several interviews with army psychologists. "I guess it was during those interviews that I figured out how much Leavenworth had changed me. Like, this one psychologist was a black dude who came on super-cool. He'd tell you to relax, make yourself at home, and then he'd toss you a pack of cigarettes and talk to you like you were just two old friends kicking it around. Now the old me would have fallen for it because basically I was used to trusting people. But in a place like Leavenworth you kind of tend to get over being stupid like that.

"So this dude looks down at my folder and says he sees I'm from Detroit, and he starts going on about what a great town Detroit is, and how many friends he's got there, and how he just happened to spend his last leave there, and what a bitch of a time he had down on Hastings Street—all this great weed and all these women, and all that kind of business.

"Well, I never hung out on Hastings Street, but I knew about it all right. It used to be the strip, the place you could get just about anything you wanted. But I also knew Hastings Street didn't exist any more. They tore it down to build the Chrysler Freeway. So here this dude's telling me about what he got on Hastings Street and I know damn well if he'd been hanging out on Hastings Street, the only thing he's going to get is run the hell over.

"So, right then I finally figure out that he's just trying to get me to tell him that I'm some kind of jive-ass nigger who knows all about Hastings Street—so then he can toss me back in my cell to rot for another six months. And the thing is, if I hadn't been watching out for something and I hadn't known about that freeway, I'd probably have been just about dumb enough to fall for it."

His lesson learned, Rhodes told the psychologists what he thought they wanted to hear and was eventually accepted for retraining and reassignment. His sentence was reduced, his dishonorable discharge rescinded conditionally, pending successful completion of his parole, and after thirty days of training that he claims "made Basic look like a Sunday School picnic," Rhodes was reassigned to active duty as a truck driver for the Army Chemical Corps installation at Fort McClellan, Alabama.

More than relieved to be quit of Leavenworth, Rhodes soon discovered that McClellan was a classic case of progressing from the frying pan to the fire. Rhodes arrived at Fort McClellan during the spring of 1963, at about the same time Jim Jones was returning from Brazil to find the country caught up in a frenzy of civil-rights activity. Most of that activity was focused in the South, where, under pressure from the federal courts and the national media, public facilities such as schools, buses, and restaurants were in the process of being desegregated. In rural Alabama white resistance had already claimed several lives, one in Anniston, a town of about thirty thousand about ten miles from Fort McClellan. If Odell Rhodes had set out to educate himself about the color of his skin, he could hardly have chosen a better—or worse—place to being.

"Alabama," he remembers, "was kind of a shock to me."

Growing up in Detroit he had lived in a peacefully integrated neighborhood. Many of his school friends had been white, and even during his summers in South Carolina he had never been acutely conscious of the color of his skin. Although he noticed that white neighbors rarely came up the path to his grandfather's house, they did, at least, stop occasionally to pass the time of day at the front gate, and, as far as Rhodes could tell, his gruff old grandfather had no more use for most of his black neighbors than the white ones. The first stirring of racial consciousness he remembers dates to his last summer in South Carolina, in 1955. That July, a mentally retarded fourteen-year-old black from Chicago, Emmet Till, visiting family in a small Mississippi town, had been lynched, allegedly for making sexual advances to a white woman. Rhodes remembers his family discussing the incident with sighs and headshakes he did not understand, but being fourteen and a visitor from the North himself as well as being acutely, pubescently aware of women, what had happened to Emmet Till frightened him. For the rest of the summer, he remembers being very careful not to let his eyes rest on any human being who happened to be white and female.

Excluding his Emmet Till nightmares, however, Rhodes claims

that when he arrived at Fort McClellan, he had never paid any particular attention to the color of his skin. Fort McClellan changed all that. The day Rhodes reported for duty the conversation in his new barracks was about a black soldier who had been dragged from his car and beaten half to death in a small town near the base, Anniston. As far as anyone could tell, the reason for the beating was that the soldier had been seen earlier in the day with a white woman in his car. The woman was the wife of another soldier whom the black soldier had volunteered to drop off at the town's railroad station.

The first time Rhodes himself ventured into Anniston he wandered into a liquor store partitioned down the middle with one door labeled "Colored" and one "White." He was genuinely shocked. A few weeks later on his way back from Anniston in a borrowed car, he had his introduction to a rural Southern sheriff. He was pulled over, frisked and told to "get your black ass back on that base in ten minutes, or I'll shoot it." Rhodes started toward the base, ten miles away, with the sheriff close behind him and an uncomfortable choice: either he broke a speed limit or he broke a time limit. Either way, he wound up in jail. Sweating, shaking, with tears of frustration running down his face, he was saved by a little-used gate at the near end of the base, opened that day for a construction project. Back in the barracks, he discovered that the time-limit/speed-limit game was a local favorite virtually every black soldier in the company had been invited to play at one time or another.

The situation did not improve. Rhodes's first summer in Alabama, 1963, also happened to be the first summer of sustained civil-rights activity in Alabama, a summer in which civil-rights workers from all over the country, led by Martin Luther King, organized a series of marches, sit-ins, and boycotts in Birmingham, Montgomery, and Mobile. They were not received warmly, and throughout the state feelings about blacks were anything but friendly.

In addition to his truck-driving duties Rhodes was assigned that summer to an Honor Guard providing military burials, chiefly to what was becoming an increasing trickle of Viet Nam war fatalities. One particularly hot summer Sunday the Honor Guard traveled to a funeral in a small town near Gadsden, Alabama, a hundred-mile roundtrip on dusty country roads. As they were forming their lines in front of the small church, Rhodes noticed a mourner arguing strenuously about something with the unit's military chaplain. Although he could not hear what they were saying, he understood immediately what the problem was: the family of the dead soldier did not want the five black members of the Honor Guard to enter the church. Rhodes watched the chaplain shrug and shake his head. The soldiers filed back on the bus.

"A lot of people felt, what the hell, what's the difference. They can bury him themselves. But I felt a little different. Hell, it's Sunday, it's about a hundred degrees, I've been on a bus for two hours—and here's this cracker telling me I can't come inside his fucking church. Well, I got a hate on; I wanted to bury that soldier and then I wanted to bury the rest of them too."

That evening Rhodes took his rifle to the rifle range and fired off several hundred shots. A chronically poor shot—he had not even qualified with a rifle during basic training—he was not a regular at the rifle range. "I just wanted to get it out of my system so when I looked at that target I was imagining it was George Wallace's face. It felt real good."

That September several young children were killed in the bombing of a black church in Birmingham. With racial tempers at the boiling point the Eighty-second Airborne Division, an elite combat unit, was sent to Fort McClellan to provide a quick federal response in the event of widespread civil disturbance. Fort McClellan itself was placed on full ready alert, and Rhodes's company was assigned to provide support services, if and when the airborne troops were called to Birmingham. The Friday following the bombing, Rhodes and three other soldiers from his company were sent to Anniston on a routine errand. On their way back, they stopped at a restaurant frequented by army personnel. Still on ready alert, their weapons, M-16 automatic rifles, were locked in their Jeep. While they ate, a group of locals entered the restaurant, spotted the black soldiers and loudly demanded that they leave. As they approached the soldiers, Rhodes put down his fork and looked across the table at another black soldier. Their eyes met and Rhodes knew that the same thought had crossed both of their minds.

"All we had to do was get up, walk outside to the Jeep, pick up our weapons, and waste those assholes right on the spot. I was to the point where I wanted to do it. If they could kill babies, I could kill them."

While the manager slowly herded the white locals away from the two black soldiers, Rhodes sat rigidly immobile, seething with anger and desperately afraid, not of the confrontation, but of what he had been prepared to do.

"After that I pretty much stopped going into town altogether. I didn't want to do anything I was going have to pay for the rest of my life. You know, there you are, wearing a uniform and you know if we ever go to war, you got to protect these assholes. It wasn't a question of wanting to live with them or wanting to marry somebody's sister, or anything like that. You just got damn tired of being harassed and not being able to do a damn thing about it."

In December, after the assassination of John Kennedy, Rhodes decided he had to leave the South. "It seemed to me like Kennedy was somebody who wanted to help black people, and even he wasn't safe in the South, so I just wanted out. I didn't care where—just out." He applied for a posting to Communication's Lineman's School, a posting he knew from scuttlebut in the barracks would take him away from the South. A month later he received his orders, but the army, in its own mysterious way, had decided to send him not to Lineman's School but Radio Repair School, and the worst part was that Radio Repair School happened to be located at Fort Benning, Georgia, a scant eighty miles from Fort McClellan, eighty almost due south, just over the Alabama-Georgia state line.

It turned out that Rhodes enjoyed Radio Repair School, and when he completed the twelve-week course, he applied for an overseas posting and looked forward to practicing his new skill in some exotic, faraway place. Once again, however, the army with its uncanny knack for giving a GI exactly what he doesn't want sent him back to Fort McClellan—to drive a truck again. With his well-practiced shrug of resignation Rhodes moved back to Fort McClellan, filed another request for reassignment, and resolved to stay close to the base in the meanwhile.

Despite its drawbacks exile in Fort McClellan had its compensations. In addition to the Chemical Corps installation the base also housed the army's major WAC training center in the South, and, since single women outnumbered single men two to one, staying close to the base was something many soldiers did by choice, quite happily.

"It was," says Rhodes, "like shooting fish in a barrel. Everybody with any sense played the field. Me, I fell in love." The object of his affections was a nineteen-year-old enlistee from Natchez, Mississippi, Paulette Blackton. "I think it was the way she walked. If she was walking with ten other women, no matter how pretty they were, she was the one you'd notice."

Rhodes and Paulette Blackton met one spring-feverish evening in May at one of the base's social clubs and married a month later when she completed her basic training. "It happened like that to a lot of people down there," Rhodes remembers. "The day we got married they had a line going around the corner at the chapel there. The South can be so damn pretty in the spring. It's easy to fall in love. Like, no matter how much I hated Fort McClellan, I'll never forget how good everything looked that spring and the way everything smelled—even the motorpool smelled like flowers."

Paulette Rhodes remained at Fort McClellan through the following summer taking a training course for office clerks, but, since the base had no housing for married enlisted personnel and since Rhodes would not move off the base, the newlyweds continued to live in separate barracks. Late in August, when her training ended, Paulette Rhodes received orders to report to Fort Ord, California. Rhodes knew that the army had a policy of honoring requests for matching assignments for married couples, so he put in a request to be transferred to Fort Ord with his wife, and the two of them began making plans to begin married life in earnest in California.

Once again, however, fate—or Rhodes's own allergy to success—intervened. One morning, quite early, Rhodes awoke to a loud Southern voice screaming "all kinds of black niggers" at a soldier a few bunks away. The voice belonged to a white mess sergeant Rhodes knew only slightly, but what he did know, he did not like. The sergeant had had grown up in a small town near Fort McClellan where, as Rhodes put it, "Those crackers must have owned that whole damn town because everything there was Cracker's Garage, Cracker's General Store, Cracker's this and Cracker's that. And that's the way he seemed to me—a damn redneck cracker who was so used to treating blacks like dogs he probably didn't even know he was doing it."

The object of the sergeant's wrath, a friend of Rhodes assigned to the company mess, had overslept that morning and Rhodes was hearing the result. Without, according to Rhodes, knowing why he was doing it—or even what he was doing—Rhodes jumped out of bed and attacked in a wild fury. At the sight of an enraged Rhodes bearing down in his underwear the sergeant chose discretion. "Nothing really happened," Rhodes says, "he ran, and I got in one good kick at his fat white ass." One good kick was enough. The sergeant reported that he had been struck by an enlisted man, and Rhodes was called before the company commander and notified of the charges against him. For his part, Rhodes was still in a fighting mood. "I didn't give a damn if they court-martialed me or not, but, if they were going to court-martial me, I told them they damn well better do something to him too."

Within the week Rhodes received new orders. But not for Fort Ord. He was, as he had requested six months before, being assigned as a radio operator—in Korea. "Maybe," he says, "they thought they were doing me some kind of favor. Or, maybe they finally got it through their thick heads that if they skinned me they'd have to take a bite out of that cracker too. I don't know, and like I say, I didn't even care. I would have done the same thing again in a minute—and I'd kick his fat ass today if I saw him on the street. As far as going back to Korea was concerned, I'd have rather gone to California—but any place that wasn't Fort McClellan was okay by me."

With his wife already in California and a twenty-one-day leave before reporting for transport to Korea, Rhodes hurried to California for a crash course in married life. Paulette had found a small efficiency apartment near the base and the two of them made a desperate attempt to settle into an instant domestic routine. "What it amounted to," Rhodes laughs, "is that she worked, and I stayed home and did the cleaning and the cooking. We didn't think of it as Women's Lib—the thing was she outranked me; she was a Spec 4 and I was only a PFC.

Although three weeks of married life did not seem nearly enough to Rhodes, he was grateful enough to have had them and enough of a soldier to accept the thirteen-month, ten-thousand-mile separation as a fact of life. If the army had taught him anything, it was that a soldier plays the hand he is dealt, and—all things considered—Rhodes did not feel he had been dealt a particularly bad hand this time. "Leaving my wife was tough, but I wasn't unhappy about going to Korea. To me Korea was a lot better than every place I'd been since."

His new assignment turned out to be only a few miles away from the first one, but this time, instead of an artillery unit, he was assigned to an infantry company patrolling the DMZ. It was dangerous and enervating duty. "It wasn't supposed to be combat, but in the time I was there my unit took casualties every week, and we lost a few, too—more than a few."

North Korean units also patrolled the bleak, unmarked hills of the DMZ, and, when contact was made, the rule on both sides was shoot first and ask questions later. Shooting at nothing was not uncommon, and shooting at a friendly patrol more common than the army liked to admit. As a radio operator Rhodes was responsible for relaying information about the locations of both friendly and hostile units in the area to the patrol commander.

"They kept reminding me that my first mistake might be my last, but I didn't need any reminding. It was scary as hell out there—especially at night."

After a night patrol Rhodes would often sleep all day and awake just in time for a hot meal and a check of his equipment. He remembers very little free time and very few excursions to the GI villages in the area. Aside from patrols, sleep, and maintaining his equipment he occupied himself chiefly by writing letters to his wife and crossing off the days to the end of his tour.

He had crossed off nearly nine months, when, one morning—totally out of the blue as far as Rhodes was concerned—mail call brought a letter from Paulette announcing that she wanted to divorce him. Rhodes sighs and shakes his head when he remembers that letter: "It was another one of those times, like when my mother died or when I went to Leavenworth. I only had a few months left and all I was looking forward to was going home. It seemed like just when everything was finally going to be okay . . . Well, anyway, I didn't know what to do. To show you where I was at, I was so shook up I even went to the chaplain."

Rhodes can not recall the chaplain's advice, but, unless it was to go out and get roaring drunk, he did not follow it. Instead, he began drinking, steadily and heavily. In the weeks that followed he drifted into a crowd of other hard-drinking soldiers most of whom shared not only a taste for oblivion but a serious distaste for army discipline. Whether as a cause or as a result Rhodes's own disillusionment with army life burst to the surface. Justly or not, he began to blame the army for the breakup of his marriage. "It was like they couldn't even give us a chance. She had to be there, I had to be in Korea—the whole damn thing just didn't seem very fair."

A barrage of calls and letters to California provided no comfort. Paulette was determined to have her divorce. To Rhodes's pleading for, at very least, an explanation she turned a deaf ear. "I knew I had to accept it, but not knowing why, what had happened, that was the hardest part.

A few weeks later a promotion Rhodes had expected went to another soldier—a white—instead. "That was the last fucking straw. I just went on the nut for a few days. To tell you the truth, I don't even remember what I did, but I know what I was trying to do. I was trying to tell the army to go fuck itself."

The army replied with a court-martial. Although the occasion had been Rhodes's binge, the specific charges against him referred to being under the influence of marijuana and opium while on duty, charges the army had been preparing against several of his malcontended comrades for several months. For the next sixty days he sat in pre-trial confinement with an almost certain dishonorable discharge hanging over his head. However, when the case finally came to trial, Rhodes, for a change, was dealt an ace. "All the evidence was about drugs and how the rest of these guys were always showing up for duty stoned. But I hadn't been messing around with drugs and nobody could say I had been. I remember the judge looking at my record and asking my C.O. how come, if I was such a rotten soldier, he hadn't written up anything against me the whole time I was there."

Rhodes was acquitted, transferred to another unit for the six weeks remaining in his tour, and then shipped back home, to Fort Gordon, Georgia. Primarily a training center for officer candidates set in the lush rolling hills near Augusta, Fort Gordon had a reputation for being easy duty, and Rhodes's assignment, to the communications training program as an instructor's aide, involved nothing more strenuous than setting up and maintaining the electronic gear used in classroom demonstrations.

With time to think, Rhodes brooded about his marriage. Despite a barrage of letters and phone calls Paulette refused to see him and—what disturbed him more—refused to satisfy his need to know what had happened between them. Although he gradually accepted the fact that there was nothing more he could do to save his marriage, he promised himself that he would never sign the divorce papers until she explained why.

That fall of 1966, at about the time Jim Jones and his handful of followers from Indiana settled in Redwood Valley to await the end of the world, Rhodes again applied to the army for a change of scenery. A few weeks later he was summoned to the company clerk's office. Assuming his new orders had come through, he bounded up the stairs of company headquarters. What had come through, however, was not a new assignment. It was a telegram from his aunt in Detroit. His younger brother, Kenneth Rhodes, had been killed in Viet Nam.

Rhodes had not laid eyes on his brother in ten years, not, in fact, since their mother's funeral, and he had no idea he had joined the army too. Barely recovered from losing his wife, Rhodes was staggered by the death of his brother. He began to brood—and to drink—and to relive the same feelings of loss he had experienced when his mother died. Like the mother he had never had a chance to know, he had now lost a brother he would never have the chance to know.

When the body came back from Viet Nam, Rhodes drove to Greenville for another funeral; once again, a funeral his father did not attend. "I remember that cemetery, burying him with a bunch of relatives I hardly knew. It was a rainy, windy day and I kept thinking to myself, what the hell is it with me anyway? Every time I even think about getting close to somebody, they either die or split."

He returned to Fort Gordon and waited impatiently for his new orders: "Anywhere—I didn't give a damn where." Within the month, they arrived. The army had decided to send him to Viet Nam. Rhodes claims that had there been any laughter left in him, he would have let it out. He knew that, as a matter of law, the army could not send the sole surviving sibling of a war fatality to a combat assignment. "They fucked up—that's what they do best." Despite the army's mistake, however, one word from Rhodes would have kept him out of the war. He said nothing, partly, he believes, because there was still enough soldier in him to want to see a war and partly, too, because he felt that avoiding combat by virtue of his brother's death was an act of cowardice, of disrespect to his brother's memory, of betrayal.

The same night he received his orders for Viet Nam, he took out the divorce papers his wife sent him and signed them. "All of a sudden it just seemed kind of stupid to make such a big thing out of it. I don't know how to describe it, but I really felt all right about going to Viet Nam—like, what the hell difference did it make anyway? It wasn't like I was leaving anything behind, or like anybody gave a good goddamn if I went or not. So, what the hell—why not?"

With the three weeks of leave the army gave to soldiers assigned to combat duty in Viet Nam, Rhodes decided to visit his aunt and uncle in Detroit. The Aikens had moved since Rhodes had last visited them two years before. They were living in a comfortable brick house in the Boston-Edison district on the west side of Detroit. Boston-Edison was an unusually pleasant neighborhood of quiet tree-lined streets and spacious, old houses, and Rhodes spent much of his leave walking around the neighborhood with his three younger cousins. He decided that if he survived Viet Nam, he would move back to Detroit, find a job, and settle down. The combat assignment would take him to the end of his enlistment, and he had already made up his mind that there was no point in re-enlisting again. With his record, he was going nowhere in the army. Except, of course, to Viet Nam.

He arrived in Saigon in the midst of the army's 1967 spring build-up, when as many as a thousand soldiers a day were passing through Bien Hoa airport. "Viet Nam," Rhodes says, "was like another planet. Like at the airport, there were mobs of guys like me, just off the plane, and they weren't doing anything but thinking about getting a weapon; and then there were mobs of guys getting ready to go home, and they were all stoned or drunk, laughing and making cracks about wood boxes."

After a few days in Saigon, Rhodes was assigned to the 11th Armored Cavalry Regiment at Long Kao Base Camp about sixty miles from Saigon. His company's principle assignment was to protect supply convoys on the main highway to Saigon. With its eight-inch, self-propelled howitzers, Rhodes's unit could do some of its protecting from right inside the base, and on some days the only evidence the unit was doing anything at all was the slow, whirring procession of the howitzers as they moved a few inches at a time following a convoy several miles away. At other times, however, the unit sought out the enemy by driving slowly down the road and offering itself as a target.

"Basically, though," Rhodes remembers, "it was more dangerous inside the camp than on the road. If you were on patrol, the worst that usually happened was some light arms fire from the jungle and we were normally in armored personnel carriers. We had a company commander who was smart enough not to send us out into the jungle. We'd just stop on the road and throw everything we had into the jungle for a few minutes. I don't know if we ever hit anybody, but we didn't take too many casualties ourselves."

Inside the camp was a different story. Surrounded by dense jungle and overgrown rubber plantations that provided perfect cover for snipers, Long Kao was a shooting gallery at night. A soldier's only protection was to stay out of groups and in the shadows. For entertainment, a soldier found the darkest spot available, lit up a stick of marijuana, and watched the flashing lightshow supplied by the helicopters that patrolled the base's perimeter. "They kept posting these movie schedules," Rhodes remembers, "but they never showed any of them—I mean with sitting all together in front of a big, white screen, you might as well just shoot yourself."

According to Rhodes, the soldiers of Long Kao rarely talked about the war they were fighting. They did, however, talk about the "other" war—the war taking place back home on the streets of cities like Newark and Detroit during the long, hot summer of 1967. The Detroit riot in particular occupied Rhodes's attention, especially after he learned it had broken out just a few blocks away from his uncle's new house. "Every black soldier in my company had something to say about what was going on at home, and most of it was pretty hard-core stuff. The way most of them felt, they'd rather have been shooting at the pigs than the Viet Cong. I used to think about what I would have done if I'd been in Detroit that summer. It bothered me, because I was to the point—after all that time in the South—where I could have part of it. And one thing was for damn sure: when you heard about the national guard driving tanks through your own neighborhood, you sure as hell didn't feel like fighting a bunch of people who never did shit to you."

After Rhodes had completed about half of his thirteen-month combat assignment, around Christmas, the army finally discovered that he was not supposed to be in Viet Nam at all. He was immediately taken off combat assignments and put to work in a radio repair shop. A few weeks later, he was sent out of the war zone, back to Korea for the third time. Despite a tense month after the North Koreans impounded the navy spy ship, *The Pueblo*, Korea seemed like a vacation paradise next to Viet Nam, and Rhodes occupied himself with women, rice, whiskey, and his short-timer's calendar—a paint-by-numbers sketch of a voluptuous woman divided into sixty sections strategically numbered from the extremities to the end of the lucky soldier's tour.

Early in May, 1968, he flew from Seoul to Fort Lewis, Washington, collected his honorable discharge and his mustering-out pay, and boarded a plane to Detroit. After eight years, two court-martials, and one conviction, Odell Rhodes was a civilian again—and happy to be one.

6

The Streets
of Detroit

June, 1968. America, the once Happy Republic, was in a state of collective shock. The war in Viet Nam had divided the country, and opposition to his war policies had forced an incumbent president, Lyndon Johnson, to withdraw from his re-election campaign. Martin Luther King, Jr., the most important black leader in the history of the republic, was dead, felled by an assassin's bullet on the balcony of a motel in Memphis, Tennessee. Robert Kennedy, running for the Democratic party's presidential nomination on an antiwar, pro–civil rights platform, was also dead, gunned down on the eve of the California primary. On college campuses and in black communities throughout the country, the two divisive, emotional issues—the war and civil rights—had galvanized segments of the population which had never before been active in national politics.

In California, Jim Jones's Redwood Valley People's Temple was growing rapidly, his apocalyptic vision of the future validated every day by the morning newspaper. Impressed by the range of Jones's appeal across racial and class lines in a climate of political polarization, Tim Stoen had just joined Jones's movement, and the young preacher and the young lawyer were beginning to wonder if together they might just do what the politicians of the day seemed unable to do: lead the country to peaceful social change.

In Detroit, Odell Rhodes's aunt and uncle, the Aikens, treated their returning nephew to a hero's welcome: his aunt cried, his cousins demanded war stories, and even his uncle, for whom a day without work was an offense against common decency, threw an arm around his shoulder and told him to take it easy for a few weeks. Rhodes took his uncle's advice and spent his first few weeks as a civilian catching up with relatives, old friends, television, and sleep. He walked the same streets he had walked during his leave before Viet Nam and stared with disbelief at the burnt-out, boarded-up buildings left over from the previous summer's riot. Everywhere he went, people talked about the riots, the tanks rumbling up and down Boston Boulevard, the assassinations of Martin Luther King and Robert Kennedy, and the angry, polarized politics that would culminate in the chaos of the Chicago Democratic Convention later that summer. He saw Black Panther posters with Bobby Seale and Huey Newton brandishing rifles and graffiti suggesting a variety of final solutions for the nation's newest political phenomenon— Rhodes's old target-practice fantasy object—George Wallace. Conquering hero or not, Rhodes began to feel as if he had missed the real war.

With the Aikens providing free room and board, there was no great pressure on Rhodes to look for work, but one morning he happened to overhear his cousin's husband mention that the Detroit Police Department was conducting a campaign to recruit black policemen. Although Rhodes had never considered a career in blue, the more he thought about it, the more the idea made sense to him. He felt he was ready to settle down and if his military experience had prepared him for anything, it just might be the police. Besides, as he puts it, "I figured police work would be people work, and that's what I wanted."

Even with a court-martial on his service record, Rhodes was confident that his honorable discharge would satisfy the recruiters that his career in the army had been successful and he believed he stood a good chance of landing a job. He filed an application, and a week or so later he was called for an interview. Although the interviewer did, in fact, pass over his service career with a quick nod at the honorable discharge, he began badgering Rhodes about whether or not he had ever been arrested as a civilian. "At the time," Rhodes remembers, "I had never been in any trouble with the police at all, not even a speeding ticket, but this guy just wouldn't let up. I guess he couldn't believe a black man could have survived twenty-six years without getting his ass burnt at least one time. I felt he wouldn't ask those questions to a white and, frankly, it pissed me off." Finally, he stormed out of the interview. His cousin's husband, subjected to a similar line of questioning, kept his cool and was accepted to the force. "Maybe he was just trying to see where my boiling point was, and I guess at that point, it was pretty damn low. It's still kind of hard for me to believe how close I came to being a cop."

But, finding other work in Detroit in 1968, a record year for the auto industry, was no problem. Soon after the police interview, Rhodes was hired on the spot at the huge Dodge Main plant on the east side of the city. The work—bolting fenders on Dodge Darts—was not demanding, but it was monotonous, the same three bolts in the same three holes several hundred times a day. "Monday morning they came across kind of slow, but by Friday afternoon, it was like trying to work on the freeway. You'd get one, maybe two bolts in, chalk the ones you missed, and get the hell out of the way for the next one. You start feeling like you're part of the machine, and not the best part either."

A few months later Rhodes heard about another job, one off the assembly line punching holes in an automatic transmission assembly with a drill press, on the night shift of a Ford Transmission plant just outside Detroit in an industrial suburb, Livonia. He took a day off from Dodge Main and was again hired on the spot. About the time he changed jobs Rhodes moved out of the Aikens' and into his own apartment a few blocks away, near Boston Boulevard.

He quickly made friends with a carpool of fellow workers who lived in the neighborhood and also commuted to Livonia for the night shift. The carpool's ride home around midnight often turned into a night on the town with stops at a string of clubs and bars on the route between Livonia and the west side of Detroit. One favorite stop was a tavern near a Michigan Bell office where telephone operators unwinded after their night shifts. The telephone contingent tended to be predominantly female, and on a good night, one thing might lead to another, sometimes outside in the back seat of a car. One such night, in the backseat of a car, as one thing was leading to another, an information operator introduced Rhodes to heroin, in the form of "penny caps"—gelatin capsules broken in half and snorted.

Rhodes soon discovered that penny caps were everywhere, even—

in fact, especially—at work, a discovery that shocked him at the time, but should probably not surprise anyone who has ever wondered why a built-in-Detroit car so often seems to give evidence of having been put together by workers with something more important than quality control on their minds.

Quite innocently at first, Rhodes became a social snorter, but as his social life continued to improve, he began to realize he was spending a substantial part of his paycheck on what he was not yet quite convinced was a habit. He was not alone, and on the way home from work one night, with three similarly strapped co-workers, an idea for a quick moonlight source of income dawned on one of them. Before the night was over, the four of them had broken into a house and stolen a television set.

Burglary soon became a regular after-hours routine. Once or twice a week, on the way home from work after midnight, the carpool rang a random doorbell in a prosperous neighborhood. If someone answered, it was a mistake; if no one answered, it was another burglary. Eventually, Rhodes and his friends made contact with a professional fence and began burglarizing on contract—filling orders for televisions or stereo equipment from homes selected and cased by the fence. On one occasion, as Rhodes was climbing the stairs of a house the fence had guaranteed to be empty, he heard a *basso profoundo* belting out "Love Is a Many Splendored Thing" in the shower. He was shaken. ("I had enough sense to know somebody could have just as easily been sitting at the top of those steps with a shotgun.") But, shaken or not, he could simply not afford to give up his moonlight income.

Throughout the winter, he continued to work his shift at the transmission plant, visit the Aikens every Sunday afternoon, and think of himself as the average working stiff—while snorting heroin and rapidly becoming a professional burglar at the same time. As far as Rhodes was concerned, heroin and burglary were simply two—essentially unrelated—forms of recreation. "It might sound strange, but even though I was using most of the money to buy drugs, I didn't really think of it like that. They were just two things I did—two things that seemed kind of exciting at the time. It was like sometimes I did a little overtime work, and sometimes I got high."

Early in 1969 Rhodes moved again. Even with his cut from the burglaries, he had fallen behind on his rent, so he moved in with one of his friends at work. For a month or so, he tried slowing down—fewer midnight excursions, less heroin. But one cold, winter day, broke, bored, and strung-out, he decided he needed some entertainment. With no money in his pocket, he simply loaded up his roommate's television set, in the roommate's own car, and drove it downtown to the fence.

"It was," he admits, "about the worst mistake I ever made. When someone offers you friendship, you either take it or you don't, but you don't fuck it over."

Realizing what he had done, Rhodes spent the next few days at another friend's house. Sunday afternoon, however, Rhodes was walking down Boston Boulevard when his roommate pulled up beside him. The two argued for a few minutes, and finally the roommate stormed back to the car, took a carbine from the backseat and threatened Rhodes. Rhodes grabbed the barrel of the gun; they struggled; and Rhodes was shot in his right thigh, just below the hip.

Four months and six operations later, his leg had been cleaned of bone fragments, broken, set, rebroken, set, rebroken again, set again, stapled, pinned, and reconstructed; and Rhodes had still not walked a step. Finally, he developed gangrene and was again taken to surgery after being told the leg might have to be amputated. It was not, but months of traction followed, and it was not until early fall, when, still encased in a half-body cast, he was released from the hospital.

He moved back in with the Aikens and tried to take stock of his prospects. He did not like what he saw. For one thing, as Rhodes puts it, "If I wasn't a junkie when I went in the hospital, I sure as hell was when I got out." For six months, he had been on a rotating regimen of pain killers "most of them a whole hell of a lot stronger than what you get on the street." Although his doctors had gradually weaned him onto non-addictive morphine substitutes, Rhodes left the hospital convinced he was already having withdrawal pains, and the first afternoon the Aikens left him alone, he hobbled downtown on his crutches and picked up a syringe and a supply of street heroin.

Whenever the moment was—if there was a moment—when the monkey took up permanent residence on Rhodes's back, the weeks immediately after his release from the hospital were probably his last, best chance to shake the monkey loose. He knew that if he confessed his habit the Aikens would be sympathetic and do whatever they could for him, and shooting up in their bathroom was making him feel horribly guilty; but, in the end, he could never quite bring himself to talk to them.

"At the time, I didn't know anything about drug programs—and I didn't even really know what I was getting myself into. I knew I was in trouble, but I was so ashamed and confused about everything, when it came down to it, what I wanted most was just to be by myself."

Although still unable to walk without crutches, he found himself a room downtown and set out to be by himself. Money, for the moment, was not a problem. Because he had been working at Ford at the time of the shooting, he was covered by a union insurance policy that paid a weekly disability benefit. In addition, during his stay at the Aikens, he had stumbled on a gold mine, an unexpected bonanza on the thin line between working and stealing. Waiting for a friend in front of a downtown bank one afternoon, he had discovered—to his astonishment—that one look at Rhodes with his cart and crutches was enough to send most people digging into their pockets.

"I think they figured I got hurt in the war, so I started hanging out downtown in front of different banks, and when someone asked me what happened to me, I'd say I just got out of the army. I was making a hundred a day just about every day, and turning it all into drugs."

For a few happy months, Rhodes worked the street during the day and spent his nights shooting heroin in his room. Just a few weeks before Christmas, however, he developed a blood clot in his leg and went back to the hospital for another operation. His bones had knitted enough in the meantime so the cast was not replaced, and for the next few months he stayed in the hospital relearning the art of walking. By early April he was able to drag himself around well enough to be released from the hospital. Although relieved to be more or less in one piece again, he was not unconflicted about facing the streets without his cast. "I tried everything I could think of to get them to put another one on, preferably one with a zipper."

With his gold mine shut down and his leg not nearly strong enough yet to go back to a factory job, he began parking cars a few nights a week at a local institution called the "Twenty Grand," an improbable blend of nightclub, bowling alley, and motel, which, at the time, was a center of black night-life in Detroit. Through the parking lot of the "Twenty Grand" passed a thick slice of inner-city Detroit, including its underworld. They were the big tippers, the ones with the block-long street cruisers, and Rhodes not only parked their cars, he cultivated their friendship and began to emulate their ways. Up until that time, he remembers, "I was into the drugs, but I wasn't really into the rest of it—the hustling drugs and hanging around with other junkies part. When it's just the drugs, you still got a chance, if you know enough to get help, but once you're part of the scene, it kind of takes over on you. Everybody you know is in the same place you are, and you never even think about people living any other way. You forget anything else even exists."

Rhodes's new circle of friends included pimps, drug pushers, professional thieves, and—especially—con men. "I was always a pretty good talker, so I guess I just naturally fell into that." With one of his new friends for a guide he began making the rounds learning the trade from a master. "Basically, it's really only two things—drugs and sex. You hang out in the right places and, believe me, you don't have any problem finding people who are looking for drugs or sex. And, once you find them, the only thing you have to do then is talk real sweet and convince them you can get it for them—the best, whatever they want."

Rhodes admits that the first time he witnessed a classic "Murphy" con game, he could hardly believe what he was seeing. "Here's some reasonable together-looking dude handing over a fistful of twenties—and I could hardly fucking believe it. I mean, he didn't know the guy he's laying the money on from Adam. But that's the first lesson. If a man wants something bad enough, you can hardly help taking his money. You know what they say—you can't cheat an honest man? Well, these people, they want something they damn well *know* they're not supposed to have, so, if they think you can make it nice and safe and easy to get it, they *want* to trust you. Hell, they can't wait to let you do their shit for them."

Once a victim was hooked, Rhodes discovered, knocking off the money was the easy part. The Murphy man simply took the victim to a building deep in the ghetto, a three- or four-story building with backstairs and a door leading to the street. The Murphy man then pretended to knock on a door and carry on a short conversation with a madame or pusher inside. After assuring the victim the women or the drugs were right there waiting to be had, he collected the money, walked back down the hall toward the same door—then took off down the backstairs, outside and away.

"Sometimes, especially if they're looking for sex, you can even talk them out of their watches or jewelry. You tell them it's kind of a private club, and since you're not going to have your clothes on, everybody leaves their valuables up front. You might even carry a little receipt book and write them out a receipt—what the hell difference does it make?"

Hanging out in the topless bars and discos around Twelfth and Woodward and Cass Corridor, Rhodes gradually began to know the bartenders and the working girls. Sitting at the bar, he would watch for "popping eyeballs," then, strike up a conversation. When the conversation turned to the dancers, Rhodes would shake his head knowingly. "That ain't nothing. It's the private action that's really something else." After a few more drinks, during which he would make a point of chatting with the bartenders and waitresses, Rhodes would offer to take his new friends to "a little private club."

Says Rhodes: "The thing most people don't understand is that hooking a mark is fun. There's no pattern to it, you have to use your head; you have to be thinking all the time. You're always trying to stay a step ahead of them and that means you're firing on all your cylinders. You learn all kinds of little tricks. For example, one thing you try to do is to get the guy to give you a few dollars to buy him a bottle, or some cigarettes, or whatever. It doesn't matter. The trick is, when you come back, you count out his change right down to the penny. And once you give a person change, nine out of ten figure you're on the level—an honest man. Then you got them. And it is a hell of a feeling. People don't understand that lots of times, you might actually work *harder* to make a buck on the streets than you would on an assembly line, but the thing about it is, on the streets, it's always *different*, every minute it's different and you're never bored."

For the drug trade, mostly composed of white suburban teenagers, Rhodes studied up on popular music, researched all the current drugs, and tried to keep a small supply of quality marijuana, hashish oil, and LSD on hand. "Mostly it was kids who wouldn't even be in my part of town if they weren't looking to buy. I'd never let on I was selling anything; I'd just strike up a conversation like we were old

buddies and then I'd lay a joint on them to take outside or down to
the bathroom, and sooner or later they'd get around to asking me if
I had any more of what I was laying on them. And when they ask,
it's all over, you got them hooked."

Hustling sex and drugs—especially sex and drugs one doesn't have
to deliver—was never the steadiest way to make a living. In dry
periods, Rhodes resorted to shoplifting, running drugs for real dealers on commission, and, on occasion, to burglary. "Nobody with a
habit can say there is something he positively will not do for money,
but after I got shot, I promised myself I would stay away from stealing. For one thing, it's too damned dangerous. I got shot and made
it, but I know more than a few people who broke into a house and
just plain got blown away. Besides, the way the law works, the difference between talking someone out of their money and taking it is
the difference between ninety days and ten years."

Nonetheless, jail did become a regular, periodic feature of
Rhodes's life—a kind of all-expenses-paid yearly vacation. His police
record lists twelve separate arrests between 1969 and 1976; however,
that total only includes occasions on which he was actually charged
with a crime. The total number of times he was hauled off the streets
is beyond both his memory and that of the Detroit Police Department.

He was convicted six times: twice on drug possession charges;
twice for Larceny by False Representation; one for Shoplifting; and
once for breaking into an automobile. With the exception of the
shoplifting charge, each of the other convictions represented a bargained plea in which Rhodes pleaded guilty in return for a reduction
of the charge from a felony to a high misdemeanor—an arrangement
that saved the state the expense of a jury trial and saved Rhodes time
and a trip to the state penitentiary. The breaking and entering conviction earned him the most time, six months. Each of the other
offenses involved either sixty or ninety days, for a grand total of 540
days—a year and a half.

His feelings about the police were basic: "I hated them. The way
I looked at it, I had no complaints when I was picked up for something I did. I never complained about that. You do it, you get
caught, you do your time. But most of the time I was arrested, it
wasn't for anything. You'd just be walking down the street, they'd

recognize you, toss you down, slap you around, and then, even if you were clean, they'd have you in and throw you in the tank. They get off on it. They like putting a gun to your head, turning the cuffs so that your hands swell up, pulling you around by your ear, elbowing you in the mouth—accidentally on purpose. You're a goddamned junkie criminal hustler. They're the law—and you know goddamned well you'd never do to a dog what they do to you."

Unpleasant as his experience of the law was, the police were not the only—or the gravest—threat to Rhodes's existence. Since his swindles almost always involved illegal sex or drugs, the victims, no matter how outraged, rarely reported the crime to the police. They did, however, sometimes decide to enforce the law themselves. Mobility was Rhodes's defense. Like most street hustlers, Rhodes moved often, from one dreary resident hotel to another, making a point never to tell anyone where he lived. If a score was big enough, he might buy a quantity of heroin and simply lock himself in his room for a few days, but usually, if he knew an enraged victim was looking for him, he simply packed up and moved to another part of town. Since the victims were usually strangers—many of them white—disappearing into the ghetto was as easy as walking around the corner and as effective as a trip around the world.

An even greater source of danger than either the police or his victims, was the heroin he shot into his own veins. Death from bad drugs (or, especially, from a "hot-shot" of unusually pure heroin) was a possibility as many times a day as Rhodes picked up his syringe.

On one occasion, Rhodes remembers sending a friend, a prostitute named Chocolate, to buy drugs for both of them. When he came to a hotel room to pick up his, he found her dead with her needle still in her arm and his bag of heroin on the floor next to her. He flushed the heroin down the toilet, covered the girl with a blanket, and promptly set off to find something less lethal for himself. "I felt bad," he says, "but I wasn't surprised. You expect it—every junkie knows that."

Death, according to Rhodes, seemed a closer presence on the streets of Detroit than in Viet Nam. "In combat, you're scared—scared shitless sometimes—but over there, at least you are always fighting it. On the streets, it's like it's part of your life; it's like you carry it around with you. You accept it. One day you see somebody, then one day they're not around anymore. You don't even think about it. A junkie's got so many ways to die, and a junkie's life really isn't any big deal."

Rhodes was often sick from bad heroin or neglecting to take care of himself; he was often on bad enough terms with somebody to make walking down the street an adventure; he has lost track of the times a gun was shoved in his face; he was always in danger of a trip to the local precinct station; but he insists that during his first few years on the street he would not have traded his life for anyone's. "Anybody who ever got off on a roller coaster ride could get off on living on the streets. You got no family, you got no time card, you got no payments to make. You do whatever the hell you feel like doing. Sometimes you're flying, sometimes you're cruising and sometimes you crash, but at least you're never bored. Whatever's happening, something else is going to happen real soon."

For him, even heroin was, in its way, a kind of liberation, as if having focused all of his dependency into a single large dependency on the drug, no other dependencies existed. As much as the effect of the heroin, he insists, the backhanded freedom it allows a junkie to care about nothing else, is a major attraction of the junkie's life. "Heroin feels good, and you always want it—but it's not because you can't stand the pain of living or some shit like that. The best thing about it is that is makes you feel like you don't need a damn thing except the feeling you have inside yourself. And the fact is, you get just as addicted to the life you're living as you do to the junk."

By the end of 1974, after six years on the street, Rhodes began to notice a change in himself. "Terminal burn-out," is the way he puts it. "Like you got holes in your clothes, holes in your arms, and holes in your head."

Lacking the energy to prowl through bars and bus stations looking for marks for his con game, Rhodes turned increasingly to petty crime for money to support his drug habit—with the predictable result. One night, crawling out of the back seat of a Cadillac with somebody else's dry cleaning under his arm, he found himself looking into the barrel of a nervous young policeman's service revolver. "He said, 'Freeze, mother-fucker'—and I was iced." Prison—six months of it—provided Rhodes with an opportunity to rest—and to think. Among the conclusions he reached was one about prison: he was determined never to go back. "The next time, it wasn't going to be DeHoCo; it was going to be the state joint. And I didn't know if I could handle it."

Gratified as the Michigan Department of Corrections might have been to know if he had a deterrent effect, rehabilitation was not exactly what Rhodes had in mind. What he needed, he decided, was a way to earn money to keep him close to drugs, but far away from the police. When his jail term ended, he looked up a friend he had made inside; a friend who worked for a big-time ghetto dealer. The friend owed him a favor. One thing led to another, and soon Rhodes was selling real drugs instead of imaginary ones.

The point was that for someone in Rhodes's position (a well-known junkie), selling real drugs was far safer than selling the imaginary ones. Big-time dealers paid big-time protection, so a dealer's runners did not worry about the law.

Predators were a far bigger problem than the police. Every afternoon, Rhodes picked up a supply of heroin worth a thousand dollars or so and every morning, he turned back the night's proceeds and his remaining inventory. At any given time, he was likely to be carrying several hundred dollars and a few days supply of heroin for the average addict. For protection, runners normally worked in pairs and in regular locations where they were more or less looked after by both the dealers' private muscle and the police.

A runner took home $125 a week in regular salary, no tax withheld, plus a daily supply of heroin. To Rhodes, it was a perfect livelihood—for a while. He began to have his doubts one afternoon when he was handed a half ounce of cocaine, along with his normal allotment of heroin. Cocaine was a drug he was even less capable of resisting than heroin, so in order to avoid doing all the cocaine himself and then "owing the man," he refused to take it. After a short discussion with the incredulous dealer, it was agreed that Rhodes's partner would handle both their allotments of cocaine.

During the night, the two of them worked the street, meeting occasionally and in the morning, Rhodes's partner offered to take Rhodes's cash and remaining drugs to check in with the dealer, a standard procedure to which Rhodes readily agreed.

A few hours later, Rhodes, innocently walking down the street, found himself surrounded by a grim-looking squad of the dealer's muscle. With a gun in his back, he was invited to take a ride, "just

like you see on television." He refused: "I figured that if they were
going to kill me, they might as well do it right there on the street in
the middle of the day with everybody looking. They probably would
have done it too, but they were waiting for the man."

By the time the dealer arrived, Rhodes had figured out what had
happened. "That dude I was working with was as big a coke freak as
I was—and he just done up all that coke and gone back and told
them I was the one who had done it."

Angry as the dealer was, Rhodes was able to remind him that he
hadn't wanted to handle the cocaine in the first place, and he eventually succeeded in convincing him that, at least, his partner's story
deserved looking into. One of the dealer's enforcers was assigned to
babysit Rhodes while the others set off to look for the partner.

After a tense night spent staring at a gun pointed in his face,
Rhodes was released the next morning. If the story sounds anticli-
mactic, it was—for Rhodes—but not for his partner. "Never saw that
dude again—in fact, nobody ever saw him again."

A few weeks later, word circulated in the street that another runner named Slim had been robbed of a day's cash of drugs. A few days
later, a revised rumor, to the effect that Slim had robbed himself,
began to circulate. Soon afterward, Rhodes happened to be loitering
on the steps of the apartment building the drug dealer used for a
headquarters. He saw the same heavies who had come after him,
leave the building with a very unhappy-looking Slim. The heavies
deposited Slim in the back seat of a car, the same car Rhodes had
refused his invitation to ride in. A few days later, a homicide detec-
tive stopped Rhodes on the street and asked him if he'd seen Slim
lately.

"Slim who?" Rhodes answered. "I don't know nobody named
Slim." Rhodes shakes his head, "It was the truth—didn't nobody
know Slim no more. His own mother wouldn't have known him—
not with five bullets in his head."

The two incidents convinced Rhodes that despite its advantages,
running drugs was "a gig that was definitely not going to end with a
gold watch and a pension. I mean, these people were perfectly happy
to waste you over a couple of hundred dollars worth of drugs—and
they weren't even worrying about whether or not they could get away
with it. Fuck, they *knew* they could get away with it. I'm not saying
every cop in the city was on their payroll, but the ones who

weren't—most of them didn't give a damn anyway; what's a dead junkie? One less to worry about, that's all."

After thinking it over, Rhodes decided to quit dealing drugs and cut his heroin consumption to a level he could support by a minimum of illegal activity on the street—some panhandling, a Murphy con now and then, and perhaps, some occasional shoplifting. "All of a sudden, everything seemed wrong to me. I guess it was kind of like an energy crisis—I felt like I couldn't take the heat, like I just couldn't keep it together anymore."

Cutting down on heroin was no great problem. As Rhodes put it, "People talk about $50 a day habits, or $200 a day habits, but the truth is that there is really no such thing. However much money you got, that is how much junk you do." Still, cutting down on heroin simply raised a new problem. As he used less heroin, he began to drink more—wine for breakfast, lunch, and dinner. He was not sure if he had done himself a favor; as he depended more and more on wine, his life turned into a blur. "Lots of times, I would wake up and I wouldn't remember anything about the day before, except where I was when I passed out—and I only knew that because I knew I was sitting there."

If it is an established truth of human nature that everybody looks down on somebody, the somebody junkies look down on is a wino. "I honestly believe an alcoholic is worse than a junkie. With heroin, you come down kind of gradually, and if you keep up your health, you can work and do whatever you have to do inbetween getting stoned. An alcoholic can't. He drinks until he passes out and then he isn't worth a shit until he starts drinking again. If wine cost what heroin costs, there wouldn't be no winos because they couldn't get the money together to get drunk."

Shortly after New Year's 1975, while crossing a street in a drunken stupor, Rhodes stumbled into a taxi coming around the corner. Although he was not seriously injured, the incident shocked him. "I felt like I really hit bottom. Living on the streets just didn't seem like fun anymore. I guess it was like a record; you buy it, you like it for awhile, and then after a while, you can't stand to listen to it anymore. Everything that really seemed like living before, all of a sudden it all seemed like dying." He decided to do something he had never done before, something drastic. He enrolled in a drug addiction program.

The Harbour Light Drug Rehabilitation Program, supported by the Salvation Army and run by ex-addicts, involved six weeks of residency and six weeks of daily out-patient follow-up. Detoxification was cold turkey—without methadone—and therapy consisted of long emotional group encounter sessions. So far as it went, the program did work. At the end of his twelve weeks, Rhodes was, in a technical sense, an ex-junkie. He had no physical craving for the drug and a substantial theoretical distaste for it.

Unfortunately, however, the problem for Rhodes, as well as for most other addicts, was simply that kicking the habit was neither the difficult nor the most important part of rehabilitation. Rhodes, for example, was a veteran of withdrawal trauma: prison, a streak of bad luck, a dry spell on the drug supply—for a variety of reasons doing without heroin was a normal part of the junkie's routine. The crucial step was not to start again, and even though Rhodes had good intentions when he left the program, he knew that if he went back to the streets, without something else to occupy his mind and his time, he would, sooner or later, begin the cycle again.

The drug counselors at Harbour Light, as aware as Rhodes of the problem, could offer him no help more valuable than free advice: get a job, get off the streets, keep busy. Getting off the streets seemed to Rhodes the most promising alternative, but the question was how? And where? After a two-week trip to visit his ex-wife in Mississippi, the first time they had seen each other in eight years, Rhodes returned to Detroit and immediately settled into his old routine.

Once again, he decided to look for help, this time in the form of a Neighborhood Service Organization program for alcoholics recommended by one of the Harbour Light counselors. Once again, he dried out, and once again, resolved to stay away from the street life. He even, for the first time in more than seven years, looked for work. "I was ready to do it, I really was; but it was winter, and it was hard to get around and there didn't seem to be much work right then. I don't know how hard I looked, but, basically, I guess it was just a lot easier to go out and buy drugs than it was to start my life over again. But I was looking—that whole spring and summer—I was definitely looking for a way out."

That summer, the summer of 1976, was the summer the People's Temple caravan came to Detroit. For Rhodes, the Temple could hardly have come at a better time. The opportunity the Temple provided to escape the streets, to escape Detroit altogether, was just exactly what he was looking for. "Man, I was so tired, so tired of hustling, so tired of looking over my shoulder all the time, that I might have gone with just about anybody."

The first time the Temple came through in early June, he was simply too stoned to recognize his opportunity; but the second time, presented with the concrete evidence of a thoroughly rehabilitated John Dine, big as life and twice as straight, Rhodes was ready.

7

San Francisco

After a sleepless night spent sweating and shaking and trying to convince his body it had seen its last shot of heroin ever, Rhodes left Detroit on a Temple bus bound for California. As he watched the cornfields, cows, and recreational vehicles of an American summer pass by outside his window, Rhodes was suddenly assailed by a legion of doubts. In the bright light of day it occurred to him that he really knew next to nothing about the People's Temple or what it might expect from Odell Rhodes, and, for a man who prided himself on his ability to figure all the angles, the realization did not sit well. Already badly strung-out, the truth was that nothing was sitting well with Rhodes that morning. His head hurt; his stomach hurt; he was nauseated; he was cold; he was hot; and, most of all, he was just not happy. And he was not at all sure if the steady stream of hugs and friendly smiles his new comrades seemed determined to bestow upon him were making him feel better or worse.

"Don't worry about a thing—Dad's gonna take good care of you now."

"You just relax and enjoy yourself, brother, you're one of us now."

"Know just how you're feeling, brother, but, remember, today is the first day of the rest of your life—and it's gonna be a beautiful day."

As much as Rhodes appreciated everyone's concern, he could not prevent dark thoughts from running through his mind. "I kept asking myself, 'What the hell do these people want from me?' When somebody did something for me, I was used to asking myself what they expected to get from me. So, I thought about these people, and then I thought about it some more, but, for the life of me, I just couldn't come up with an answer. I mean, what did I have they could possibly want?"

Eventually, somewhere in Nebraska, Rhodes finally decided to relax: "I figured, what the hell, if it doesn't work out, at least I got myself a free ride to California."

When the free ride to California arrived at the Geary Street Temple early on a perfect California morning, Rhodes was shown to a free bed on the balcony of the Temple auditorium, fed a free breakfast, introduced around, and left to rest up from the trip. That night, after dinner, Marie Lawrence borrowed a Temple car and began showing Rhodes the sights of San Francisco. For the next few days, he toured the city: Fisherman's Wharf, the Cable Cars, Chinatown, North Beach, the Golden Gate Bridge. Between excursions, he was introduced to the Temple's version of social services: an appointment with a specialist to check his chronically inflamed leg; another specialist to check his eyes; a trip to the dentist. He was given money to buy a special orthopedic shoe, new eyeglasses, and new clothes. "I couldn't believe it," Rhodes remembers, "anything you needed, all you had to do was ask for it. It wasn't just that you didn't have to pay, it was the difference between trying to get something out of welfare, standing in lines and filling out forms, and just asking for what you needed."

At night, there were Temple meetings, but with Jones away in Cuba, the meetings were bland discussions of routine Temple business punctuated by an occasional testimony—someone thanking Jim Jones in absentia for that particular day's blessings.

Rhodes watched and waited. He was not quite sure of what, but something; at very least, some indication of what the People's Temple expected of Odell Rhodes. He thought he saw it coming one afternoon when he was visited by Lee Ingram, a member of the Planning Commission, who was one of the group running the Temple's daily affairs while Jones was away. Ingram, however, only wanted to introduce himself and add his welcome to the new brother. A few days later two counselors, Vera Young and Frances Johnson, called Rhodes into an office and went over a short list of Temple rules. When they came to the prohibition against alcohol, drugs, and tobacco, they slowed down and took special care to ex-

plain the reason behind the prohibition. Rhodes, who thought he
had heard it all before, was surprised to learn that the People's Temple's objection was on the grounds that mind-altering substances
were means by which the ruling class controlled and exploited the
poor. Rhodes simply nodded and filed the explanation away for future reference, but he was beginning to realize that this "church" he
had joined was somehow different than other churches. And, as for
its leader, there was no mistaking the fact that Jim Jones was something more than a minister. Both publicly, in meetings, and pri-
vately, during the course of a day, Rhodes heard an endless stream
of testimonies to the power and goodness of "Dad"—Jim Jones.

Without understanding much more than it was somehow expected of him, Rhodes caught on quickly enough to stand up and
offer his own testimony. "I said how grateful I was that I was saved
from drugs and I thanked Jim Jones. It seemed a little strange to me,
since I had only seen the man that once in Detroit, but you couldn't
be around there very long at all without picking up that you didn't
thank God, you thanked Jim Jones."

As far as Rhodes was concerned, thanking Jim Jones was hardly
an exorbitant price to pay for what the Temple had done for him.
He still expected something more, but in the meantime, he was
content enough to eat, sleep, and wander the halls of the Temple
waiting. But, while he relaxed, he could hardly help noticing that
he seemed to be the only person in the Temple with a minute to
spare. Day and night, virtually everyone he saw seemed to be in
perpetual motion. Every corner of the building seemed to be filled
to capacity at any given minute. People his own age would stop to
talk to him for a few minutes, then excuse themselves to go off to
work or to some chore within the Temple. Even the elderly members seemed to be constantly busy, helping out in the kitchen or on
a cleaning crew, or on their way to some planned group activity.
And although the legions of children who filled the Temple did not
work, they never seemed to have any free time either. They were
constantly supervised, and even if they were only playing, it seemed
to be purposeful play. "It was one of those things," Rhodes remembers, "that really blew me away. You never saw kids hanging around,
crying, or whining for somebody to pay attention to them. They
were always busy and cheerful and real careful not to get in anybody's hair."

From top to bottom, everyone Rhodes ran across in the Temple impressed him, and by the time Jim Jones returned from his tour of Cuba, Rhodes was already congratulating himself for choosing a winner. Along with several hundred other members (whom Rhodes was already pleased to think of as comrades), he piled aboard one of the Temple's fleet of buses for an overnight drive to Los Angeles where the combined congregations of the San Francisco and Los Angeles churches would welcome their leader at a special Saturday night meeting.

The meeting consisted of a three-hour lecture by Jones on life in Cuba. Rhodes, who had nodded through his only other exposure to Jones in Detroit, was entranced. "He talked about the way they did things in Cuba, and after a few minutes, you wanted to be in Cuba. It was like you were standing right there next to him—the way he explained things—he could make you see it exactly the way he saw it. I never ran into anybody who could explain things the way Jones could."

One of the topics Jones discussed that night was the way in which, in Cuba, people enjoyed their work—and felt useful doing it—because they believed they were working for each other. Rhodes was so impressed that the following Monday back in San Francisco, he approached Lee Ingram about a job. "You can do anything you want," Ingram told him. Rhodes didn't know what to say. Work was not an area in which he felt confident to express an opinion, even—or especially—when it concerned himself. Finally, Ingram suggested that Rhodes might try helping out in the Temple Day Care Center for a few days. "You like kids?" Ingram asked him. Rhodes shrugged again. On the streets of Detroit, his experience with children had been severely limited.

Ingram explained that the Day Care Center had been looking for a male staff member for quite some time and urged Rhodes to give it a try, for a few weeks at least. Rhodes agreed and spent the next few weeks discovering that he did indeed like children and that, furthermore, the Cubans had the right idea: when you liked what you were doing, work wasn't so bad after all. In fact, spending the day driving children to the park or the beach, playing with them, teaching them how to catch a ball, or build a sandcastle seemed more like vacation than work.

After a few weeks, in the course of a regular Tuesday night meeting, Jim Jones himself singled out Rhodes and thanked "the new brother from Detroit for the fine work he's doing with our children." Rhodes was stunned, overcome with surprise and satisfaction. "I guess at that point, I couldn't even remeber the last time somebody told me I was doing good at anything, and for Jones to take the time from everything else he had to think about to notice me—well, it meant a lot to me right then."

Until that night, Rhodes had not even known if Jim Jones knew who Odell Rhodes was. Rhodes was carefully keeping as low a profile as possible, watching, trying to figure out just exactly what the People's Temple was all about; and although he had not yet satisfied himself about the Temple, he had formed an opinion about Jim Jones. Jones reminded Rhodes of a type he had known on the streets. "He impressed me as a man you wouldn't want to mess around with. There was something about the way he carried himself. You see it on the streets sometimes. There was this old con in Leavenworth Jones reminded me of quite a bit. This guy was tough as nails. He didn't mess with anybody; in fact, he'd try to help you out if he saw you making a mistake, but he was the one guy on the whole block nobody ever even thought of messing with. Jones handled himself like that—like you wouldn't ever want to be on his bad side."

Although Rhodes had never spent much mental energy thinking about capitalism or the socialist revolution, the more he listened to Jones, the more he felt as if Jones was expressing his own feelings, feelings he had never been able to put into words. When Jones vented his rage at the racism of white America, Rhodes remembered Alabama, and, when Jones jabbed his finger in the air and told the congregation that "This system is the reason you are where you are," Rhodes nodded his head as if there was nothing more that needed to be said. "He'd say," Rhodes remembers, "that slavery had never really ended. It just painted up its face, but in its heart, it had never really changed. Then he'd ask people to get up and tell about the things that had happened to them.

"I remember one night, this little old lady, she must have been in her eighties, she stood up and started talking about what happened to her when she was a girl in the South. I don't remember all the details, but one night something happened down on this farm where she was sharecropping, and the white man who owned the place came into her house and started throwing things around. This woman had just had a baby—it wasn't but a few weeks or maybe a few months old—and this cracker just picked up its crib and threw that too. Anyway, the baby died eventually—and nothing ever happened to the white man.

"When she got done telling the story, I remember Jones just sat there and cried, and pretty soon everybody there—hundreds of us—everybody was just weeping like all hell, and, finally, Jones said, 'We can't let things like this happen to us anymore—we can't live in a place like this. It's like living in hell!'"

Rhodes's own reaction was, for once, uncomplicated. "Even if it hadn't been Jones saying it—no matter who might have said it—you don't have to try very hard to convince black people they're still treated like slaves. I mean, when he said living in this country is like living in hell, believe me, you sure as hell didn't see anybody stand up and start waving a flag."

Rhodes had never heard anything remotely like Jones's Bible lessons. "He said," Rhodes remembers, "that the Bible wasn't worth the paper it was printed on." According to Rhodes, Jones liked to conduct classes in which he took a selected passage from the Bible and exposed its "logical inconsistencies." "Maybe it would be the story about Adam and Eve. He'd read it up until the part where they have two sons, Cain and Abel, and then when Cain goes to the Land of Nod, he'd look up and say, 'Now, if Adam and Eve were the first people, and Cain and Abel were their only sons, where in the hell did these folks from Nod come from?' "

With a disgusted look on his face, Jones would then throw the Bible on the floor, making sure to remind the congregation that the King James whose name graces the classic English translation of the Bible was none other than the same King James who brought the slave trade to the new World. "Are you gonna sit there and read this garbage?" Jones would demand. "Are you gonna sit there and read this slave Bible?"

For good measure Jones would then point his finger in the direction of St. Mary's Cathedral, a spanking new white marble building a few blocks up Geary Boulevard, and ask the congregation, very rhetorically, "How can they call themselves Christians? They spend five million dollars of poor people's money on a lot of concrete and glass, when people in this city are going to bed hungry at night. How can they dare call themselves Christians?"

According to Rhodes, Jones's own personal catechism consisted of a very few simple propositions: "I don't believe in any damn God I can't see. There ain't no heaven in the sky; and the only hell is the one we're living in." Rhodes remembers Jones claiming that he, Jim Jones, was God. "But, when he said that, he was usually talking about that part in the Bible where it says there's a little bit of God in everybody. I always took it like he was trying to impress people that they shouldn't depend on some God in the sky. Like, what did He ever do for you? He wanted people to depend on themselves, and on each other—and on him—instead."

But more than anything else Jones did, Rhodes watched his faith-healing miracles in utter fascination, not because he believed in miracles, but because as a fellow professional, Rhodes recognized a class act when he saw it. For the small-time street hustler from Detroit, watching Jones cure cancer and bring the dead back to life was like Knuckles O'Toole watching Horowitz play the piano. "He was," Rhodes says flatly, "the best con man I ever saw—and I've seen quite a few. I knew guys who could talk you out of anything in your pocket and Jones would have taken any of them to the cleaners. I mean, he just got done telling them what a crock the Bible was, and then he'd turn around and pull off a miracle they wouldn't dare put in the Bible, it was so outrageous. And he'd have people eating out of his hand."

A week or so after the meeting in which he praised Rhodes from the pulpit, Jones stopped Rhodes in the hall, threw an arm around his shoulder, and thanked him again for working with the children. Then he pulled Rhodes aside and in a low, comforting voice, told Rhodes not to worry because the children were calling him "Dad." "I'm their 'Dad,' " Jones told him, "but I can't be everywhere—so you have to stand in for me."

The incident, his first personal contact with Jim Jones, chilled Rhodes to the bone. "It was true, those kids I was taking care of, they were calling me Dad sometimes. Well, I knew the only person in the Temple you called 'Dad' was Jones, so I didn't know what to do about it. I didn't want to tell them they couldn't, but I didn't feel right about it. What blew me away was, to this day, I don't know how Jones knew about the kids calling me Dad. I was thinking about it a lot, but I know for damned sure I didn't tell anybody it was bothering me, because I was still thinking about whether I *wanted* to tell anybody. So, even if somebody heard the kids calling me 'Dad' and told Jones about it, there was no way in hell he could have known it was bothering me. No way in hell—and all of a sudden, there's Jones and he's telling me he knows it's bothering me and not to worry. I damned near thought I must have been talking to the devil."

"Maybe," says Odell Rhodes, "he was just so tuned into people, he could look at you, and he'd always have a pretty good idea of what you were up to, so maybe he could just guess about what was likely to be bothering you. I don't know, but if that wasn't it, I'd hate to think what the hell else it could have been."

Whatever power Jones did possess, he was careful not to depend on the supernatural alone. He kept copious files on every Temple member, complete with family histories, medical records, and miscellaneous data of every variety; some of it supplied by the members themselves through self-confession letters each member was required to write periodically, and some of it from informers who were charged with striking up friendly conversations with members whose files were found lacking in personal secrets.

Odell Rhodes knew enough about confessions, informants, and files to understand the uses to which Jones put the information he gathered, and he admired Jones for it. "I guess I'd seen enough of the army and of jail to know that when you're dealing with a few thousand people, you need discipline, and the best way to get discipline is to convince everybody you know everything there is to know. As far as I was concerned, he wasn't doing anything I hadn't seen before."

Even the most skeptical members, those who knew how Jones used information and how he staged his exhibitions of supernatural power, retained a residual sense of awe about Jones's capacities. "Even if he had somebody listening to everybody twenty-four hours a day," Odell Rhodes says, "he had to have some kind of photographic memory to keep it all straight." Dale Parks, who served several years as Jones's personal secretary, believed Jones did have a photographic memory. "He could repeat conversations you'd had with him years ago, word for word, and he could read something through one time and repeat it to you virtually word for word."

Parks knew about Jones's filing system and helped in the preparation of many of his miracles. He was not a believer, but even Parks wonders about the times he drove Jones over the steep, winding two-lane mountain roads around Redwood Valley. It was standard procedure for Jones to tell Dale when he could pass another car blindly in the lane of oncoming traffic. "I don't believe in ESP; I don't even believe in astrology, but I drove those damn roads with him a hundred times, and whatever it was, nobody will ever convince me it was pure, dumb luck."

Jones himself liked to explain his powers by claiming he had been born on another planet, like Superman, an explanation that may not be particularly more far-fetched than any other, but whatever the source of his powers, he convinced virtually everyone in the Temple, at every level of sophistication, that there was something quite special about his abilities. "You had to know the man," Dale Parks says, "he could go for days without sleep, and you'd never know the difference. One minute he was this hard-headed politician, running some meeting of the Housing Authority, the next minute he was pulling rabbits out of his hat, and before you could catch your breath, he was doing something else. I don't know what it was, but he could get more things done than any two people I ever saw. Maybe it was his glands."

After two months in a dormitory at the main Temple building, Odell Rhodes moved to a communal Temple family house a few blocks away from the Geary Street building on Sutter Street. The house, a two-story Victorian building in a mostly black neighborhood, was typical of the living arrangements of Temple members. Rhodes lived on the first floor in the front of the house with six boys between the ages of seven and twelve, three black, three white. In the back, on the same floor, the mother of three of the boys lived with three young girls, two of them her own. Upstairs, four other adults and three teenage girls, none of them related by blood, lived in four other rooms. Rhodes was charged with complete responsibility for all of the boys including those whose mother lived down the hall. The household took all of its meals at the main Temple's dining hall on Geary Street, and the Temple paid all household expenses. Two of the adults had outside jobs; Rhodes and two others worked at the Temple.

"Basically, we had nothing but good times. It was like one big family, and there was always something going on. I never spent so much time laughing in my life.

"Frankly, it was just about my idea of a perfect way to live. None of those people in that house, if they lived by themselves, could have lived nearly as well. Neither of the women who worked could have held down jobs—they would have been shut up in some tiny room some place, living with their kids on welfare—and I don't know how the rest of us would have lived at all. This way, we were all comfortable and not only that, we were all together and having a damned good time."

In addition to his housemates, Rhodes ran with a crowd of young people, many of whom lived in apartments in the same building on Divisadero Street, a few blocks from the Geary Street Temple. Two or three nights a week he spent in Marin County, across the Golden Gate Bridge, with a woman, a Temple member with whom he was having an affair. "There wasn't anything weird about sex at that time," he remembers. "It did get a little weird later on, but at that time if you met somebody and you hit it off, you just did whatever you did. You'd only hear about it if you started hitting on a lot of different women, or going out with two at the same time, or something like that."

Relationships with outsiders were actively discouraged; the stated reason being that "anyone who wasn't one of us was likely to be against us," but Rhodes felt anything but isolated. "There were three or four thousand of us and I had more friends than I ever had in my life, so I never thought much about people outside of the Temple."

He ventured outside the Temple's orbit only once. In the late spring, he developed an infection in his crippled leg and spent a few days in a hospital. While in the hospital, he met a nurse, an exchange student from Equador, whom he began dating as soon as his leg healed. Rather than being discovered, an offense that would have meant a public reprimand and some sort of penalty, Rhodes went on his own initiative to Jimmy Jones, one of Jim Jones's adopted sons and a power in the Temple, and confessed that he was having an affair with an outsider.

"First he asked me if I talked about the Temple with her, but when I said she didn't even know I was a member, he didn't seem to care very much. He told me if I were serious about her, I'd better make damned sure she was Temple quality, and if I weren't serious about her, well, it was like, if you have to do it just for sex, it might as well be an outsider; but don't forget what you're doing here, and don't let it go on for too long. She went back to Equador not too long after that, so there wasn't any problem."

The year he spent in San Francisco, Rhodes could hardly have been happier. With a job he liked, friends, and a rising sense of his own worth, he felt he had gone a million miles farther than the distance between Detroit and San Francisco. While life in the Temple might have seemed a bizarre deviation from the normal to outsiders, to Rhodes it was exactly the opposite: the best way by far he had found yet to lead what he considered a normal life.

However, as pleased as he was with his new life, there were moments in which he had his doubts, if not about life in the Temple, at least about its leader. "I loved the Temple, and I really respected Jones—after what he had done for me, how could I help but respect him. But, every once in a while something would hit me not quite right. One thing I remember is how Jones would always talk about trusting him. He'd always make a point of telling us we might not be able to trust anyone else, but we should always trust him. Well, basically I did, but, hell, I'd made my living for years telling people to trust me—I mean, those were my words, 'trust me.' So I knew damned well the last person in the world you would want to trust is the one telling you to trust him.

"Sometimes when he would talk like that, I'd start remembering this blind man I used to know in Detroit. Just a little old blind man with a tin cup and a fat, old dog. I knew him for years; then one day I'd happened to see him in an alley counting out his money: dollar bills here, fives there, tens someplace else. Well, now, you know that they don't make money in braille—so it blew me away. I promised myself right then and there, I was never going to believe anybody was who he said he was, no matter what. And sometimes—not always—but sometimes that blind man came back to me when I listened to Jones.

"I learned the hard way that there's sharks, and then there's food for sharks, but the thing was, when I joined the Temple I was so damned tired of watching out for sharks, and trying to be one myself, that I wanted to believe the Temple wasn't like that. I wanted so damn bad to believe it that I guess I did."

8

The Promised Land

Odell Rhodes does not remember the first time he heard about Jonestown. "But, it wasn't right away, I know that much. I guess I might have heard some seniors talking about going to the Promised Land, but damned if I knew what they were talking about. Nobody actually talked to me about it for quite some time. It wasn't like it was a secret, or anything like that, but it wasn't on everybody's mind at the beginning either."

There was, in fact, not a great deal to talk about. When Rhodes joined the Temple, the Agricultural Mission (it was not yet called Jonestown) amounted to only a handful of temporary buildings, less than fifty acres of cleared land, and a population of about forty. Although building a utopian community had been an ambition of Jim Jones for years (since his boyhood in Indiana, in fact), it was not until 1973 that he actually began to do anything about it.

Jones had visited Guyana in 1963 on his way back from Brazil, and in 1966, when the country won its independence from Great Britain and elected a black socialist government, he marked it off on his atlas as a place to go back to. When he did go back seven years later, after discussing the possibility of establishing his utopian community with Guyanese diplomats in the United States, it was to negotiate a lease for a larger chunk of undeveloped jungle someplace near the Venezuelan border.

The Guyanese were immediately receptive to the idea. A grossly underdeveloped country, Guyana was always willing to listen to schemes involving foreign capital, especially from an organization whose leader's political views were as sympathetic as Jim Jones's were. Furthermore, the aim of the proposed settlement, to experiment with agricultural diversification projects on cleared virgin jungle, happened to coincide with a major unrealized objective of the government's own development program. The Guyanese had something else in mind too. The land the government offered to lease to the Temple was situated in a largely unsurveyed strip of jungle along the Venezuelan border, a strip claimed at various times, by both Venezuela and Guyana which had become the object of a steadily—if slowly—simmering dispute. By allowing a sizable population of American citizens to settle there, the Guyanese government felt it could, with a single stroke, not only establish documentation of its sovereignty, but also insure against any impulsive attempt by the Venezuelans to annex the region by force.

Between 1973 and 1976, while negotiations between the Temple and the government dragged on, the Guyanese allowed the Temple to begin settling on a small scale and finally, in February 1976, a long-term lease for a part of the land under negotiation—3,843 acres—was signed. For the year following the signing of the lease, the settlement remained quiet, essentially a caretaking operation; then, abruptly, early in 1977, large quantities of building materials, supplies, and—eventually—settlers began to arrive by boat via the nearby riverport of Port Kaituma.

Although preparing the settlement to receive several hundred settlers must certainly have required some time after the signing of the lease, it just as certainly did not require a year; in fact, the effort to prepare the settlement for large numbers of settlers did not even begin in earnest until the early months of the new year, 1977.

It was not a good year for Jim Jones. Although the Temple continued to flourish, Jones's behind-the-scenes problems were also growing. During 1976 several Temple members had followed the lead of Elmer and Deanna Mertle and Grace Stoen and left the Temple. Jones called them traitors, and in his mind they represented nothing but problems. By far the biggest problem was Grace Stoen. Early in the new year, she finally tired of negotiating with Tim Stoen for custody of her son and hired a lawyer to initiate custody proceedings in a San Francisco court. It was exactly what Stoen and Jim Jones had feared most.

Although the Stoen case did not immediately receive extensive

news coverage, it obviously had lurid potential: the well-known religious and civic leader, the Reverend Jim Jones, involved in a
steamy sexual scandal with a member of his congregation (who also
happened to be the wife of an assistant district attorney), was a pot of
rich yellow ink waiting to be splashed across somebody's front page.

Beyond the publicity was the even more disturbing fact that the
outcome of the case was a foregone conclusion from the moment
the suit was filed. But, although Jones had been told many times
that fighting Grace in court would be hopeless, he was still having
difficulty reconciling himself to giving up without a fight. His feelings about John-John were so strong that the question of custody was
a highly emotional issue for him—one that was difficult for him to
remain rational about. To Jones, John-John was something even
more valuable than a son; he was a symbol of the future of Jones's
cause. The custody case was therefore a matter of principle, as if not
contesting the right of a traitor like Grace to take custody of his symbol would somehow be both a private and public admission of failure. Despite the contingency plan to spirit John-John out of the
country (which Jones and Stoen had devised over the summer to
insure that Jones could keep John-John), Grace's suit rankled Jones,
and he remained deeply conflicted about whether to contest the case
or not.

Nonetheless, whether he fought or not, Jones did understand that
in the long run the only way to keep John-John was to send him to
Guyana where he would be beyond the court's jurisdiction. With
the child safely out of reach Jones could then, if he so decided,
contest the case, and the worst that could happen would be that the
court might cite Jones for contempt when he refused to hand the
child over to Grace. In that case Jones could simply put himself
beyond the court's jurisdiction as well. He could simply move the
entire People's Temple—lock, stock and barrel—to Guyana while
the court issued as much legal paper as it wanted. Without finally
making up his mind if he would fight in court or not Jones took
Grace's decision to file suit as his signal to set the wheels of the
Temple's flight to the jungle in motion.

Early in March, 380 Temple members applied to the Guyanese
embassy in Washington for immigration visas, and shortly after they
were issued a few weeks later, the first substantial contingent of Tem-

ple members left for their new home in the jungle. Among the new settlers were John Victor Stoen and his new guardian, Maria Katsaris.

In the meanwhile, the Mertles (now legally Al and Jeannie Mills) were busy trying to sell their version of life in the People's Temple to the press. After several failures, they managed to interest Marshall Kilduff, a reporter for the *San Francisco Chronicle* and Phil Tracy, an editor of *New West* magazine. Kilduff and Tracy began researching the Mills's allegations and interviewing other former Temple members.

At the same time, the father of a young Planning Commission member, Bob Houston, who had been found dead in the San Francisco railroad yard, where he worked, after an argument with Jones, was threatening an investigation of the Temple.

Next to Grace Stoen, the Mills and Sam Houston were minor inconveniences, but to Jones it all added up to something more than the sum of its parts. He began to believe that he was the object of a conspiracy that included not only Grace Stoen, the Mills, and the other former Temple members, but the CIA, the FBI, and all the other forces of political reaction in the country as well. Convinced as he was that he was a radical leader of the stature of a Martin Luther King, a Malcom X, a Bobby Seale, or a Daniel Ellsburg, Jones was certain that the Temple had become the target of a witch-hunt, the same sort of concerted effort he believed the government and the press had directed against the Black Muslims, the Black Panther party, the Chicago Seven, or any of the other martyrs of the New Left.

Throughout the winter and spring, Odell Rhodes was only vaguely aware of Jones's problems with the Mills and Grace Stoen. "I'd heard about those people who were supposed to be our enemies," he remembers, "but I didn't really pay too much attention to them. I guess I was just plain too busy with what I was doing to think about it very much."

What he knew of the Mills's charges, which centered around the repressive discipline inside the Temple, did not impress him. "There was discipline all right—no doubt about it. But, to me, it wasn't any big deal. You put a thousand people together and you damn well better have a little discipline. There's discipline in the army that's a hell of a lot worse—and then there's prison, which is a whole different ball game altogether. I don't doubt that the things those people say happened might have been true, but the discipline I saw just seemed like the price you expect to pay for something like the Temple. I guess I figured if the Temple wasn't right for them, they shouldn't be with us. All I knew was that it was right for me."

The Stoen case did not impress him a great deal more: "I never knew Grace Stoen, but the way people talked about her was that she had run off and abandoned John-John. That was all I knew about it, and I never doubted it. You could tell how much Jones loved him just by looking, and to me, when I looked at John-John, I saw Jim Jones."

Throughout the early spring, these two subjects, the Temple's enemies and the Promised Land in the jungle, gradually began to dominate Temple meetings. Jones told the congregation that the defectors were merely the visible tip of an enormous iceberg of Temple enemies. "The way he presented it," Rhodes remembers, "was that we'd been too successful. He'd talk about how the power structure in the government felt threatened whenever a group of poor people, especially black people, got themselves together. He compared us a lot to groups like the Black Panthers, and he talked a lot about how the FBI and everybody else was getting ready to harass us just like they harassed the Panthers."

According to Rhodes, Jones rarely attacked the defectors personally. "He said he felt sorry for them—because they didn't have any more sense than to sell their brothers and sisters down the river, but he didn't seem angry about it. He said he had more important things to worry about—like what was going to happen to all of us now that the government was on our case."

Throughout the spring, Jones told the congregation that the movement was in serious danger. "He said we were at war, but because we were committed to nonviolence, there wasn't any way to fight back. Besides, we were just a few poor people, how the hell were we going to fight back anyway?"

The only way out, Jones told the congregation, was to leave the racist hell of America behind, to start again someplace else. In Guyana, he promised, the congregation would build for themselves the society that America had failed to become.

"He started talking about how beautiful it was there, and how, most of all, over there a person could be free. He talked about how

there was no pollution and no crime on the streets too, but, basi-
he kept saying that over there a person wasn't judged by the color of
his skin, or the way he talked, or who his parents were. Over there,
you could be anything you wanted to be, do any type of work you
wanted, make yourself the kind of person you always wanted to be—
anything, just so long as you were working to help your brothers and
sisters, that was all anyone was judged on over there."

Even the Temple's own discipline, Jones promised, would melt
away in the workers' democracy of Jonestown. "Like the only reason
we couldn't smoke or drink here was because here everything you
buy is made off the sweat of poor people and things like drugs are
just a way of oppressing people who don't know any better. But, over
there, we wouldn't be oppressed by anybody, and we'd be able to do
anything we wanted. It all made a lot of sense to me," Rhodes admits, "because I knew that since I'd been with the Temple, since I'd
found something that made sense to me, I didn't even want to do
things like drugs—the things that fucked me up."

If Rhodes was attracted to Jonestown by the prospect of starting a
new life in an environment free of temptation and full of possibili-
ties, other members found other attractions in the picture Jones
painted of the new society in the jungle. In fact, with his character-
istc genius for selling his followers' fantasies right back to them, the
picture Jones painted was a coloring-book cartoon to be filled in
according to one's heart's desires.

For many of the Planning Commission group, several of whom
had come to the Temple directly from communes or other experimental communities, Jonestown was the ultimate communal fantasy—a last, best chance to build a new society on the principles of
love, peace, and cooperation. Dick Tropp, the intellectual ex-Berke-
ley graduate student, even circulated a tract comparing the Temple's
flight from persecution in the United States with the settlement of
the New World by persecuted religious minorities and America's
long tradition of utopian pioneering.

To many of the older black members, the faith healing constituency, the Promised Land echoed with memories of the Old Testa-
ment Land of Milk and Honey and the Promised Land of black,
slave spiritual music. "I went over there," Grover Davis says, "because I wanted a place to live out my days in peace and then die in
peace." To many of the black members, whom Jones had convinced

that America had never been home for black people, it represented simply the opportunity to go back, to live finally in freedom.

To everyone, with the possible exception of Jim Jones, Jonestown was a great adventure. Jones himself was deeply conflicted about Jonestown. On the one hand, it represented a way to escape his enemies and to hold onto John-John—and the rest of the community. But, on the other hand, it also meant abandoning ten years of hard work and everything he had accomplished in California. In Jones's mind, there was, for every utopian dream and promise of peace, a countervailing sense of defeat. The Jim Jones who moved to Guyana was not going to be a major political figure in the United States.

In the end, Jones's own feelings about Jonestown must have been colored by his abiding sense of the apocalypse. He had moved from Indiana ten years before to escape the end of the world. Now, once again, Jones saw the beast slouching toward Bethelehem. The sinful colossus America was once again about to destroy itself; the persecution of the Temple was enough evidence of that. On the one hand, Jonestown promised Jones that he would save his followers from the holocaust, and perhaps one day inherit the earth; but, on the other hand, it also meant that Jones had failed; he had failed to save the rest of the world.

Throughout the spring the move to the jungle proceeded with scores of settlers and tons of supplies leaving San Francisco every week. At the Geary Street Temple a permanent work crew of some forty members packed and crated everything from food and clothing to sophisticated short-wave radio and enough medical supplies to furnish a small hospital.

Meanwhile both Jim Jones and Tim Stoen visited the settlement on several different occasions. Their reactions could hardly have been more different. The jungle—and the prospect of building the jungle paradise that bore his name—exhilirated Jones. The more he saw of Jonestown, the more convinced he became that leaving America was the right move to make. Stoen was not nearly so sure. While Jones enthusiastically embraced the move to the jungle as a solution to all his problems, especially the problem of holding on to John-John Stoen, the move to the jungle did nothing to solve Tim Stoen's problems.

Stoen's biggest problem was the looming court action for custody of John-John. Even though both he and Jones knew that Jones had nothing to gain by contesting the case, there was still the possibility that Jones might decide, as a matter of principle, to air Grace's betrayal in court anyway. If that happened, the affidavit Stoen had signed attesting to the fact that Jones was John-John's father would undoubtedly become a matter of public record. A court fight was bound to attract public attention, and the part of it that involved Stoen would not be pleasant, especially if, as Jones would expect him to do, Stoen supported the contention that Jones was in fact the boy's father. If that happened, Stoen would, in effect, be put in the impossible position of dragging his own good name through a public mudpile.

There was no way around it. If the fight over custody of John-John became public knowledge, Stoen was likely to spend the rest of his life trying to explain a situation no one was likely to understand. More than once Stoen expressed his misgivings to Jones. The court fight, Stoen told Jones, could well destroy both of them. And the worst thing about it was that, as the child's mother, Grace was bound to win the courts decision eventually, no matter what Jones and Stoen did. The court would then order Jones to return the child. If Jones refused, he would be held in contempt—and he would then be trapped in Guyana permanently, unable to return to the U.S. without facing arrest.

Stoen outlined a plan whereby Stoen would claim the child was his and arrange with Grace for joint custody to be awarded. He would then allow Jones to see John-John on his time. Jones was not interested. He was not prepared to bargain about custody of John-John. As far as Jones was concerned, John-John was his child, period. To Jones, John-John was a living symbol of everything Stoen and Jones had worked so hard to accomplish: the new society, the extended family, the ideal of communal living, the struggle against bourgeois repression—everything. It was out of the question.

With Jones unwilling to compromise Stoen was left with a decision to make. Either he stood by Jones and effectively gave his life over to the Temple permanently, or he cut his losses, denied that Jones was John-John's father, and left before it was too late. As the weeks passed the pressure increased. The court case was now scheduled to be heard during the summer. And looming on the horizon was the matter of the forthcoming *New West* magazine exposé.

Both Jones and Stoen knew that the New West article was in preparation and both knew that its authors, Marshall Kilduff and Phil Tracy, had interviewed a number of ex-members, including the Mills and, even more ominously, Grace Stoen. Stoen also knew that, even if Jones had not already decided to abandon California permanently, the New West article was likely to clinch the decision. Having now spent some time in Jonestown himself, Stoen apparently decided that—unlike his leader—he was not prepared to spend the rest of his life in the jungle a thousand miles away from civilization. He was too well educated, too sophisticated, too attached to the pleasures of the world. He had never intended to be a pioneer; after all, he had joined the Temple and worked with Jones at least partly because Jones and the Temple had seemed to offer a unique opportunity to do something important with his life—to build a grass-roots movements that might someday become a political force on a national scale. He had signed up to play political hardball—and Guyana was a great deal less than what he had bargained for.

While Jones was shuttling back and forth between Jonestown and California trying to accelerate the move to the jungle, Stoen spent most of his spring trying to put a bit of distance between himself and the Temple. He flew from Guyana to London, returned briefly, and then, after spending a few weeks in San Francisco, took off again for London without telling anyone in the Temple where he was going.

The news of Stoen's disappearance upset Jones enormously. For at least a month several members of Jones's staff—especially Eugene Chaikin, another Temple attorney who had gone through some of Stoen's files that had been shipped to Guyana—had been warning Jones that Stoen was thinking about leaving the Temple. At first Jones refused to believe it. After all, Tim Stoen was almost as much a part of the People's Temple as Jones was himself. Next to Jones he had done more to build the Temple than anyone; next to Jones there was no one who knew more about the Temple's affairs than Stoen; he was the one man whose loyalty Jones had never thought to question. But, now Stoen had disappeared, and suddenly visions of an inconceivable betrayal danced in Jones's head. He sent Eugene Chaikin back to the files to search for evidence that Stoen had connections to the CIA or the FBI, and he spread word throughout the Temple leadership that—wherever Stoen was—Jones wanted to see him.

Meanwhile, before Stoen left San Francisco, he had arranged

with a friend—his superior in the U.S. attorney's office, G. William Hunter—to send a suitcase to Stoen in London. Hunter evidently had some question about the arrangements and, without realizing Stoen had made a point of not telling the Temple that he had gone to London, let that crucial piece of information slip out. Jones quickly ordered the San Francisco staff to tell Hunter they would arrange to ship the suitcase. Two Temple members were then dispatched to London, and when Stoen arrived at Heathrow Airport to claim his baggage, he was told that Jones wanted to see him in Jonestown—immediately.

Stoen flew back to Guyana, met with Jones and tried, once again, to explain his dilemma to Jones. The two men talked for days, first in Jonestown, then in Georgetown, the Guyanese capital. The conversations were full of anger and misunderstanding—mirror images of their conversations in Redwood Valley eight years before. Stoen pleaded with Jones to give the boy back to his mother. Why ruin both their careers over a child? It was a simple matter of priorities. The greatest good for the greatest number—that was the principle they had always been guided by. Why desert it now?

From Jones point of view, however, it was Stoen who had deserted first principles. If Stoen refused to stand by him now, he was nothing but a traitor, a traitor to everything they had both worked for. Stoen insisted that Jones did not understand. He had no intention of hurting Jones or the cause; he was simply trying to salvage the best from a bad situation. Jones shook his head sadly. It was Stoen who obviously did not understand. Stoen had signed on to build a movement that was more important than any individual. If he left in the middle of the struggle, he was no better than Grace or the Mills, or any of the others who had betrayed the movement. In fact, Stoen was far worse than the others. They might plead ignorance; but, Tim Stoen knew what the fight was about. He understood better than anyone. The problem, according to Jones, was that Stoen was a coward. He had convictions without courage. He was incapable of sacrifice; selfish; bourgeois; weak. Jones understood; he understood only too well.

Stoen returned to San Francisco, his differences with Jones still unresolved. Then, on August 1, the long-feared *New West* magazine article finally appeared in print. The article detailed charges by the Mills and others, charges which included mistreatment, physical abuse, extortion, embezzlement, and blackmail. It also outlined the basic facts of Grace Stoen's relationship with Jones.

A few days later Jones dictated a statement denying the charges and resigning from the San Francisco Housing Authority by short-wave radio from the jungle.

Odell Rhodes meanwhile remained alone in the house on Sutter Street. Everyone else—the six boys he had cared for and the nine others living in the house—had already left for Guyana. "Was I lonely? Damn right I was—ain't nothing in the world lonelier than a house that used to be full of people."

A few weeks later Rhodes picked up the telephone in the Sutter Street house late one afternoon.

"Are your bags packed?"

Although Rhodes had no bags to pack, he answered that they were.

"You need anything before you go?"

"Go where?"

"Over there—Guyana."

"That," says Rhodes, "was what I wanted to hear."

He hurried to the Temple where he was given money to buy boots, blue jeans—and a suitcase. Later that evening, he reported back to the Temple and shortly before dawn the next morning, boarded a Temple bus for the cross-country trip to Kennedy Airport in New York.

"I remember the morning we left real well. I guess Jones was still kind of a hot news item because there were reporters hanging around the Temple all the time, even real early in the morning. I remember as we drove through the gates, there were all these reporters snapping pictures and screaming at us about where we all going to. I think somebody picked up the window and told them, but me, I just smiled and waved at them. Damn, I was happy to be leaving all that behind."

9

Summer: Leaving Your Chains Behind

After a frantic nonstop three-day bus ride to New York, Rhodes and his twenty-odd traveling companions boarded their flight to Guyana, by way of Trinidad, early in the evening of Sunday, August 21. To Rhodes's astonishment the six-hour plane ride turned into a party. "And it wasn't your typical People's Temple party at all. I mean, we were letting it all hang out—drinking and smoking—and I do mean everybody. I could hardly believe I was seeing some of those folks toss down the whiskey, but it was like just being on our way, everybody felt like celebrating."

After the plane left Trinidad for the final leg of the journey only a few seats were filled by travelers other than those in the Temple group, and the cabin echoed with some of the most unlikely toasts ever heard at thirty thousand feet:

"Free at last—free, at last!"

"Goin' to the Promised Land—God Bless Jim Jones, we're goin to the Promised Land!"

"Hallelujah!"

When they finally landed at Timehri Airport in Georgetown, the Guyanese Temple, the new settlers were met by a reception committee from the Temple's Georgetown headquarters and taken back to the headquarters building, a converted hotel, the Lamaha Gar-

dens. After a few hours of fitful sleep in the hot, unfamiliar Caribbean climate the group returned to the airport and spent the rest of
the morning clearing Guyanese immigration.

Since the last leg of the journey, by coastal steamer up the Caribbean coast through the Mora passage and down the Kaituma
River to Port Kaituma, was not scheduled to leave until sundown,
Rhodes and the others spent the rest of the day wandering through
the city taking in the sights. Georgetown is a picturesque city, very
much the former colonial capital, whose chief distinctions—before
it became a dateline synonymous with the People's Temple—were
rum, fine dark Demerara rum served in countless grog shops, and
pickpockets, also countless, and reputed to be the most brazen in the
Caribbean.

As he wandered through the Stargrove, the city's main open-air
market, Rhodes happened to bump into a Temple member he know
slightly from San Francisco, the athletic twenty-four-year-old graduate of the Santa Rita Correctional Institution, Stanley Clayton.
Clayton enjoyed a richly deserved reputation within the Temple for
irrepressibility, and Stanley the clown, the good-natured cut-up and
lover of good times, had been on the loose in Georgetown for nearly
two weeks waiting to join up with Rhodes's group for the trip to
Jonestown. Clayton had spent most of those two weeks exploring the
grog shops and was in the midst of a farewell tour of his favorites
when he happened upon Rhodes. A few words about the glories of
Guyanese rum were all that was needed to convince Rhodes to join
him, and without wasting any more time the two prospective pi-
oneers set off to fortify themselves for the voyage to Jonestown.

They arrived at the docks shortly before sundown full of good spirits—and amply supplied for the trip upriver. They were not the only
ones. "Seemed like just about everybody had the same idea," Rhodes
remembers. "There wasn't hardly anybody down there who wasn't
holding on to a bottle or two."

As the small coastal steamer headed out into the Caribbean under
a fine orange sunset, the party began all over again with bottles passing from mouth to mouth against the beat of loud rock music blaring
from several competing portable cassette recorders. Six hours and a
long wake of bottles later the boat turned up a jungle river to the
cheers of the partygoers.

"Yes, sir, we're almost home."

"Don't look like the River Jordan, but I know it's the Promised Land."

"Pass me that bottle—I'm gonna drink to freedom!"

When dawn broke, those in the group who were still conscious watched in amazement as the boat came around in a long, slow U-turn and began steaming back the way it had come. The Guyanese captain, it happened, had piloted his floating houseparty up the wrong river. He was toasted warmly for the mistake; and, as the boat backtracked to the coast and finally found the right river, the Jonestown pilgrims stretched out under the sun, emptied their last reserves of rum, and took in the scenery.

"There we were," Rhodes remembers, "going deeper and deeper into the jungle until the last afternoon you didn't see anything but jungle and a few Indian houses—and it was like every mile we went you could feel your hassles getting left behind, like you were taking off your chains."

One teenage girl, full of rum and the spirit of freedom, developed an immediate and irresistible crush on one of the Guyanese boatmen. With Clayton and others assuring her that since she was now in the Promised Land she was free to do whatever she wanted, she marched down to the crew's cabin and did it.

When the boat finally docked at Port Kaituma early the next morning before daybreak, the settlers were picked up by a Temple truck, driven the twelve miles into the jungle, and welcomed warmly with peanut butter sandwiches and hugs from their leader, who had stayed up into the morning waiting for the new arrivals. A few hours later, however, while the members of the group were sleeping off their excesses of travel and good spirits, the welcome took on a different tone when the captain of the boat appeared at the settlement to assure Jones that his boatman would do the right thing and marry the girl.

Jones listened to the captain's account of the voyage in a cold fury and then immediately had everyone in the group rousted out of bed and brought to the main pavilion. He told them they had disgraced their community, their cause, and their leader, and, for some reason, he singled out a very tired and hung-over Stanley Clayton in particular for having "a slave's idea of freedom." Clayton could hardly believe his ears: "He said we were here to build ourselves a new life and all I could think about was women and drinking and such things like that. Well, I felt he promised me I was going to be able to enjoy myself. He said we were going to be happy over there, and free—and there he was taking it away the very first day. I felt like turning right around and walking the hell out of there—I mean, I was so depressed I didn't think I could stand it."

Odell Rhodes had suspected all along that the Promised Land would not be a party and he was neither shocked nor depressed: "I just wanted to get out of there and have a look at the place in the daylight, find my old friends, get myself settled. I felt like I'd come home, and whether or not I could drink or whatever, it just didn't seem that important to me. I just wanted to pitch in and help do my share."

There was an enormous amount to do. Completely cut off from the outside world, Jonestown had grown from a primitive camp with less than a hundred settlers to a bustling community of nearly seven hundred in less than six months, and new settlers were arriving at a rate of thirty to forty per week. Jones's avowed goal was complete economic self-sufficiency within a year, and to that end virtually everyone who was physically able put in a workday that began at sunrise and ended at sundown, most of them at one of three vital projects: clearing the jungle, farming, and building new cabins.

As Rhodes walked around Jonestown for the first time he saw an instant city of plain frame cottages, thirty or so of them, all but a few constructed in the past three months. There were cottages for children, cottages for single men, single women, and married couples, all constructed out of rough-cut lumber, with shutters for windows, open porches, and wooden plank runways laid between them in defense against the thick, impermeable clay mud that lingered after every rain. Inside, the cottages were as alike as their exteriors, with the same built-on-the-spot bunk beds, tables, and chairs, and the same compulsive use of every inch of space. Living space was chronically overcrowded, primarily because of the difficulty and expense of importing building materials. Although surrounded by a virtually limitless supply of timber, without a mill to turn the timber into lumber, Jonestown was forced to import virtually all of its building materials, in effect carrying coals to Newcastle.

Beyond the cottages were the fields, several hundred acres planted with bananas, kasava roots, pineapples, melons, mangoes and citrus trees. In addition, smaller, experimental plots of North American crops—beans, cabbages, potatoes, carrots, greens—were in various states of preparation and cultivation. By far the largest part of the work force tended the fields, preparing the ground, plowing, weeding, watering, and harvesting. Following what he had read about China and seen firsthand in Cuba Jim Jones had made it a firm policy that everyone who arrived in Jonestown took a turn in the fields. "We're all field niggers," Rhodes remembers him saying, "and none of us is any better than a field nigger."

Where the fields ended the jungle began. Endless jungle, stretching thousands of miles through the great South American rain basin in one direction and all the way back to the Caribbean coast in the other. Even in Viet Nam Rhodes had never seen anything remotely like it—tall deciduous trees rising a hundred feet from the jungle floor and spreading a canopy of damp, dark shade over everything below. At the edges of the cleared land, where the sun penetrated, there was dense underbrush—exotic flowering plants and razor grass—but farther under the canopy only shade ferns, bamboo, and ground moss grew.

Rhodes spent the balance of his first day moving into a partially completed cabin with a group of young men, including Stanley Clayton. Clayton was in a sullen mood, moping around the settlement, still upset by Jones's tongue-lashing and disappointed that the Promised Land had not delivered what he expected. Although Rhodes spent several hours before dinner trying to explain to Clayton how fortunate they both were to be part of such a unique experiment, Clayton was not convinced. Rhodes, however, was so excited he forgot to sleep, and as he sat on the half-finished porch of the new cabin watching the stars fade into a spectacular jungle sunrise, he decided Jonestown was the most beautiful place he had ever seen.

A few hours later, after breafast, Rhodes and Clayton were both assigned to a work crew preparing a field to be planted with kasava roots. "It was," says Rhodes, "by about a million miles the hardest work I ever did, but it wasn't like you kept waiting for the day to end or anything like that. You were out there with all your friends and you knew you were doing it so people you loved would have food to eat—and I didn't mind it all. It felt good to me."

Late in the afternoon, after an eight-hour shift in the fields,

Rhodes's crew was called to form part of a bucket brigade laboriously watering one of the experimental gardens. Jones himself took a turn in the line, and after about an hour, as Rhodes remembers it:

"There was this big commotion down the line. Turned out Jones had emptied a bucket of water over somebody's head, and then somebody got him, and all of a sudden there was one hell of a water fight going on. Most people couldn't wait to get into it, but there was this one, kind of older man who was bitching about getting his clothes wet—hell, you were already soaked with sweat—and Jones just took out after him laughing and shouting about how he hoped he never got so old and sour he couldn't have fun like a kid every once in a while. It was fun—and damned if that water didn't feel like just what you needed."

When the water fight finally ended, Rhodes wrung out his shirt and went off to dinner marveling at Jones's ability to turn work into something more than work. "It was like he knew just how far he could push people, and when you had to let off some steam—and how to make you feel everybody, including him, was all in it together."

Rhodes settled easily and happily into a spartan routine consisting mostly of work and sleep. At night, after work, he might spend a few hours on his porch talking with friends, or perhaps stay at the Central Pavilion watching a movie or a viedo cassette of a television program; and, on Sundays, there were picnic excursions to Camp 1 or Camp 2, swimming holes at jungle streams; but his chief form of recreation on any given day was likely to be eating. "I never," he says, "ate so much in my life. I guess it's what working can do to you, but the food was damn good too, and you could have as much of it as you wanted. I piled it on so high people would tell me I needed a tray with sides on it."

After a ten-hour day in the fields and a marathon encounter in the mess tent Rhodes often found himself wandering back to the fields he had just left. "It was like I didn't even need entertainment. I could have been listening to the band rehearse or watching TV, but lots of times I just wanted to have a look at what we'd accomplished that day. There was so much satisfaction in it; I mean there I was, thirty-three, thirty-four years old or whatever, never done a damn thing worth shit in my life, and all of a sudden I'm watching myself make 10,000 banana trees into 70,000, watching us push the jungle back a few feet more every day. I could hardly believe I was lucky enough to be a part of building something like that with people I cared about—it was just entirely different than working for money. I'd be tired as hell, but I felt like I couldn't wait for it to be morning again so I could get back at it again."

Pioneer spirit—or whatever it was—eventually even Stanley Clayton caught it. "You just couldn't be there," Clayton admits, "and not want to be part of building it." In fact, after a few weeks in the fields Clayton volunteered for the jungle clearing crew, the most demanding and difficult work at the settlement. Jonestown's master plan called for clearing a mile of jungle in every direction from the Central Pavilion—2,500 acres. Although less than a third of the planned total actually was cleared, even 800-odd acres was an achievement, the largest successful jungle reclamation in the country, in fact; and Clayton's clearing crew managed it; with no machinery more sophisticated than chainsaws and hand axes. "You just cut for a while," Clayton shrugs, "then you chop for a while. Chopping is fun. It's the damn stumps that can drive you crazy."

Clayton's adjustment to life in Jonestown was also aided by his discovery that the pioneer spirit was not the only spirit available at the settlement. Along with many others he quickly mastered the art of brewing "jungle juice," a mixture of pineapples, yeast, and sugar, in gallon jugs. But, although "jungle juice" was both plentiful and potent, Clayton was not a man who could easily turn his back on a new friend like Guyanese rum. Fortunately, he discovered that the local Guyanese, who sometimes guided the clearing crew in the jungle tended to be men after his own heart—hard-drinking, generous, and not overly punctilious about rules. "I'm no alcoholic," Clayton insists, "but I did get a lot happier when I found a way to relax over there."

Although Rhodes did not feel the same need for alcoholic relaxation Clayton felt, there were times, especially when he was with Clayton, that Rhodes relaxed too. On one occasion Clayton and Rhodes were assigned to overnight guard duty at the front gate. As soon as they had settled into the small gatehouse, Clayton produced a pack of cigarettes—a gift from one of his Guyanese friends—and offered one to Rhodes.

"When he took it," Clayton remembers, "I figured we were going to have a pretty decent evening."

"He told me," Rhodes remembers, "he was going to get us something to drink. I thought he meant water."

Clayton walked the half-mile to the Temple's closest neighbor, one of the hard-drinking Guyanese farmers who moonlighted with the jungle-clearing crew, and returned with a nearly full bottle of fine dark Guyanese rum.

Says Rhodes, "He didn't have to pour it down my throat."

Says Clayton, "We just sat there looking at the stars, hooking that bottle now and then."

By morning they had hooked all but a few fingers. "Neither of us," they both agree, "could walk back up the hill to breakfast."

In the morning, when Rhodes and Clayton failed to report for work, a crew supervisor drove down to the gatehouse and poured them in the back of a truck. When they had sobered up sufficiently to be able to stand without external support, they were brought to the pavilion where Jones took one look at them and began sadly shaking his head. They received extra work details as punishment; but, under the circumstances, both felt they had gotten off lightly. Clayton, in fact, began to feel that, although Jonestown might not be exactly what he had been promised, Temple discipline was, at least, for a change as honored in the breech as in the observance.

The discovery cheered him and encouraged him to make a further test of Temple rules. The Jonestown code of sexual conduct prohibited casual sexual encounters. A couple who desired to enter into a sexual relationship was obliged to apply to a Relationship Committee, then endure a three-month nonsexual waiting period, at the end of which, if suitable accomodations could be found, the relationship could finally be consummated. Clayton and his long-time girlfriend from San Francisco had applied to the Relationship Committee but were still nine or ten weeks short of legally spending a night together. Secret brief encounters in the jungle were a temptation, but Clayton had been told that jungle animals were attracted by the scents of lovemaking, and, ardent though he was, he was not quite ardent enough to risk an *in flagrante* encounter with a jaguar. Now, all but convinced that everybody in Jonestown was so involved in building the community "you could do pretty much what you wanted as long as you showed up for work in the morning," he resolved to ignore his eight roommates in the cottage where he lived.

In turn, Rhodes, who was one of the roommates, tried to ignore Clayton: "But, it started to make me kind of nervous, because Stanley was having her over there every night. I tried telling him, 'Hey, man, don't do it—please. He'd say okay, and the next morning I'd see her sneaking out the door. So I tried going to sleep real early and getting up real early so I could say I didn't see anything. But, I was worried anyway because we had some people in that cabin who were so gung-ho, I was sure somebody was going to turn him in. But, what happened was, after a while everybody started doing the same thing—and I mean *everybody*. I mean it got to be a regular pajama party in there at night—and I never did believe it."

The relaxation of discipline came straight from the top, according to Rhodes: "It was Jones. Everything that happened there, it was always Jones's attitude that people followed. At that time, he was so much into seeing the place grow, and he knew everybody was working hard, so I don't think he gave much of a damn about anything else."

Even when it came to the question of allowing someone to leave Jonestown, something Jones had told the congregation he would not permit as long as there were still others in California waiting to be brought over, Jones's response was milder than Rhodes expected. During the early fall three Temple members left the settlement. One, a drifter named Leo Broussard, drifted out into the jungle one day and, despite rumors that he had been eaten in the jungle, surfaced eventually in Port Kaituma. Jones sent one of his adopted sons, Jimmy, to escort Broussard to Georgetown and buy him a ticket back home. Two others, a San Francisco street hustler named Chris Lewis and his wife, left by the front door. The Lewises were favorites of Jones; Chris Lewis, a powerful, charismatic street hustler, was later killed in a San Francisco street fight. Rhodes remembers Jones weeping at the news of his death. When Lewis decided Jonestown was too tame for him, the Lewises were sent off with a party in their honor. Rhodes remembers the party well, because Michelle Lewis chose him to receive a much coveted half-carton of cigarettes, the Lewises' goodbye present to their nicotine-starved comrades.

Leaving Jonestown was the last thing on Odell Rhodes's mind. By the end of September, after a month in the jungle, Rhodes was as addicted to the life of a pioneer as he had ever been to the street life. "It wasn't perfect—I'm not saying it was. Sure we missed things, like I remember I kept my last piece of chewing gum alive for about a month, and it was crowded, and the work was kind of rough sometimes, but when you stacked it up against everything we were accomplishing, the bad things didn't amount to shit. I know for myself, personally, I felt like I'd never been happier, and I didn't feel like I was in some lonely place all this great distance away from home—I felt I *was* home, finally."

On the rare occasions when he left the compound (if the truck was headed for Port Kaituma to pick up settlers or supplies at night or on Sunday he sometimes jumped in back for the ride) "the ride back was always the best part. Everytime we passed the front gate I felt like cheering." If he happened to be working in the fields when a truckload of new arrivals came bounding up the dirt road, he would look up, and wave and feel his spirits soar, "like I was personally responsible for bringing them to a better life."

Rhodes not only came to think of Jonestown as his home, he also came to think of the small, isolated jungle settlement as a new, emerging nation, and he shared with most of the rest of the community the dream that they were building the capital city of a country that would someday spread through the great jungle and attract thousands—perhaps hundred of thousands—of oppressed refugees from America. Like most of the community, Rhodes ceased thinking of himself as an American and gradually came to have little or no interest in anything that happened outside of Jonestown.

Although Jim Jones encouraged the community to forget about the past—and was, of course, the ultimate source of the fantasies about the future—Jones himself was anything but oblivious to the outside world. As much as he hoped that the thousands of miles of ocean and jungle between Jonestown and San Francisco would insulate the community, he still continued to worry about his enemies. He made keeping track of their activities the primary responsibility of the staff that remained in San Francisco and he personally kept in daily contact by short-wave radio.

For the first few months the reports were evidently reassuring. Although Jones rarely shared the details of his intelligence with the community, his mood was so buoyant and optimistic most of the community simply assumed they had left their tormentors behind forever. The conspiracy, which had been such a subject of concern in San Francisco, was mentioned only rarely, and, although Jones did speak occasionally of vigilance and self-defense, America seemed so far away and Jonestown so isolated that hardly anyone took the warnings seriously. Odell Rhodes, for one, was so convinced that worrying about Jonestown's enemies was a closed chapter that the community's first alert shocked him.

Rhodes remembers that he was just finishing his work in the fields when he heard three quick shots from a rifle, the pre-arranged panic alarm for everyone in the community to drop everything and assemble immediately at the Central Pavilion. Rhodes ran the half-mile to the pavilion just in time to hear Jones announce that the settlement was about to be attacked. "He didn't say much, and I didn't know what the hell was going on, but just the fact that he didn't say much had me worried because you knew that if he wasn't talking something had to be wrong. I think all he said was something about how the prime minister was out of the country and the people he'd left in charge were against us, and they'd been bribed or something so they were going to look the other way and the CIA was going to take the opportunity to assassinate him and kidnap John-John Stoen back for his mother.

Within a few minutes virtually all of the community's 700-odd members, including all but the youngest children and seniors who could barely walk, were deployed around the perimeter of the settlement in a defensive line armed with whatever was close at hand— machetes, axes, hoes, shovels, and rocks. A few cutlasses and the handful of firearms in Jonestown at the time were distributed to a platoon of bodyguards who accompanied Jones as he stalked the lines exhorting the troops. For six days everyone in Jonestown stared nervously toward the jungle waiting to be attacked. "That's all we did, all day, every day—we just sat there. We even slept there. It started raining and we just stayed there sleeping in the mud."

Once a day, in rotation, sections of the line were sent back to their cottages for dry clothes: "They told us they didn't give a damn if men showered with men or men showered with women—just get the hell back as quick as you could." Rhodes was called off the line for other reasons on two occasions. The first time, after somebody remembered his army background, he was called to have a go at disassembling a carbine no one else had been able to clean. A few days later he was sent to one of the nursery cottages to help care for some of the small children, who along with the elderly and infirm were the only members not on the picket line. Accustomed as he was to drills, alerts, and just plain following orders after eight years in the army, Rhodes had not given much thought either way to the seriousness of the situation. What he saw at the nursery shocked him. The children had been tranquilized and many of them were cranky and disoriented—and extremely difficult to comfort. For a few minutes he was angry that the children had been made to suffer, but it soon occurred to him that his anger might be misplaced. "If there was any one thing I thought I knew about Jones it was the way he felt about children, and I just couldn't see him doing that to them unless he thought he had to. I don't know exactly what I thought before then, but that convinced me—I thought they were coming."

A few days later, with no more ceremony than it had begun, the Six-Day Alert ended. Although rumors that the enemy had been sighted in the jungle circulated periodically, as well as one rumor of an actual skirmish, after six days of waiting no one could say for sure if the threat had been real or not. All Jim Jones would say was that through the combination of the community's vigilance and the intervention of Jonestown's friends in the Guyanese government the assault had been forestalled—for the time being. The danger, however, according to Jones, had only just begun. Through his "sources," Jones told the community, he had learned that the Temple's enemies, primarily Grace Stoen and the other defectors, had joined with the CIA and hostile elements in the Guyanese government in a plot to destroy Jonestown. A CIA trained force of mercenaries remained in a staging area across the Brazilian border waiting for marching orders. "We only want to be left alone," Jones told the congregation, "I've told them that. But it's not enough that we've come all this way to get away from them. They want to destroy us."

10

Fall/Winter:
State of Siege

When Jim Jones announced to the community that the conspiracy which had driven the People's Temple from California had now followed them to Guyana, Odell Rhodes believed him.

"I didn't think about it all that much, but it did make sense to me. We all knew what the FBI did to the Muslims and the Panthers, and we heard all the time about the CIA in Chile and them trying to assassinate Castro with a poison cigar and basically wasting people whenever they felt like it, so I guess we all believed you couldn't put anything past the CIA."

As plausible as what Jones told the community sounded to Rhodes, he did not know the entire story about the Six-Day Alert. In fact, very few members of the community, aside from the circle of advisers closest to Jones, knew anything about the rest of the story. In the eight weeks Jones had been in Guyana the Stoen case had taken several turns for the worse. In July, shortly before Jones left, Tim Stoen had reached an agreement with his wife and joined her in the court action to regain custody of John-John; with the husband and wife united against Jones (and both now claiming that John-John was their natural child), a California court had wasted no time awarding temporary custody to the Stoens. The decree was issued on August 26 and two weeks later the Stoens sent their San Francisco lawyer, Jeffrey Haas, to Guyana in an attempt to serve Jones with documents ordering John-John's return.

Haas chartered a plane and flew to Jonestown on September 12. He was allowed to enter the settlement but not to see Jones or serve him with the court order. When Haas returned to Georgetown, he conferred with the Stoens by telephone, and then hired a local lawyer to pursue the case in the Guyanese courts.

When Jones learned that Haas had initiated legal action in Georgetown, he reacted with something very close to panic. Moving to Guyana had been painful enough; Tim Stoen's defection in the midst of the crisis had been even worse; but, at very least, Jones had consoled himself with the belief that moving to Guyana would end the custody problem once and for all. It was, after all, Tim Stoen's own plan, guaranteed to be foolproof. Now both Eugene Chaikin and the Temple's Guyanese solicitor explained to him that although the California court order was indeed unenforceable in Guyana, there was nothing to prevent Stoen from starting all over in a Guyanese court.

Jones moved quickly. Guyana is a small, poor country where hard currency—especially dollars—is scarce and the things it can buy expensive. It is also a country with a delicate political balance, in which a minority black government rules an Amerindian and East Indian majority. A few dollars and a block of six or seven hundred immigrant voters can go a long way, and Jim Jones had not neglected to make powerful friends in the Guyanese government, among them, Claude Mingo, the minister of home affairs; Ptolemy Reid, the deputy prime minister; and Frederick Wills, the former foreign minister. As soon as Jones learned of Stoen's intention to carry the fight to the Guyanese courts, he called on his friends.

For openers he demanded that the government revoke Jeffry Haas's visa. The response was lukewarm, even after Jones claimed to have documentary evidence that Haas was a CIA agent who had been dispatched to assassinate him. The most Jones's friends would promise was that the charges would be investigated. Jones was livid. He attempted to reach Ptolemy Reid, the deputy prime minister, who was his most important government contact. Reid, he was told, was not available; the deputy prime minister was in the United States on business. Jones panicked. Putting together Haas's presence with his protector's absence, he was certain that both events were part of the same conspiracy. Stoen, Haas, and the CIA had obviously arranged for the court to issue an order to produce John-John immediately while Reid was out of the country. Armed with the court order, the CIA's mercenaries would then invade Jonestown, kidnap John-John, and assassinate Jones.

Evidently convinced that an attack was imminent, Jones then sounded the alarm that sent the people of Jonestown into the trenches. He then contacted the Temple's San Francisco office by short-wave radio and instructed his staff to track Reid down and inform him that unless Jones received assurances that the court would not act, the people of Jonestown would respond to any attempt to recover the child by killing themselves in protest.

Reid responded that he had never heard of a Guyanese court acting quickly about anything, but promised to look into the situation nonetheless. Six days later, the Guyanese court ruled against the Stoens' lawyer's motion for an immediate writ ordering Jones to hand John-John over to the Stoens and scheduled a preliminary hearing on the merits of the case for November 18—six weeks away. Jones then called an end to the Six-Day Alert.

He did not, however, call off his attempts to pressure the government. Through his staff in Georgetown he began an intensive lobbying campaign to convince the government that the custody case was actually a CIA plot. Whatever the Guyanese thought of that contention, the matter of Jim Jones vs. Tim and Grace Stoen was placed before Prime Minister Forbes Burnham and discussed with the U.S. embassy. A few weeks later, Jones was informed of the government's decision. It would not interfere in a court proceeding; it would, however, informally guarantee that whatever orders the court issued would not be enforced as long as Jones and the child remained in Jonestown.

If the Guyanese thought it had formulated a reasonable compromise, it did not anticipate the depth of Jones's fears. To Jones, the compromise was evidence that the CIA had its own agents inside the government, evidence that the CIA had as much clout with the Guyanese government as he had. Furthermore, although the Guyanese court had so far refused to issue an order honoring the California court's order to return John-John to the Stoens, it had issued a writ ordering Jones to produce the boy to the court pending its hearing of the case. Since Jones was terrified that he could be arrested for refusing, the compromise had the effect of making him a prisoner in Jonestown, with the result that he was now unable to lobby his case personally in Georgetown. He also believed that by effectively restricting his movements, the compromise made him a sitting duck for whatever adventures the Stoens and the CIA had in mind. Instead of accepting the compromise, Jones redoubled his efforts to convince anyone who would listen that he was the victim of an unprovoked, politically motivated attack whose ultimate aim was not merely to steal his own child, but to destroy Jonestown.

Inside Jonestown, the community was thoroughly ignorant of Jones's legal and political problems. All the people in Jonestown knew was that the enemy had reappeared and their community was threatened. That much Jones made abundantly clear. In the community's regular meetings, formerly low-keyed affairs devoted chiefly to routine business, Jones began to speak more and more of Jonestown's enemies. "Somebody might start talking about some problem we were having with our chickens, and all of a sudden, Jones was telling us the problem wasn't chickens, it was snakes—and then he'd start in on Tim Stoen or the CIA or somebody else who was against us," Odell Rhodes remembers.

In response to the threat, Jones preached readiness and matched words with action by drilling the irregular team of bodyguards formed during the alert into a permanent, full-time security force patrolling the settlement day and night.

Although he did not doubt the danger, Odell Rhodes was not worried. "If they were out there, I figured we'd see them sooner or later, but I'd lived in combat zones enough so it didn't bother me all that much." Beyond the formation of the security forces, he noticed no particular change in Jonestown's daily routines. "I guess maybe we started having a few more meetings, and there was a lot of talk about being ready for anything, so every time a plane flew by, you kind of wondered who it was, and if you saw somebody running someplace, it made you wonder what was going on, but basically, things didn't seem any different to me. They sure didn't seem any worse, I know that."

A month or so after the Six-Day Alert, Jones announced a further security precaution. In the future, Jonestown would be closed to unannounced visitors. Up until that time, every Sunday had been an open house, primarily for the benefit of Jonestown's Guyanese neighbors who flocked the settlement to take advantage of Jonestown's free medical clinic, a festive Sunday dinner, and a movie or dance at night. Rhodes was disappointed; he liked the Guyanese he had met, admired their open, easy-going manner, and—frankly—enjoyed showing Jonestown off to them. But if the enemies had made some small sacrifices necessary, neither Rhodes nor anyone else was about to complain.

Within a few weeks, Jones also began practice alerts to prepare the community to react instantly to an emergency. Although Rhodes was not sure that staying awake all night practicing security measures and then going out to the fields to do a day's work actually increased anyone's alertness, he was not about to complain about that either.

"I think everybody felt like it was too damn bad they couldn't just leave us alone, but nobody was too uptight about it at that point. We were all basically just working hard and having a pretty damn good time. Even Jones. Even when something happened, lots of times he'd make it into kind of a joke. Like I remember one night, it was kind of late; I was down by the pavilion and I heard gunshots—I'd swear it was automatic rifle fire, and I was in the army long enough to know what an automatic weapon sounds like. Now, I also know I never saw an automatic weapon at Jonestown, and I don't believe anyone ever found one. But, anyway, it came from the direction of Jones's house, and the security went down there and they said that everything was all right—nothing to worry about.

"At the time, what was on everybody's mind was that the supply boat was a day late and we didn't have any meat. But the next day, we had some kind of stew for dinner and then, after dinner, we had a meeting and Jones started talking about what a fine dinner it was. Then he told us that last night—when we heard the shots—someone had broken into his house and tried to kill him. But the security had killed whoever it was instead. Then he said that it seemed a waste to bury this person when his people had been without meat for a couple of days—and I don't think he actually came right out and said we had just eaten somebody—but the way he was talking, we knew for damn sure that that's what he meant. In fact, I remember there was this old lady, Birdie Rogers, sitting in the front row and she was about the blackest person in Jonestown. I mean, she was the blackest person I have *ever* seen and all of a sudden, she turned green—I mean, you could see her turn green—and Jones took one look at her, and he started to ask her if anything was wrong, and he just plain broke up. He damn near fell off the platform laughing.

"Eventually," Rhodes remembers, "the meeting turned into a joke with people talking about who ate what parts." Rhodes had nothing more to say about the incident except to swear that he saw the truck bringing the shipment of groceries the following day.

While Odell Rhodes and most of the rest of the Jonestown community went cheerfully about their everyday business, the battle in Georgetown between Jim Jones and the Stoens continued. Jones's Georgetown staff, composed chiefly of members of the old San Francisco Planning Commission, including Sharon Amos, Deborah Touchette, Mike Prokes, and Tim Carter, worked long overtime hours lobbying Jones's case with anyone who would listen—foreign diplomats, Guyanese politicians, journalists, bureaucrats, and other Americans visiting Guyana. They kept Jones informed of their efforts with mountains of paper describing each and every contact they made, and Jones communicated his strategy to them directly by short-wave radio from Jonestown. Within the capital the staff was accepted as a sort of unaccredited foreign embassy—even on the regular diplomatic social scene—and through their entreaties with the Guyanese government Jones succeeded in securing promises from the Guyanese government that the judge hearing the Stoen case would be informally "briefed" on the Temple's version of the background of the case. Perhaps as a result of the "briefing," the November 18 hearing produced nothing more substantial than the decision to schedule another hearing early in January.

Emboldened by his success Jones then ordered the Georgetown staff to mount a blitzkrieg public-relations campaign against the Stoens in preparation for the January hearing. Through his contacts in the Foreign Ministry he also managed to have the Stoens' visitors visas limited to two weeks. To that point the U.S. embassy had carefully refused to take sides in the dispute, but it did protest the curtailment of the Stoens' visas, and eventually the Stoens were allowed to remain in the country through most of January. When the January hearings finally ended, the court reserved its decision, setting no date for any further action. Although the court's non-decision once again represented a victory—of sorts—for Jones, it was, as it turned out, a victory bought at a substantial cost; and, ironically, virtually the entire cost was credit thrown away.

All of Jones's contacts in the government had assured him that the court was unlikely in the extreme to issue a definitive ruling in a complicated case known to be of interest to powerful parties inside the government and out. In view of their assurances, the lobbying campaign seemed to many a tactical mistake, at best; and there were some who openly resented his overt attempt to exert pressure on a matter pending before a Guyanese court. Even among Jones's closest friends, many of whom understood the depth of his concern about John-John, there was a feeling that by making the case into such a highly charged public issue, Jones had put them—totally unnecessarily—into a potentially embarrassing situation, in which the very appearance of any special treatment for Jones could be viewed as bowing to pressure.

The result was that a number of small concessions Jones had won from the government were now called into question by nervous bureaucrats and junior ministers who had previously looked the other way when politely asked by some unofficial third-party emissary known to be close to both Jones and one or another of his powerful friends in the government. The powerful friends, in turn, found themselves in a position in which countermanding decisions to require Jonestown to abide by the same rules as the rest of the country, were simply not worth the trouble it would cause—especially since the concessions themselves were all relatively minor matters such as exemptions for the Jonestown clinic and school from Guyanese licensing procedures.

Although this negative trade-off between political damage and bureaucratic inconvenience was carefully explained to Jones's staff on several occasions, Jones—by now beginning to feel the effects of his exile in the jungle—chose to interpret his friends' exercise of elementary political self-interest as yet another betrayal—in effect, over-reacting again to a situation he had created in the first place by over-reacting.

In Jones's peculiarly Manichaean mind, anyone who was not with him in every battle, right to the end, was against him; and, if there were those in the government who were now unwilling to help him, there could only be one explanation: the conspiracy against him had penetrated the Guyanese government and was now creeping inexorably through the ranks of his friends.

According to Odell Rhodes, Jones's attitude toward his Guyanese hosts changed drastically during the early part of the new year. Without any attempt to explain why, he told the members of the community that they could no longer count on the protection of their black socialist brothers, and he began to raise the possibility that when the inevitable attack came, the Guyanese Defense Forces might be among the attackers. "Up until then," Odell Rhodes remembers, "when we talked about an attack, we generally talked fighting. But when he started to talk about the GDF, he said they'd come in with tanks and automatic weapons and we wouldn't stand a chance. People would say they'd fight anyway—and he liked that— but he'd tell us we couldn't fight against the GDF. He said no matter what happened, they were still our brothers. They were poor black people just like us, and if they came, it would be because some of their leaders had been bought off, and they wouldn't understand what they were doing. He said it would be better to kill ourselves than to let them kill us."

Trapped in the jungle, betrayed yet again, and now, in his mind, more vulnerable than ever, Jones was clearly beginning to lose some of his enthusiasm for his jungle paradise. The confident, optimistic leader, who had worked as hard as anyone to build Jonestown, who had stayed up until morning to welcome new arrivals and made a daily habit of joining the workers in the field for at least a few minutes every day, was now more likely than not to be found in the radio shack conferring with his staffs in Georgetown or San Francisco about legal strategies and public-relations campaigns. In Jones's mind the political situation was now a full-blown crisis.

He was especially troubled by what he perceived as the betrayal of his Guyanese allies. As he brooded about their treachery, he began to come to the conclusion that if Guyanese socialism was insufficiently dedicated to the cause and incapable of resisting the blandishments of his enemies, it might well be time to seek out a more powerful and constant protector. Early in January, he instructed the Georgetown staff to contact the local Soviet embassy with an eye toward discussing the possibility of moving the community—lock, stock, and barrel—to the Soviet Union. Although it seems difficult, at best, to imagine a Soviet diplomat with much enthusiasm for the prospect of one thousand—mostly black—Americans immigrating to Mother Russia, the Soviets were evidently at least polite enough to encourage Jones to make the subject of moving to Russia a favorite

130 AWAKE IN A NIGHTMARE

topic at nightly meetings. "He talked about it quite a bit," Rhodes remembers. "He said somebody might go over in the spring and look around, and if it looked all right, we might just go because that would be one place we could be damn sure nobody was going to hassle us." Although Rhodes considered himself as curious as the next man about life in Russia, "I didn't think about it as much as most people. It seemed like kind of a waste to me to talk about moving after all we'd accomplished. I guess I didn't see why we couldn't try to make Jonestown work. We'd done so damn much already."

Rhodes's realization that his leader might be prepared to give up on Jonestown troubled him almost immediately, not so much because of what Jones said, but because by the middle of January he began to notice that Jones's mood had filtered down and affected the spirit in which the people of Jonestown approached their work. "It got so nobody was really working very hard anymore. You couldn't put your finger on it exactly, but it was like nobody thought it was very important anymore." But, although Rhodes did sense that the long discussions about enemies and attacks, the increased security, and the talk about moving to Russia were all somehow tied to the passing of the old pioneer work spirit, he was not at all sure *how* they were tied together; and he was, in any event, inclined to attribute the problem in the fields to a more immediate problem.

New settlers had been arriving steadily throughout the period Rhodes had been at Jonestown, but beginning in December, perhaps because he suspected his enemies closing in, Jones felt the need to surround himself with as many supporters as possible. Jones instructed his San Francisco staff to step up recruitment, especially among the more substantial members, those with skills, education, and property who had been most reluctant to uproot themselves. In some cases recruitment bordered on conscription. In the case of one family in which a son had left home and broken contact with his parents, Jones instructed his staff to tell the parents the son was in Jonestown. When the parents arrived expecting a reunion with their son, Jones had the staff tell the son that his father was critically ill in Jonestown and languishing because he feared he would die without seeing his son again.

Others were told that their skills were desperately needed and warned that refusing the summons would be considered an act of betrayal equal to the treachery of a Deanna Mertle or a Tim Stoen.

Scores of Temple members succumbed to the pressure and when they arrived, Jones was so happy to see them, he excused many of them from the once obligatory stint in the fields. The effect on the morale of the field workers was predictably devastating. Odell Rhodes felt that Jones had broken a promise, and for the first time since he joined the Temple he felt like complaining about something.

"It hurt, because here you are working your ass off to bring people over, and they step right off the boat and slide right in to some easy job—maybe even a job you wanted."

As resentment about exceptions to the everybody-works-in-the-fields policy grew, productivity declined. But by now less interested in productivity than with tangible evidence of his following, Jones allowed the community to divide into classes of workers and managers. His response to the grumblings in the fields was to institute a system of Production Reports kept by members of the Security Force who roamed the community taking notes on workers. The result, again predictably, was anything but an increase in productivity:

"Maybe you're just comming off a break, and just getting ready for one, but either way you're not moving real fast—and they happen to see you right then and all of a sudden you got to answer for loafing off even though you're busting your stones the whole damn day. It gets to you real quick. You stop really caring about what you're doing and you start spending more time looking for who's watching than you do working. And when you're supposed to be growing your own food that ain't the way to do it."

Sure enough, Rhodes's fears were soon vindicated at the dinner table. Jonestown's food, formerly one of its glories, soon became a bland, monotonous medley of rice and vegetables. Jonestown never really had even approached agricultural sufficiency, a goal that even under the best of circumstances may have been impossible given the problems of jungle farming and the fact that well over half the population was either too young or too old to be productive at farming or much of anything else; but until January, what it did produce had been supplemented regularly with fish, meat, and staples like rice and flour. By early spring, only the staples and an occasional shark or swordfish, caught by local fisherman, found their way to the Jonestown dinner table.

Jones told the community that with the ever-growing population, the reason for the restricted diet was simple economics. But in view of the fact that Temple bank accounts in the Caribbean continued to increase steadily to something in excess of ten million dollars eventually, the reasons, if they were economic at all, were certainly not simple.

In all probability, they were not economic at all. Like most of what happened after the winter of 1978, the explanation begins inside Jim Jones's mind. In Jones's mind, Jonestown had become a community fighting for its very survival. Abandoned by his allies, surrounded by his enemies, Jones had begun to view Jonestown as a kind of Stalingrad of the jungle—a city under siege. Whether or not the enemies were real or the attack anything other than fantasy, the simple fact was that Jones possessed the rare power to invest his fantasies with reality. Through a combination of circumstances, including the force of his personality, the structure of the community, and its isolation, if Jim Jones believed Jonestown was under siege, it was the simplest thing in the world for Jim Jones to make Jonestown into a community indistinguishable in every respect from a community actually under seige. All he had to do was tell the community an attack was imminent, seal the perimeter, restrict visitors, and begin to provide the hardships that accompany a siege—hardships like crowded quarters and short rations.

The compulsion to act out fantasies in order to make them seem more real is common enough, especially among schizophrenics and politicians, both of which Jones probably was; and, in fact, the person Jones probably wanted most to convince may well have been none other than Jim Jones. In any event, whatever his intentions, by early spring he had succeeded in creating a very real sense of danger within the community.

When Odell Rhodes looked down at a dinner plate full of rice and gravy—and not much else—he simply shrugged his shoulders and accepted what seemed to him the perfectly natural consequence of the danger surrounding the community—a fact of life under siege. "The food didn't bother me at all. Jones explained it to us, and I believed him. Besides, I've had worse food lots of times. Hell, I was used to having no food lots of times. I sure as hell wasn't about to get down on anybody about the food."

If there was anything Rhodes *was* about to get down on anybody about is why it was becoming impossible to defend Jonestown and to build it at the same time. Rhodes simply did not understand why the building program had all but stopped, why the jungle-clearing project had stopped entirely, and why farming had slowed to a crawl. "It just kind of seemed to me like everybody was starting to worry about everything except what we were there to do—to make Jonestown a good place to live."

11

Spring:
The Serpent's Tooth

By early spring, Odell Rhodes knew that Jonestown was a far different place than the happy, busy pioneering community of the previous August. The constant threat of attack, the strain of living under siege, and the growing sense of isolation had combined to create an atmosphere of fear and a general mood of hopelessness. Convinced that the world that began at the edge of the jungle contained nothing but danger, the people of Jonestown were beginning to believe that their enemies had driven them to a corner from which there was no escape.

Even the pace of daily life was changing. The heroic effort of carving the settlement out of a wild jungle had been all but abandoned, and more and more a typical day was one endless community meeting—a marathon of routine meetings, practice alerts, and a new species of group encounter sessions called White Nights.

A White Night was a kind of crisis rehearsal that might last a few hours or an entire day, but however long it lasted, its distinguishing characteristic was numbing emotional intensity.

"They would usually start," Rhodes remembers, "with the traitors—the Stoens and the rest of them back in the States. That's the way he got your attention. He'd get real sad and talk about how he just couldn't understand how people who'd been our brothers and sisters could turn around and do these things to us. He'd talk about what kind of people could sell out their comrades for a fancy car and a pocket full of credit cards. Then he'd shake his head and he'd say they'd broken his heart—made him feel like life just wasn't worth living.

"When he started talking like that, then people would start jumping up and down and shouting about how much *they* loved him— and finally, he'd say he knew they did and that was the only thing that made him want to go on—that made him want to go on living."

More and more, according to Rhodes, the dominant subject of the White Nights became the question of whether or not life was worth living. "It would always come around to what we were going to do when they attacked us. Sometimes we'd talk fighting; and then he'd remind us that we couldn't fight the Guyanese, and then other people would bring up various alternatives, but he'd just keep shaking his head and ruling them all out for some reason or other, whatever they were. What it usually came down to in the end was that no matter what happened, they'd send us all back home. Then he'd talk about all the reasons we left America, and he'd ask if anybody wanted to go back to that. And then it'd get real quiet, and finally he'd just throw up his hands and say there wasn't any way out for us."

To Rhodes the point was clear: "He was trying to make people understand how serious it was—to let them know we were all in this together, and we damn well better be prepared to see it through all the way to the end—whatever it was.

"He wanted people to say they were willing to die. There was a whole lot of talk about whether people were willing to die for their beliefs or not and he was always telling people there were a whole lot of things worse than dying for your beliefs. He said living against your beliefs was living in hell—and, if you were dead, well—at least you were free.

"I don't know if I agreed with all that exactly, but to me it was real simple. Shit, I spent eight fucking years in the army ready to die for a country that hadn't done balls for me. I was damn well ready to die for Jonestown—if that's what it came down to."

Although Rhodes considered himself as firmly committed as anyone to seeing Jonestown through to the end, the pressure of constantly reaffirming his commitment at a frantic emotional pitch had a complex effect on him. Strong emotions tended to unsettle him, and, as a White Night shuddered to the inevitable emotional climax, Rhodes often felt as if he were watching an event he was not quite a part of. While others screamed and cried, Rhodes studied his shoes: "I don't know what it is about me, but since I was a kid I think I've cried maybe twice in my life—I guess it just got kicked out of me somewhere along the way."

Unlike many of the others for whom the shared catharsis amounted to a much-needed release from the tensions of living under siege, Rhodes left the White Nights feeling simply drained, and instead of the feelings of communal solidarity the events stimulated in many others, he felt mostly confusion. "It was just that, to me, I knew in my heart I was in for the whole trip, so talking about it didn't do anything for me. The only thing that bothered me was Jones. You could see how depressed he was about the way things were going. He just didn't seem to have the energy he used to have. He didn't laugh and make jokes about things the way he used to. And he looked terrible. I figured maybe he was sick."

While Rhodes and perhaps some others of his street-wise friends were confused about the direction in which Jonestown was moving, there were a few others for whom the changes in community stimulated not confusion but serious dissatisfaction. There were not many; but a few people, especially among the group of middle-class Planning Commission–level members Jones had made a special effort to bring to Jonestown during the winter, were openly unhappy.

Dale Parks, Jones's former personal secretary, was one. Parks had left the Temple in San Francisco because he wanted a taste of what life was like outside the People's Temple. He was convinced to come to Jonestown only after Jones swore to him that his skills (he was a respiratory therapist) were desperately needed. When he arrived and discovered he was not needed for anything but his presence, he felt ill-used. "Jones lied to me. It was as simple as that. He lied to me, and he lied to my family, and I knew from day one it was going to be hell over there."

Debbie Layton Blakey, an attractive twenty-five-year-old from a prominent Temple family, also arrived in Jonestown during the winter, at about the same time as Dale Parks. Until that time she had been a key member of the San Francisco staff responsible for keeping track of the organization's financial records as well as a variety of other sensitive tasks, including at one point offering Tim Stoen a bribe of five thousand dollars not to join his wife in the legal fight to regain custody of John-John.

Debbie Blakey was a member of the Temple's ruling inner circle, one of a dozen or so people in the Temple closest to Jim Jones. Along with the Stoens, her two sister-in-laws, Carolyn and Karen Layton, Maria Katsaris, Terri Buford, and a few others, she belonged to the Temple's family of families, the small group who called Jones Jim and spoke freely to him, at least in private.

Less than eager to travel to the jungle in the first place, Debbie Blakey was shocked by what she saw at Jonestown—the overcrowding, the food, the constant psychodrama, the close, heavy atmosphere of depression. The Jim Jones Blakey found in Jonestown frightened her. What had seemed to be strength of character and a commitment to an unpopular but just cause in San Fransico seemed more like paranoid megalomania in the jungles of Guyana.

What had happened to her brother, Larry Layton, was especially disturbing. Layton had, in succession, married two women and brought them into the Temple. Jim Jones had, in succession, appropriated both of them to his own household. Layton worshipped Jones, and now, little by little, he seemed to be losing his ability to tell where Larry Layton stopped and Jim Jones began. Debbie Blakey was horrified, and to her peers in the inner circle she made no effort to hide her feelings. Although she was reluctant to even ask Jones to be sent back to San Francisco, largely because her mother was at the same time wasting away with terminal cancer in the Jonestown infirmary, her unhappiness was a matter of common knowledge.

Dale Parks and Debbie Blakey worried Jones enormously. Especially Debbie Blakey. Nothing he could say seemed to comfort her, and he was beginning to have the awful feeling that once again, someone close to him, someone he had trusted implicitly, someone who should have been closing ranks behind him, was at the point of betraying him.

Jones had other reasons to be worried as well. Although the issue of who would eventually win custody of John-John Stoen still rested peacefully with the Guyanese judge who had long since decided that in this particular case judicial discretion was the better part of judicial valor, all was definitely not quiet on the home front of the Stoen war. For months the Stoens had tried unsuccessfully to convince the U.S. State Department in Washington to conduct a full-scale investigation of living conditions inside Jonestown. The State Department refused, claiming that its routine consular visits showed no reason for any further investigation and citing a department legal counsel's advice that an investigation would constitute interference with the "rights of privacy and religious freedom of U.S. citizens."

Discouraged by the State Department's response and the no-news-is-bad-news-news from the courts in Guyana, the Stoens decided to pursue their fight along other avenues. Along with the Mills and some twenty other relatives of Jonestown members, they formed a group called the Committee of Concerned Relatives, raised a war chest, and decided to mount a public-relations campaign.

Their ultimate goal was to destroy Jonestown by provoking enough public outrage about living conditions in the settlement so the U.S. government would pressure the Guyanese government to expel Jones from the country. To that end they hired a San Francisco firm of public-relations consultants to organize a media campaign charging Jones with kidnapping John Stoen, holding the people of Jonestown prisoners under concentration-camp security, and various other acts of terrorism and brutality. Although some members of the committee, including the Mills, also wanted to highlight charges of embezzlement and mismanagement of Temple funds against Jones, it was finally decided to concentrate on Jonestown, perhaps because Tim Stoen and, to a lesser extent, Grace, had been so intimately involved in the Temple's financial dealings that charges against Jones would probably only result in countercharges against them by Jones. Furthermore, whatever the Mills thought of Jones's financial dealings, Stoen was in a position to know that personal greed was not one of Jones's vices, and despite the ill will between them he may still have respected Jones for that much at least.

While the Committee of Concerned Relatives planned its campaign, Jones had his staff keep close track of the Committee's members. He had also, in the meanwhile, hired Charles Garry, a colorful San Francisco trial lawyer, to act as a spokesman for the Temple. Retaining Garry, who had successfully represented unpopular political causes (including the Communist party and the Black Panthers) for more than thirty years, was Jones's way of letting the Committee know that he was fully prepared to fight in any arena the Committee might choose. But deep in his heart Jones continued to hope that in the end the Committee would choose not to fight at all; and throughout the winter he confined his staff's activities to observation (with perhaps an occasional vaguely threatening telephone call) and he had Garry do nothing more hostile than give speeches and make himself available for interviews.

Then, suddenly, on April 11 the situation changed dramatically when the Committee issued a blistering statement to the press (with copies to every member of the U.S. Congress). Signed by the Stoens and some twenty other relatives of Jonestown residents, the statement accused Jones of "flagrant and cruel disregard for human rights," including threatening the lives of the entire community during the Six-Day Alert; using "physical intimidation and psychological coercion as a part of a mind programming campaign; preventing members from leaving Jonestown by confiscating passports and stationing guards around the community; and depriving them of their right to privacy, free speech and freedom of association."

The statement went on for three thousand words to paint a picture of coercion, repression, and insanity. The night it was issued one of the San Francisco staff read the entire text to Jones by short-wave radio. When he heard the names of those who had signed it, he broke down and cried; he then summoned the entire community to the Central Pavilion and announced that the end had come.

"We can't win no matter what we do," he told them, "because no matter how hard we try to live our lives in peace, they won't leave us alone. They've followed us here, they lie about us, and they won't rest until they destroy us. We'd be better off dead than living with all this pain."

Ignoring shouts of support from the crowd, Jones shook his head sadly: "Are we afraid to die? Is it worse to die than to live in hell?"

Odell Rhodes remembers what happened next:

"He sent one of the nurses to the medical tent and told us she was going to get the poison, and we were going to do it right then and there. Then he started calling on people, calling them out by name, and asking them if they were afraid to die. I wasn't sure if it was for real or not, but the people he was calling on, they were all people who'd stood up before when we talked about dying and admitted they were afraid, so I kind of figured, if he really meant to do it, he wouldn't be calling on those people, he'd be calling on people he'd know were ready to do anything he said.

"Then, when the nurse came back, he said she was going to demonstrate how easy it was, and she took one sip out of this bottle and just kind of keeled over and crumpled up. Well, right then I stopped being worried. I mean I'm no medical expert, but I never heard of any poison that takes a person as quick as that."

Confident that he was witnessing only another piece of Jim Jones's theater of the absurd, Rhodes began to look around to see who else had come to the same conclusion. "There were some people who looked real worried, and some people who didn't. It was kind of hard to say how many of each there were, but a lot of the old people and a lot of the children were sitting there with their eyes all bugged out, so I guess they believed it."

Meanwhile Jones continued to call the roll of those he knew were afraid to die. "A lot of them were crying and you could see how hard it was on them but eventually they'd all say they'd do it if that's what he decided we had to do. But, then he got to this one teenage girl, and she said she'd do it just like the rest of them, but she wanted to say goodbye to all her friends first. Well, she started going on naming damn near everybody in Jonestown. It might not sound real funny now, but it was like she was reading the goddamn telephone book, a mile a minute, without even breathing, and after a while you just couldn't keep a straight face. I don't remember who laughed first, but after a while even Jones was laughing, and that was about the end of it. Even the dead nurse got up and started laughing."

Rhodes gave the suicide performance very little thought. "I didn't necessarily see the point of scaring hell out of the children, but aside from that, I just thought of it as one more way of getting it across to people how serious things were. In a way I was almost surprised he hadn't done it before; I mean one thing about Jones you could count on was that he never passed up an opportunity to make everything as dramatic as possible."

But if the suicide drama seemed only barely out of the ordinary to Odell Rhodes, it meant a great deal more to Debbie Blakey. However reluctantly she had come to Jonestown, however oppressed she had felt trapped in the jungle with a leader whose sanity she questioned, the suicide rehearsal was something entirely different—a loud alarm warning her to get clear as quickly as possible.

A few days after the rehearsal she asked Jones for permission to fly to Trinidad for a few days to visit a sister who, she said, was flying through on her way to South America. Jones understood immediately that once she had a passport and a plane ticket in hand Debbie Blakey was not likely to be back. He refused. They argued. Finally, Jones relented. Trinidad was out, but he would assign her to the Georgetown staff. There, back in civilization, surrounded by the creature comforts of Lamaha House and a group of close friends, her attitude might soften.

Although Jones certainly knew that in Georgetown, defection was as easy as a stroll to the U.S. embassy, if he was afraid Debbie Blakey might defect, he may have believed two factors would dissuade her: the first was her mother, Lisa Layton, who was terminally ill with cancer in Jonestown; the second was Jones's claim that he had a "spy" inside the embassy who could delay any attempted defection long enough to get word back to Jonestown.

Debbie Blakey, however, was not to be dissuaded. On May 15, after arranging for an airplane ticket to be wired from California, she marched into the embassy and requested an emergency passport (her own was locked away in Jonestown) and embassy protection until she left. With standing orders to assist Jonestown refugees, the embassy readily agreed, requiring of Debbie Blakey only that she confirm her intention to leave the Temple in writing:

"I have decided to leave the People's Temple Organization," she wrote, "because I am afraid that Jim Jones will carry out his threat to force all members of the organization in Guyana to commit suicide if a decision is made in Guyana by the court here to have John Stoen returned to his mother."

That evening, when Debbie Blakey did not return to the Lamaha Gardens headquarters, a radio call went out to Jones. He instructed the staff to find her. The following day, the staff spread out through the city, and when one of them, Deborah Touchette, came across Blakey in the Georgetown post office waiting for her wired ticket in the company of an embassy official, the scene spoke for itself. With a few brief words, Deborah Touchette confirmed it, then hurried back to Lahama Gardens to report the bad news over the radio. Jones instructed two other staff members, Terri Buford, a close friend of Debbie Blakey, and Karen Layton, her sister-in-law, to get to the airport immediately and wait there. The following day, when Blakey arrived to board her flight home, the two women made one final appeal, urging her not to blame Jones for "personality conflicts," to consider the pain she would cause him by leaving, and, finally, to consider the affect on her ailing mother. Debbie Blakey cooly replied that she had considered everything, hugged them goodbye and boarded the plane while two embassy "pukes," as Karen Layton later described them to Jones, looked on.

There had been no violence, no threat of violence—nothing more than a moderately emotional leave-taking, but back in Jonestown, Jim Jones was waiting with emotions anything but moderate.

For several days, Jones locked himself in his cabin and brooded, telling no one in Jonestown what had happened. When he finally did speak, he announced only that an anonymous member of the staff in Georgetown had absconded with, as Odell Rhodes remembers it, "something like twelve thousand dollars of our money." The charge was, as Jones knew perfectly well, a fabrication from whole cloth, but it was not a lie without a purpose. It allowed Jones to convince the community (and perhaps himself) that the same old enemy, Bourgeois Capitalism, had struck again. The same greed, which had caused the Stoens and the Mills "to sell out their brothers and sisters for a pocket full of credit cards and a fancy car," had once again claimed one of their comrades.

In a barrage of angry meetings, Jones vilified the defectors as "murderers"—defectors not merely from Jonestown but from social-ism, who would rather "pay taxes which buy guns to kill black ba-bies" than stand with the poor and oppressed trying to build a better society in Jonestown. With a no-more-Mr.-Nice-Guy edge in his voice, he announced the beginning of a campaign to fight dangerous bourgeois backslipping within the community; and then fell silent for another few weeks.

This time Jones was not merely meditating on his latest betrayal; he was anxiously awaiting news from San Francisco. Since the pros-pect of Debbie Blakey joining with the Stoens in their effort to pub-licize the situation in Jonestown disturbed him as much as the de-fection itself, Jones had decided he was more than willing to trade his silence for her silence. He would not, he told Debbie Blakey through intermediaries, break her mother's heart by naming her as the traitor if she would agree to keep quiet—absolutely quiet—about the Temple's affairs. It was essentially the same offer Jones had made to Tim Stoen (as it happened, through Debbie Blakey), and the an-swer from Debbie Blakey was only slightly different than Tim Stoen's answer. Debbie Blakey did not want to spend her life fighting Jones; that would be too much like still being in the Temple; but she would not remain silent. Early in June she made available to the Committee of Concerned Relatives an affidavit, which contained her version of life in Jonestown, questions about Jones's sanity, and a chillingly accurate predicition of Jonestown's future.

On June 15, when some of the contents of the affidavit appeared in the *San Francisco Chronicle,* Jones finally decided to tell the community about its latest traitor, not only who she was, but the full story of her betrayal.

"He told us," Rhodes remembers, "that it was Debbie who left—which surprised a lot of people. I know it shocked the hell out of me. I mean, I knew she wasn't happy here, but it was hard to think of her as a traitor."

According to Rhodes, Jones seemed unusually subdued, more anguished than angry, as he told the community that he had kept the secret of the defector's identity in order to spare her mother and because he had hoped to convince her to leave in peace. But now that she had joined the enemy, the people of Jonestown had a right to know.

"He said if she had to leave, that was one thing, but we were willing to let her alone, so why couldn't she just let us alone? Why couldn't she live and let live; why did she have to go and tear down everything we were trying to build?"

Finally, with tears in his eyes, Jones did something he had never done before. He confessed that the defection was his fault.

"He told us the reason she was doing it was because she hated him—she hated him because he wouldn't have sex with her. He said she freaked out when he wouldn't have sex with her, and that was why she was doing it—to get even with him."

Jones had never been bashful about sharing his sexual life with the community. There were no secrets in the new socialist family; secrecy was a sign of bourgeois repression. Everybody in Jonestown knew about Jones's sexual powers; they were as much a matter of common knowledge as any other basic fact of nature. According to Jones, he had been granted superhuman endurance ("twelve hours is a warmup for me") as well as extrabiological potency. His seed, he claimed, was so powerful it produced only male offspring. It was also more powerful than any contraceptive ever devised. There was nothing Jim Jones could not do in bed, and nothing he would not talk about. But this time, the words came tumbling out in a strange, sad jumble. He had tried to explain to her, he told the community, that sex was a political act, that he had never engaged in sex for the sake of mere sensual pleasure. He had always used sex to further the revolution, as a reward to a good worker, or as a tool for stimulating revolutionary zeal. He had tried to explain to Debbie Blakey that his rejection was an act of love, but she was so madly infatuated she would not listen. She had developed a bourgeois attitude to sex, she wanted only pleasure, she wanted to possess him. He hated to hurt her, but what else could he do?

As the monologue turned into a medley of self-accusations, with Jones in obvious pain, woman after woman began to stand up from the audience and offer testimonials to the purity of his motives and the splendor of his performance.

"Jim Jones is love."

"He opened my eyes—he changed my life, and I don't care who knows it, once you have Jim Jones you don't want no other man."

"That man, he lasts all day and all night, and there still ain't no way in hell you can get enough of him."

"I say you never been fucked until you been fucked by Jim Jones."

Within a few minutes there was so much commotion in the pavilion, so many women competing to be heard, that Jones himself put a stop to it. Odell Rhodes remembers, "First he said something about how he couldn't let any black women get up because it might humiliate a black woman to admit having sex with a white man. But the thing about it was, a lot of the women who were saying those things were like little old ladies, and you really wondered if they were talking about something that had happened, or just trying to make him feel better. I mean he was down about it, he was as down as I'd ever seen him."

While neither Odell Rhodes nor anyone else in Jonestown had anyway of knowing what had really happened between Jones and Debbie Blakey, no one in the community was any more inclined to doubt Jones's version of the event than they were to doubt his version of Grace Stoen's defection, or Tim Stoen's defection, or the CIA conspiracy, or anything else Jones insisted on. Besides, it was anything but a secret that the women Jones surrounded himself with—Debbie Blakey, Carolyn and Karen Layton, Maria Katsaris, et al., were Jim Jones's women. "I never did know, or care very much, what he did with whoever he did it with," Odell Rhodes says, "but I think most people pretty much assumed they were all kind of special to him."

Whatever the facts about their relationship were, Debbie Blakey's defection was an enormous blow to Jones, a nightmarish *déjà vu* of Grace Stoen's defection and a serious affront to his tender vanity as well as a betrayal of his cause. Brooding alone in his cabin Jones may well have convinced himself that, whatever Debbie Blakey thought her reasons were, the real reason was hidden, frustrated desire. It may have been the least painful explanation we could imagine, especially if he feared that the truth was that he had lost his sexual hold over her. Sex and power are anything but uncommon bedfellows, and for Jim Jones they were all but indistinguishable, two faces of the same compulsion.

"His strongest supporters," Odell Rhodes says flatly, "were always women." Another ex-Temple member—a woman—says, "I never did understand how any self-respecting man could even stand to be around Jones."

In principle, Jonestown's rules for sexual conduct were simple enough and no different for men than for women. As a species of political behavior sex was not to be casual, it was not to interfere with work, and, for very practical reasons, it was not to result in new mouths to feed. In practice, however, the limits of acceptable social conduct were complicated by several factors, among them the predominantly female population and the fact that—especially for males—sex was frequently employed as a means of social control. A male worker accused of virtually any misconduct was routinely charged with paying more attention to his sex life than to the revolution. "Jones would tell you," Odell Rhodes remembers, "your trouble was you had your head between your legs—and you weren't worth shit to nobody with your head between your legs."

As a matter of routine discipline Jones encouraged the mates of poor workers to deny sexual access, an arrangement that not only tended to alienate the men but also to concentrate power in the women, who were generally more responsive to Jones in the first place, by making them allies with Jones against their mates. On occasion, Jones indulged in even more brutal forms of sexual shaming. According to Jones, bisexuality was a revolutionary virtue, a virtue he naturally possessed, and a male's willingness to enter into a homosexual relationship was sometimes used as a test of his commitment to the cause. Although sexual shaming and punishment were more common, good workers and Jones's favorites were sometimes rewarded with sexual favors, preferential matchmaking, or even, on a few occasions, outright pimping. The Jonestown doctor, for example, who gained Jones's favor during the day by supporting his claim that nonrevolutionary sex caused cancer, was rewarded for his zeal at night by being regularly indulged with a succession of teenage girls.

Odell Rhodes found the entire subject of sex a cause for bewilderment. "Most of what he said about it I could relate to pretty well. I mean with so few men and so many women it's pretty obvious you have to keep kind of a tight leash on things so you know people aren't going to lay up all day screwing. And it was pretty obvious to me that we couldn't afford to have a lot of babies popping up. All that made sense to me, but it did seem like there wasn't much rhyme or reason lots of times to who was allowed to do what with whoever—like there were different sets of rules for different people."

Rhodes himself, after several attempts to establish what he thought would be acceptable relationships and several consequent admonitions about "hitting on the sisters" and "having his head between his legs" finally threw up his hands in defeat. "One time, in the middle of the night, I got dragged out of my cottage and Jones put his hands around my neck and started strangling me because I was supposedly hitting on some woman I wasn't supposed to. Far as I knew I wasn't hitting on anybody at that time, so it really confused me. Seemed like, if you just went around trying to get to know somebody, you might get called out for that. But, if you didn't seem friendly, then you might get asked what you had against women. I never really did get it straight what you were supposed to do and who you were supposed to do it with."

If a bachelor like Rhodes had his set of confusions, a man in a supposedly approved relationship had a different set. Since Jonestown was, first and foremost, supposed to be one enormous extended family, the first rule of personal relationships was non-exclusivity. No relationship was ever permitted to separate a couple from their obligations to the larger community, and any relationship that threatened to produce a bond between two individuals stronger than those individuals' bond to the community, ran the risk of summary dissolution. Routinely, for the sake of the community and the cause, Jones separated husbands and wives, young lovers—any relationship with the potential to generate its own momentum.

Through it all, there was one member of the community to whom no rules applied, the same man who made the rules for everyone else. A few weeks after he announced Debbie Blakey's defection, Jones made another announcement: a young black woman, Chanda Oliver, had had an "accident." "He told us she'd taken some medication—she was a dental assistant in the infirmary so she had access to drugs, and he said whatever it was she took, blew her mind." Chanda Oliver was a friend of Rhodes, and he had difficulty believing what he heard. "It just wasn't like her. She wasn't the type. She was the sort of person who lit up a room when she walked into it. She was bright, she was friendly, she cared about people—she was one of the best-liked people in Jonestown." She was also, according to Rhodes, one of the most beautiful. "I didn't know anybody who didn't have some kind of thing for her—she was that beautiful. She could take your breath away. But, I never knew her to mess around with anybody. She'd had kind of a rough time with her father, and a rough time with her boy friend, and she just wasn't into that sort of thing."

Shortly after he heard the news of her breakdown, Rhodes developed an infection in his chronically bad leg and was admitted to the infirmary, to the same ward where his friend was kept sedated, and isolated behind a curtain. The first night, around midnight, he watched—somehow not believing what he saw—as one of Jones's aides and a member of the security staff helped the heavily sedated patient from her bed and led her away. "Jim's waiting for you," he heard someone say.

For about two weeks he watched the same procedure every night. "They'd come and get her around midnight and then somebody would bring her back the next morning. From what I heard I knew they were taking her to Jones's cottage. Now, I don't know what went on up there, but I think I have a pretty good idea. I also think I know what she felt about Jim Jones—he was kind of like the father she never had. She told me that. I'm no psychiatrist, but I damn well don't believe she'd take drugs—not willingly anyway. And you sure as hell don't need to be a psychiatrist to know she was never the same after that. So I wonder, I wonder what it would be like if you were real sweet, and basically pretty innocent, and somebody you really trusted and respected, just like he was your own father—if that person spent a couple of weeks getting off on you every night."

12

Summer:
No More Traitors

With Debbie Blakey's defection life in Jonestown entered a new phase. Before her escape, Jim Jones had been content to believe that the threat to Jonestown was exclusively a threat from the outside. Now he was convinced that the serpent had entered paradise itself. Struck twice by lightning, betrayed once again by a follower he had trusted, Jones turned his energies to a massive campaign to insure that Jonestown would never again suffer another defection.

He resolved for openers to attack the problem of defection at its root cause—in Jones's mind the root cause of all evil—political reaction. The campaign against bourgeois tendencies would begin with political education. Even before he informed the community of the identity of the new defector, Jones had already instituted a system of mandatory political education classes for everyone in the community from school children to seniors.

"We'd have films about Russia and Cuba," Odell Rhodes remembers, "and lectures about what was going down in Chile and Angola—things like that. It wasn't so bad, except by that time, with all the meetings and alerts and everything, you hardly had any free time left as it was, so, to me, I guess it was kind of like one more thing I could have done without."

Others felt differently. For many, in fact, the lectures, discussions, quizzes, self-analysis letters, and general political ferment provided both a welcome distraction and an education. Rhodes, how-ever, had long since decided that a blanket skepticism about politics in general was the healthiest political education of all, and to him the classes were a luxury Jonestown could ill afford.

Time spent in classes was time that could have been better spent working in the fields or building new cottages—or even, perhaps, taking a day off from the ceaseless struggle against capitalism, perhaps for a picnic, or something else to lighten the ever-darkening mood of the community. By the middle of July, two months after Debbie Blakey left and a month after the community was told of her defec-tion, there was no doubt at all in Rhodes's mind that Jonestown was on the edge—and to his way of thinking there was no doubt about the reason either.

A few weeks after the political education classes began, as a further means of rooting out bourgeois tendencies, Jones announced the formation of something he called the Committee for the Defense of the Revolution. The Committee, Jones explained, would be charged with monitoring "negative thinking" within the community. It's membership would be secret—absolutely secret—so secret that no one in Jonestown would ever know when he was in the company of a member of the Committee. Furthermore, the members of the Committee had been instructed to express bourgeois sentiments themselves in order to test the revolutionary vigilance of those hear-ing the remarks. Anyone who failed to report what he heard would then be presumed guilty of the passive crime of insufficient revolu-tionary zeal.

Up until the very end, Odell Rhodes never did find out if there really was a Committee for the Defense of the Revolution, but he quickly realized that the point about the Committee was that it didn't matter if it existed or not; its effectiveness was quite independent of its existence. As long as there was the barest possibility that it existed, the fear it generated exerted strong pressure to turn everyone into an informer. Within a matter of days, Rhodes and most of the com-munity realized that it was a matter of simple common sense to be very careful about everything one said to anyone. A member who came back to his cottage after a day's work and flopped down into a chair with an audible sigh of fatigue and an "Oh, my aching back," ran the risk of being reported for negative feelings about Jonestown. Even acts of God were not exempt: "You might," Odell Rhodes discovered, "bitch about the fucking mud—and all of a sudden, there you are up on the floor being called out for being negative."

In addition to any and all complaints about life in Jonestown, the category of negative thought also included any and all conversation about life back in the capitalist hellhole of America—no matter what its content. While guarding the front gate one night, Rhodes and another guard, who also happened to be an ex–street hustler, passed the time exchanging what Rhodes thought to be memories of a life they were both happy to have left behind. "He was the kind of guy I figured I could say just about anything to. He'd done drugs and done time just like me, and he smoked a cigarette when he had the chance and drank jungle juice now and then, so I always felt like we both knew where the other one was coming from. Well, that night I guess we did talk about the old days—being out on the streets and all—but I know I never said anything about wanting to be back there, because I damn well *didn't* want to be back there. But, anyway, the very next night, there I was, up on the floor answering for myself. And I couldn't even get mad at him, because I knew he was just afraid if he didn't turn me in, I might turn him in."

Denounced roundly for harboring latent bourgeois sympathies, Rhodes resolved "I just wasn't going to say shit to anybody—I wasn't going to say one fucking word I wouldn't say to Jones himself."

Rhodes remembers the first few weeks after the formation of the Committee for the Defense of the Revolution (or the planting of the idea for the Committee) as a time of near hysteria. "It got weird—it really did. It was hard to figure out what the hell was going on for a while." Within a month, by the beginning of August, Jim Jones's war against the enemy within had succeeded in deflecting the community's fear of Jonestown's enemies into fear of one another.

"It got to be," Rhodes explains, "that, like when you were maybe a little down, and you just needed to talk to somebody, you were afraid to do it." With virtually everyone afraid to talk to anyone else, especially about his feelings, the opportunity to vent one's minor frustrations with a therapeutic dose of sociable bitching became an enormous risk, and minor everyday depressions began to fester into persistent feelings of unhappiness and loneliness independent of any immediate cause. The result was something like mass depression, an atmosphere of despair almost impossible to withstand, even for those with the sunniest of dispositions.

Already isolated from the outside world, the people of Jonestown now found themselves isolated from each other. It was, however, isolation with a twist, an isolation that actually—peversely—tended to drive the community closer together. Although they were alienated from one another, the people of Jonestown were not alienated from their community—or from their leader. In fact, with husbands and wives informing on each other, children informing on their parents, and everyone afraid to talk openly to friends, the only channel of communication left open—the only emotional relationship still available—was the same for everyone, the one that went straight to the top, to everybody's Dad, Jim Jones himself.

Once again, like so much that happened in Jonestown, the process was insidiously circular. In the manner of what theorists of social interaction call a "zero-sum" game, as personal relationships— including family ties—became more difficult, most people's relationship to Jones became more important; and, as the relationship to Jones grew more important, all other relationships began to seem relatively unimportant. Eventually, for the vast majority of the community, what mattered above all else was pleasing Dad, at any cost, even when it involved denouncing or informing on a husband, wife, mother, father, or friend.

Surrounding everything was the thick, bleak sense of hopelessness, the feeling that nothing mattered—feelings that both mirrored Jones's own mood (and thereby tended to confirm it) and also tended to leave most people so emotionally on edge they were even more vulnerable to Jones's increasingly bleak view of Jonestown's prospects. Nowhere was the sense of common desperation more evident than in the nightly meetings, which had now become a routine orgy of harangue, confession, and catharsis. With virtually everyone too confused and too afraid to conduct close relationships in private, the overwhelming bulk of the community's emotional life was now conducted at the same time and in the same room—at the public nightly meetings.

For Odell Rhodes, it was simply too much. More accustomed than most to living on a meager diet of emotions and sensitive as ever about displaying his emotions in public, Rhodes decided he preferred no emotional life to the public hysteria of the meetings, and he began to contrive a way to avoid them. Early in August he succeeded. After several months of petitioning the Work Committee to allow him to leave the fields in order to work with young children, he was finally assigned to teach craft classes in the community school.

He could not have been happier, but, since the craft classes only amounted to an afternoon's work, he was also afraid that, if he did not fill up his day with another task, one was likely to be found for him. Knowing that his old friend, Marie Lawrence, the woman who sponsored him when he first joined the Temple, was looking for someone to help her man the night shift caring for invalids in a nursing-care cottage, Rhodes volunteered to help, fully aware that if he was working in the nursing-care cottage at night he would not be attending the meetings.

His new schedule suited Rhodes perfectly. Working afternoons with his craft classes satisfied him deeply both because he genuinely loved being around children and also because being a schoolteacher was something close to a dream come true, for a junkie about a year removed from a park bench, success and status beyond any reasonable expectation.

"I ran the whole crafts program from start to finish," he says proudly. "I decided what we were going to make, I found the things we needed to work with, and I taught everybody what to do. If you ever saw a kid's face when he finishes something he made himself—even if it's only a little necklace made out of beads and shells—you'd know how I felt about it."

He considered his work in the nursing cottage at night a blessing of equal proportions, for different reasons. The nursing-care job not only allowed him to pass up nightly meetings, it also allowed him something very few people in Jonestown had nearly enough of—time to be by himself. The work itself was thoroughly undemanding—a few trips to the kitchen for special diets, a few bedpans to empty. For most of the evening Rhodes sat at a table while the patients slept. In Jonestown it passed for solitude, and it gave Rhodes the opportunity to think.

He found himself thinking a good deal about his leader. "He was looking worse every day. Maybe he was doing drugs—I don't know, but he looked like he was made out of old spaghetti. I started having these funny feelings about him. Like I'd always respected Jones for what he'd done, and I was grateful to him for what he'd done for me, but I didn't necessarily feel he always did the right thing. I guess I'd always kind of felt Jonestown was more important to me than Jones—which I guess made me different than a lot of people—and right about then I guess I was kind of looking around and dividing people into those who really wanted Jonestown to work out for us and those who'd given up on it, and I just wasn't sure about Jones. In fact, there were a lot of times when I began to think maybe we'd be better off without him."

One of those times came one night in the nursing-care cottage when Rhodes realized that in addition to the Cultural Revolution— the Chinese approach to preventing defections—Jones had also adopted the East Berlin solution. That night, while Rhodes was on duty alone, several security guards dragged three teenagers—two boys and a girl—into the cottage, and while one of the guards went to find a nurse to sedate them, another of the guards explained that the three had been caught attempting to escape and were to be sedated and confined to the cottage indefinitely. It turned out that the attempt to escape had amounted to wandering off into the jungle and staying out all night. As a veteran of many jails, Rhodes found himself face to face with an uncomfortable shock of recognition. "All of a sudden it just hit me. There was all this security, and it wasn't so much to keep people out as it was to keep people in. All these things Jones had been saying about how he didn't want people to leave because there were still people who wanted to come over, and even everything else about how everybody who left just made trouble for us, I could accept it up until a point. But when it gets to where you start doing the things you're supposed to be getting away from—when you have to start worrying about ypur own security people dragging you around and locking you up, you got to start to wonder if it's worth it. It just seemed wrong to me. Like even if the people who leave do make trouble for you, you're better off without them in the long run, because if you're always worrying about them you're going to make things a lot worse for everybody else."

Stanley Clayton, another prison veteran, made the same association at about the same time. "Got so people were telling you when you could take a shit and when you couldn't. And I said to myself, I said, Stanley, this is just like the fucking jailhouse. And I said it out loud, too, and people'd come up to me and say, 'Stanley, now don't you talk like that—you gonna get your ass burned.' But I felt it was the truth, and I was supposed to be free over there, so I figured I could say any damn thing I felt like."

Clayton was wrong. For several months he had worked in the kitchen, as a crew chief, with a group of other irreverent, street-wise young people who took most of what happened in Jonestown a good deal less seriously than the majority. With his friends in the kitchen Clayton was used to saying and—within limits—doing pretty much what he wanted. Even defecting was something the kitchen crew discussed among themselves. "You know, like somebody might say, shit, let's split this fucking hole, and everybody'd say right on, right on, but then something always came up and we'd never do it."

As Clayton began telling anyone who would listen how Jonestown was beginning to remind him of the jailhouse, however, even the kitchen crew succumbed to fear of the Committee for the Defense of the Revolution. He was reported, called up before the community during one of the nightly meetings, and very nearly treated as if he had, in fact, defected. In addition to being denounced by Jones and assigned an extra work detail he was also threatened with physical punishment.

"They had this bunch of punks," Clayton recalls, "who liked to go around saying they were going to do this and do that to people who got in trouble—and sometimes they did it. Well, I got up there and one of them started talking real tough about what he was gonna to do to me. I mean, shit, he was nothing but a rookie and I told him—I just whispered it real sweet in his little rookie ear—that if he touched me, he best go on and kill me, 'cause no matter how bad he hurt me, I'd find him, and I'd give him every bit of it back and a lot more besides, which I would have.

"I mean I never could see abusing people for something they said, and I never did understand why Jones allowed it. But, shit, all you had to do was stand up to them 'cause, like I say, they were nothing but a bunch of punks."

Clayton insists that, except for the shock of discovering that one of his friends was a fink, the incident meant very little to him. "I didn't stop talking and I didn't stop trying to enjoy myself, and I didn't stop thinking about leaving." In fact, from the middle of the summer on, Clayton says he thought about leaving Jonestown constantly, and he was confident that if he attempted an escape he would succeed.

Although Jonestown's official mythology held that escape was impossible, primarily because of the jungle, Clayton was not convinced. Slipping through the security guards into the jungle presented no problems and, to Clayton, the threat of the jungle was far overrated. "I worked in the jungle, and I knew people who lived in the jungle, so I knew it wasn't like they said. I could have made it and anybody who ever spent any time being in it by himself could have made it too."

Odell Rhodes agreed with Clayton about the jungle, but he doubted Clayton or anyone else could have escaped: "Sure, you could've have gotten out, but what then? You had no passport, no money, no way to get to Georgetown—so what good is it going to do you to walk out? You'd get to Kaituma or Matthews Ridge and they'd bring you back and put you on tranquilizers."

Whatever the deterrent effects of the security force or the jungle, the fact was attempted escapes were less than rare. Aside from the three teenagers Rhodes saw being dragged into his nursing-care cottage, he never saw—or heard about—another attempted escape. "It wasn't," Rhodes says, "something most people thought about. To most people Jonestown was home and they weren't about to run away from home just because things weren't perfect. Besides, no matter how bad it was getting, I think most people still felt it was better than where they came from. I know I did. I knew things were getting pretty bad in a lot of ways, but, to me, I never stopped feeling like I was doing a lot better than I would have been doing someplace else. I mean where the hell was I going to go—back to the streets?"

As much as Clayton thought about leaving, the reasons he stayed were similar to Rhodes's reasons. "I sure as hell didn't feel like I had any commitment to hang in there or anything like that, but there was something about the fact that what you were leaving wasn't just Jonestown, it was all your people—and that kind of slowed you down. Besides, I wasn't doing so bad. Basically, the people I ran with were having a pretty good time, and the other thing was, even though it kept reminding me of the jailhouse, when I thought about it I had to admit I was getting my shit together. I was working and getting along with people, and I didn't really know if I could go back and cut it over there—I didn't know if I was ready."

Neither Rhodes nor Clayton feels comfortable speculating about why others made no attempt to leave, but both insist that by the late summer, virtually everyone did know that something was seriously wrong in Jonestown. "It wasn't," Rhodes says, "that people didn't know. I don't know what it was, but it wasn't that. Like people talk about brainwashing, and maybe we were, but not the way most people think, not so that we didn't know what was happening to us."

Whatever they felt had gone wrong, Rhodes, Clayton, and most of the rest of the community were inclined to place most of the blame on the enemies they heard so much about—and not to look any farther (or nearer) for other reasons. If they had questions about Jones, they were questions about his health, perhaps even his mental health, but never about his motives.

"Besides, you have to remember," Odell Rhodes says, "I wasn't sitting around thinking about what was wrong with Jonestown. I might have had those kinds of thoughts, but I didn't sit around trying to have them. Most of the time, I was with the kids, or with my friends, or working at night, or listening to the band rehearse—or whatever. And when I did start thinking about how bad things were, I'd say to myself: 'Damn, I've seen this place when it works. I know it can work, so I can put up with it for another day. I can hold out until we get through all this bullshit and get things moving in the right direction again.'"

Fully aware that the Jonestown he was living in was not the Jonestown he had been promised, he preferred to remember the Jonestown he had once seen and to contemplate the Jonestown of his mind's eye. Whether or not others responded in a similar way, the fact was that as things in Jonestown grew progressively worse, the people of Jonestown, by and large, simply adjusted to them; and as they began to use more and more of their energies adjusting, they cared less and less what it was they were adjusting to. Bound by their fear and their isolation, and by their memories and dreams, they settled into their misery as if the possibility of leaving it simply did not exist—as if they were living on the edge of the world; as if leaving Jonestown was as much a real possibility as flying to the moon.

13

Fall:
The Enemy Arrives

Looking back at his life in Jonestown, Odell Rhodes is sometimes struck by how little he remembers, how few incidents stand out from the background of his daily routine. "Maybe its some kind of amnesia or something," he says half seriously, "but, I guess the truth of it is that most days I just got up in the morning and did what I did every day—just like anybody else with a regular job".

His memories of the hot, humid dog days of the late summer and early fall are almost exclusively of the craft classes he taught in a small tent near the main pavilion. He remembers, for example, the shy, frightened teenager, a girl of about fourteen, who arrived in Jonestown late that summer and had difficulty making friends. One afternoon in class, off in a corner by herself, she began making strange, stunning flowers out of scraps of fabric. As the other children crowded around her, demanding to be taught how to make the flowers themselves, it seemed to Rhodes he was watching her blossom as brightly and unexpectedly as her creations.

Gradually, something of the same sort was happening to Rhodes. By mid-September he was not only spending as much time out of class researching projects, scrounging materials, and borrowing tools as he was in the classroom tent itself, he was also spending most of what remained of his free time with his students.

Groups of them took to following him around Jonestown, wherever he happened to be, and two in particular, two young ladies, ages fourteen and fifteen respectively, Niki Mitchell and Judy Houston, began to seem like unattached appendages. "Niki came over on the plane with me and Judy didn't have a real dad, so they just kind of adopted me".

Between his classes, his students, and his work at night in the nursing-care cottage, Rhodes had suddenly become a very busy man. What little leisure time was left over, after work and the extracurricular demands of Niki Mitchell and Judy Houston were subtracted, amounted to a few hours on Sunday and a few minutes most other days, barely time enough to lend a hand in the electronics shop tinkering with broken equipment or catch a few minutes of band rehearsals now and then.

Late in September Rhodes moved into the nursing cottage along with the other two night orderlies, Marie Lawrence and her husband, Bob Rankin, and, for the rest of the fall, he saw very little of Jonestown except the school tent and his cottage. Aside from his roommates, he had very little contact with other adults. Occasionally, he listened to music with a young woman, Monica Bagby, a bright eighteen-year-old who had arrived in Jonestown during the summer with a collection of jazz on tapes—Bob Adams, Al Jarreaux, Minnie Riperton, and Phoebe Snow—music Rhodes liked as much as she did.

"Most people were more into rock and roll, the kind of music the band played, and I liked that too, but I kind of missed jazz until Monica came over".

Monica Bagby knew very little about Jonestown the day she arrived. Although her mother had been a long-time member, Monica was not, and she had only gone to Jonestown because her mother wanted a firsthand report about the jungle paradise Temple members in San Francisco heard so much about. Jonestown confused Monica. She was impressed by the way whites and blacks treated each other, but the lack of privacy and the constant emotional pressure of meetings and alerts frightened her, and from one minute to the next she vacillated between thinking she really had found paradise and wanting to go home.

Rhodes was also taking as many opportunities as he could find to get to know another young woman, Juanita Bogue. Although he was fifteen years older than Juanita, Rhodes, and most everybody else who knew her, thought of her as much older. Everybody in the Bogue family enjoyed a reputation for being sensible, hard-working, and useful, the kind of people who came immediately to Rhodes's mind when he thought about who was committed to making Jonestown what he dreamed about. Juanita's father, Jim Bogue, was an unusually talented man who had helped design and build many of Jonestown's cottages and had spent a solid year setting up a sawmill to take advantage of Jonestown's most important natural resource.

Rhodes saw the same good-natured competency in Juanita, and if there was anything on his mind that summer besides work, she was it. "The truth was, she was on my mind a whole lot, but that's mostly where it was, on my mind. I thought about her a whole lot more than I saw her."

For most members of the community the early evening hours— the period between work and the nightly meetings—was usually time for socializing, but Rhodes had barely enough time to clean up after his class, escape his students, eat, and rush back to the cottage in time to begin work again. He was not, however, inclined to complain about his schedule. If working at night meant fewer opportunities to see Juanita Bogue, it also meant fewer opportunities to listen to Jim Jones, and Rhodes was by now firmly convinced that missing nightly meetings was worth whatever price one had to pay. Although the meetings were usually broadcast throughout the community over loudspeakers, Rhodes heard them only as background noise and, sometimes, he would manage to block out everything but the voice of the crowd and then imagine he was outside Brigg's Stadium while the Tigers were winning the World Series.

Jim Jones was barely even a presence in his life. After September, Rhodes remembers catching only the briefest glimpses of Jones hurrying to or from the radio room, his face hidden by dark glasses, his mouth set down at the corners.

If it seemed to Rhodes that very little was happening in Jonestown, on the surface, as far away from Jones as it was possible to be in Jonestown, he was right. On the surface, there was very little happening. All of the major projects—land clearing, farming, and building—had virtually ceased to exist in anything but name, and for many members of the community, Rhodes not included, work had turned into make-work.

Although there were occasional announcements that enough

lumber to build fifty new cottages had been ordered, or that a thousand new breeding hens for the chickery would be arriving any day, new supplies rarely actually appeared. "It was," says Rhodes, "like you kind of expected nothing much was going to happen even when he said it was." Although Jones had given up actively building Jonestown months before, by September his lack of interest was so obvious that most of the community—with the exception of a few dreamers like Odell Rhodes—recognized that Jonestown was now a transient camp. Far from committing resources to building program, Jones was now not even interested in building new cottages if they cost nothing at all. Jim Bogue's long-awaited sawmill for turning jungle timber into usable lumber had been successfully tested at the beginning of the summer. Completely functional, it sat unused while living conditions continued as unpleasantly over-crowded as ever.

In place of building Jonestown the community's attention had gradually focused on re-establishing Jonestown in the Soviet Union. By September all but the most essential tasks were replaced by classes, especially classes in conversational Russian, Russian history, and Russian customs. Jones periodically, reported on the state of his negotiations with the Soviets and finally even set a date, January 1, for the departure of the first advance party.

As much as he titillated the community, however, with the prospect of moving from Guyana, for Jones himself the move was either a fantasy that never quite got off the ground or a myth for internal consumption only. Jones's correspondence with the Georgetown staff mentions the move only sporadically and the staff's contact with the Soviet embassy were on a far smaller scale than Jones led the community to believe.

If Odell Rhodes had the impression that Jones was living in the radio room that fall, it was not because he was busy negotiating with the Russians. Jones had other things on his mind. The long hours he spent with his short-wave radio in the corrugated tin radio room were devoted to desperately trying to keep up with events in the outside world. Jones, in fact, was so busy directing his staffs in Georgetown and San Francisco that nobody in Jonestown saw much of him during the fall, not even his wife, Marceline, his mistresses, or the two sons, John-John and Kimo, who lived in his cabin.

John-John, now eight, had grown into a sturdy, serious, obviously

precocious child. "Nobody treated him special," Odell Rhodes remembers, "but you could see there was something special about
him. There was something real deep about him—just the way he'd
talk to adults, it was like he was a lot older than he was. I don't know
if anybody ever said it, but I think most people took a lot of pride in
him. Like raising kids like John-John who weren't mean or selfish or
prejudiced or anything like that was what Jonestown was all about."

As he wandered about the settlement, first among his peers and an
eight-year-old symbol of the community's idea of itself, John-John
was blissfully ignorant of the storm whose center he had become.
During the summer the conflict between Jones and the Stoens had
escalated into a war with battlefields in two different continents. On
the Guyanese front Jones was not doing badly at all. Despite pressure
from the Stoens, the United States embassy continued its policy of
strict neutrality, which left Jones's influence with the Guyanese government unchallenged. Although Jones would never have believed
it, the truth was that the embassy was as frightened of Jones's charges
of interference as Jones was of its interference. The Lamaha Gardens
staff had lobbied effectively in Georgetown, and, by and large, the
press and the diplomatic community were sympathetic to Jonestown.

Lacking specific directions from Washington, neither the ambas-
sador, John Burke, nor his deputy, Richard Dwyer, saw any reason
to invite local criticism or to stir up nasty rumors about the CIA by
pleading the Stoens' case with the Guyanese. Aside from helping to
repatriate anyone who happened to escape, the embassy was not
about to go out of its way to involve itself in Jonestown's affairs.

With the embassy staying out of it, the war in Guyana was largely
a paper-war in which both sides deluged the judge hearing the case
with mountains of letters, newspaper clippings, and legal briefs, all
presumably intended to clarify the issue of whose son John-John was
and where he should be brought up. On August 10 the judge finally
threw up his hands in despair. Claiming his impartiality had been
compromised by pressure from both sides, he resigned from the case.
His nondecision, however, amounted to a victory for Jones, since
the entire case, already ten months in the pipeline, now reverted to
square one and a complete retrial.

Discouraged by the State Department's policy and the bad news
from the court, the Stoens decided to concentrate their efforts on the
home front. Their plan was to stir up as much trouble for Jones back

home as possible. Tim Stoen knew Jones well enough to know that the more pressure he exerted, the more irrationally Jones was likely to behave. By putting on the pressure and then putting Jones's responses under a searchlight, Stoen hoped to create enough public concern to force some kind of action in Washington.

Under the umbrella of the Committee of Concerned Relatives, Stoen developed a three-pronged strategy: harass Jones in the courts; publicize conditions in Jonestown; and press for a full-scale Congressional investigation of the People's Temple. During the summer, as attorney for the Committee of Concerned Relatives, Stoen filed a variety of lawsuits on behalf of both former members and relatives of current members. The specific charges differed from suit to suit but in general the allegations all covered the same ground: harassment, intimidation, deprivation of civil rights, libel, and slander. The largest of the suits, which the Committee hoped to make into a media event, was filed on behalf of a former member, Jim Cobb, most of whose family had stayed with the Temple and were living in Jonestown. According to the Cobb suit, Jones had attempted to intimidate Cobb by various threats and slanders in order to frighten him away from publicly opposing the Temple. The suit called for damages in the neighborhood of twenty million dollars.

While Tim Stoen waited for the lawsuits to come to trial, Stoen and other members of the Committee were also busy in Washington pounding the corridors of Capitol Hill. Since direct pressure on the State Department had failed to elicit response, the Committee decided to outflank the State Department by lobbying directly with members of Congress in the hope of drumming up enough Congressional interest for a full-scale legislative investigation.

By the end of the summer the Committee had obtained pledges of support from some twenty-odd Congressmen, the most vocal of them, a 53-year-old Democratic representative from a suburban San Francisco district, Leo J. Ryan. Ryan's district south of San Francisco included several former and present Temple members, making the Temple something of a local issue, but, more importantly, it also happened to be something of a personal issue for Leo Ryan.

Ryan had an old drinking buddy, a retired Associated Press photographer in San Francisco, Sam Houston. Sam Houston had a son who as a youngster had played with Ryan's own children. The son, Bob Houston, grew up, went to college, and then joined the People's

Temple. After several years, late in 1976 Bob Houston died at the age of thirty-three in a grisly railroad accident near the San Francisco waterfront. When Sam Houston, who had never approved of his son's commitment to the Temple, learned that a few days before his accident Bob had had a violent argument with Jim Jones, he began to suspect that his son might have been murdered.

Although no evidence of foul play or any Temple involvement was ever uncovered, Sam Houston continued to blame the Temple, if only because at the time of his death Bob Houston had been working two eight-hour jobs every day—as a parole officer during the day and a railroad laborer at night—in order to both support his family and turn over large sums of money to the Temple. At the very least, Sam Houston was inclined to blame the Temple for the physical fatigue and mental stress which he believed might have contributed to Bob's death.

Despite Sam Houston's feelings about the Temple, his daughter-in-law and two grand-daughters (one of whom, Judy Houston, was close to Odell Rhodes) remained in the Temple, in Jonestown. As early as October of 1977, Leo Ryan promised his old friend he would do whatever he could to make sure the two girls were not being held there against their will.

With the formation of the Committee of Concerned Relatives, Houston put Tim Stoen and other members of the group in touch with Ryan. Shortly before Christmas Ryan wrote the State Department in the Stoens' behalf, expressing his interest in the custody case and urging the Department to aid the Stoens in whatever way it could. Throughout the spring he continued to advocate the Stoens' cause with the State Department and to meet periodically with members of the Concerned Relatives group. When it became clear during the summer that the State Department would not intervene in a custody matter and that the Guyanese court would not decide the case for several more months, if ever, Ryan agreed to work for a Congressional investigation of the Temple. In order to press the issue with his colleagues armed with firsthand information he decided, late in the summer, to visit Jonestown himself.

Firsthand investigations in hostile environments did not frighten Leo Ryan. A feisty, physically courageous man with a taste for activism, Ryan had a track record of confronting sensitive issues with his body. In 1964, while a California state legislator, he had spent several weeks researching the Watts riots by teaching in a Los Angeles ghetto high school. Six years later, now a member of Congress, he posed as an inmate in Folsom prison, educating himself about the prison reform movement. In the early seventies, he chained himself to baby seals in Newfoundland, making him—as Leo Ryan himself liked to claim—the only member of Congress ever to chain himself to a baby seal.

While Leo Ryan planned his firsthand look at Jonestown, Jim Jones sat locked inside his radio room listening to daily reports of the Committee of Concerned Relatives' activities via short-wave radio from San Francisco and planning his counterstrategy. To protect the Temple's U.S. assets against the possibility that one or another of the pending lawsuits might result in a judgment against Temple property, he ordered his San Francisco attorney, Charles Garry, to begin liquidating the Temple's real-estate assets and transferring the proceeds out of the country, beyond the reach of a court judgment.

Early in September he also began a direct counterattack against the man who had become his arch-enemy, Tim Stoen. Once and for all Jones was determined to prove that the conspiracy led by Stoen was linked to the CIA and to unmask Stoen as a CIA agent. Although Jones himself had never doubted Stoen's connection with the intelligence community, the idea of proving the connection and publicly discrediting Stoen was sparked by a visit to Jonestown during the first week of September by a California private investigator, Joseph Mazor. Mazor told Jones that he had worked for the Committee of Concerned Relatives for several months on, among other projects, a plan to kidnap John-John Stoen from Jonestown, and he convinced Jones that he could obtain documentary proof of Tim Stoen's CIA connections.

Although Jones had no particular reason to believe Mazor, whose motives for changing sides (beyond working both sides of the street) are unclear, he evidently found the prospect of unmasking Tim Stoen so attractive that he retained Mazor on the spot without even pausing to entertain the possibility that Mazor might be a double agent. In fact, Jones found the project so exciting he also retained a lawyer from Memphis, Tennessee, Mark Lane, who claimed to be the country's foremost authority on intelligence conspiracies. Lane, who had built a career alleging conspiracies in the assassinations of John F. Kennedy and Martin Luther King, was now to search for evidence of the conspiracy against Jim Jones. While Mazor worked through his contacts with the Committee of Concerned Relatives, Lane would file suit under the Freedom of Information Act in order to secure and search government documents for evidence of the conspiracy.

In late September, shortly after Jones unleashed Mazor and Lane on Tim Stoen, Jones's San Francisco staff began reporting rumors of a high-level defector in the Temple organization. Whether or not the rumors originated with Stoen, perhaps to discredit Mazor, or perhaps simply to grate on Jones's nerves, Jones's response was to dispatch a Jonestown aide, Tim Carter, to San Francisco to pose as a Jonestown defector, infiltrate the CCR, and report the identity of the defector back to Jones.

As Jones and the Stoens played out their private mini-power version of international intrigue with agents, double agents, and, undoubtedly, triple agents, the situation in the early fall fit perfectly into Jones's delusions of persecution. Having long since convinced himself that the fight for custody of John-John was merely the visible tip of the conspiracy against him, Jones now had the Committee's summer offensive for evidence.

Throughout the fall the pace accelerated. On October 3 Tim Stoen sent a telegram to the State Department, which was forwarded to the U.S. embassy in Georgetown and in all probability eventually leaked to Jones's Georgetown staff. The telegram informed the government that because of the government's failure to act in the custody matter, Tim Stoen was now prepared to use "any means necessary,"[8] presumably including force, to regain custody of John-John.

On October 24 Leo Ryan received authorization from the House Foreign Affairs Committee to travel to Guyana. On November 1 he informed Jones of his intention to make that visit during the week of November 14–20. Jones promptly authorized Mark Lane to reply to Ryan's letter with a list of conditions to be agreed to before Ryan would be admitted to Jonestown. The conditions included the presence of Jones's lawyers, the presence of a member of Congress sympathetic to the Temple, and assurances that Ryan would not bring the press or members of the Committee of Concerned Relatives with him.

According to Lane,[9] Lane discussed these conditions in a telephone conversation with an aide to Ryan, James Schollaert. Schollaert and Lane agreed, according to Lane, that the presence of Jones's lawyers was Jones's business; they also agreed that, as a practical matter, finding a Congressman sympathetic to the Temple was likely to be impossible; but, again according to Lane, Schollaert did assure him that Ryan had no intention of bringing the press or members of the Committee, and Lane was left with the impression that if he could convince Jones to drop the demand for a sympathetic Congressman, he could tell Jones that Ryan would honor the conditions about not bringing the press or the Committee. None of the negotiations, however, were conducted in writing; and, in fact, Ryan's sole written response to Lane was a thoroughly uncompromising declaration of his intention to investigate Jonestown—period.

From Jones's point of view, Ryan had painted him neatly into a corner. Convinced as he was—not entirely without reason—that Ryan was another agent of the conspiracy against him, Jones would have preferred to slam Jonestown's gate in Leo Ryan's face. He realized, however, that refusing to allow a Congressman access to the community would tend to lend substance to the Committee of Concerned Relatives' charges and might result in a major public-relations disaster.

At the same time, during the first week of November, while Jones wracked his brain for a way out of the Ryan dilemma, he was stunned by news of a more immediate disaster. One of his most trusted aides, Terri Buford, a long-time principal in the Georgetown staff whom Jones had sent to San Francisco in September to coordinate the assignments of his lawyers, Mark Lane and Charles Garry, had suddenly disappeared—vanished from sight in the midst of the Lane-Ryan negotiations. With the rumors of an informer ringing in his ears, Jones could only conclude the rumors were true and the informer was Terri Buford.

Lightning had now struck for a fourth time. A member of the same inner circle to which Grace and Tim Stoen and Debbie Blakey had once belonged, Terri Buford was a defector of the same magnitude. There was practically nothing about the People's Temple, Jonestown, or Jim Jones personally that Terri Buford did not know. She knew the situation in Jonestown intimately; she knew the details of Jones's campaign to prove Tim Stoen's CIA connections; she knew Jones's defense strategy in the lawsuits brought by the members of the Committee of Concerned Relatives; she knew Jones's political contacts in Guyana, bribes and all; and she knew the location of virtually every dime Jones had squirreled away in foreign bank accounts. If Terri Buford had joined his enemies, Jones not only had the psychological trauma of a fresh betrayal to cope with, he also had to contend with the horrifying prospect that his enemies were now in possession of his secrets.

Already in a state of near panic about Ryan's impending investigation, Terri Buford's defection was far more than the mere straw required to break Jones's fragile mental health. In the context of the Committee of Concerned Relatives' summer offensive and the Ryan visit, it could hardly have helped seeming to Jones that his enemies had finally gained the upper hand—that the conspiracy that surrounded him was at the point of drawing tight, into a noose.

Although the truth was that Terri Buford evidently had no intention of joining Tim Stoen in anything, much less a conspiracy against Jones, her defection was still a paranoid's nightmare. During the negotiations for Ryan's visit, Terri Buford had simply decided that Ryan's trip, all by itself, might well be enough to push Jones past his limits—limits she knew he was fast approaching. She confided those fears to Mark Lane, the same Mark Lane who was simultaneously negotiating the conditions for Ryan's visit. Fearing for her own safety, she wanted a place to hide, and Lane, who seems to have been unaware of the effects Terri Buford's disappearance might have on his client, encouraged her, even to the point of hiding her in his own house. Whatever Lane's motives, he had now heated an awkward situation. Having involved himself in Buford's disappearance, there was now no way for Lane to reassure Jones about her intentions since, were Lane to confess his role, he would immediately, in Jones's mind, be counted as another conspirator.

Leo Ryan's plans to visit Jonestown went forward during the second week in November. On November 9 he discussed the investigation with State Department officials and, on November 13, met again with the State Department and members of the Committee of Concerned Relatives, including the Stoens and Debbie Blakey. Given the collective knowledge of the participants in that meeting, especially Debbie Blakey, whose affidavit six months before had predicted the potential for disaster in Jonestown, it is inconceivable that Ryan left the meeting unaware of Jones's state of mind or Jones's probable reactions to Ryan's visit.

On November 14, the following day, Ryan left Washington accompanied by eight members of the Committee of Concerned Relatives, including Grace and Tim Stoen, as well as reporters from both San Francisco daily newspapers and a film crew from NBC-TV news. The Ryan party arrived in Georgetown early in the morning on the fifteenth and waited in Georgetown until November 17. On the morning of the seventeenth, Thursday, Ryan met with Jones's lawyers, Mark Lane and Charles Garry, and two members of Jones's Lamaha Gardens staff, Deborah Touchette and Sharon Cobb, to discuss what the Temple representatives considered to be a breach of Lane's understanding with Ryan that his party would not include members of the press or of the Concerned Relatives.

Ryan replied that as far as he was concerned he had no agreement with Lane, and, furthermore, that the relatives and reporters were, in any event, not "official" members of his party. When the Temple contingent argued that, given the presence of the press and the relatives, and the fact that the group contained individuals Jones considered to be his enemies (especially the arch-enemy, Tim Stoen, and Jim Cobb, who was suing the Temple for twenty million dollars), Jones could hardly be expected to believe in Ryan's impartiality. According to Mark Lane, Ryan simply made it clear that Jones's sensibilities were at the bottom of his list of priorities. He told Lane and the others that he was determined to leave for Jonestown that afternoon and listed the visiting party; Ryan, his aide, Jackie Speir, the NBC film crew, reporters and photographers from the San Francisco dailies and another reporter from the *Washington Post*, and four members of the Committee of Concerned Relatives, Jim Cobb, Carole Boyd, Beverly Oliver, and Anthony Katsaris. Were Jones to bar the party at the gate to Jonestown, Ryan continued, the television film crew would record the event and Ryan would return to Washington more convinced than ever that a full-scale Congressional inquiry was in order.

The Temple representatives then returned to the Lamaha Gardens headquarters, conferred with Jones by radio, and eventually decided they would proceed with Ryan to Jonestown and attempt to work out a further compromise there.

Late that afternoon, the Ryan party boarded two small chartered airplanes and flew to the airstrip at Port Kaituma, a few miles from Jonestown. They were met, coldly but politely, by Jones's adopted son, Johnny, and after the two lawyers went on ahead to confer with Jones, the entire visiting party entered Jonestown in the back of the Jonestown dump truck shortly before sundown.

14

Apocalypse Tomorrow

Inside Jonestown Jim Jones was hardly even listening to Mark Lane and Charles Garry. Jones already knew what the two lawyers were trying to tell him, knew it all to well: Leo Ryan had backed him into a corner. Finally, Jones nodded. The Ryan party could enter the settlement. Then he stood up and headed back to his cabin. After a solid year of preparing himself and his followers for an armed attack, Jones was not about to watch his enemies stroll peacefully through the front gate.

All of the events of the preceding year, especially the custody battle with the Stoens, the defections of Debbie Blakey and Terri Buford, and the efforts of the Committee of Concerned Relatives, had convinced Jones of the power and reach of the conspiracy against him. Now the Ryan visit, which for Jones represented the conspiracy's boldest step yet, threatened disaster. And, as if the threat of disaster were not bad enough in itself, there was also the galling image of Tim Stoen, sitting safely in Georgetown, waiting to gloat over Jones's humiliation.

Sitting alone in his cabin preparing himself for that humiliation, Jones's thoughts were already racing ahead. For more than a year Jones had used Jonestown as something very much like his own private repertory theater specializing in full-dress performances of the fantasies of Jim Jones. With his enemies at the gate and Jones pow-

erless to stop them, he was now scripting his most spectacular production, the all but inevitable sequel to The Siege of Jonestown. It
would be entitled The End of a Dream; it would be a tragedy; and it
would have an unbelievable last act.

If Leo Ryan and the other members of the Committee of Concerned Relatives assumed that Jones's decision to admit them (with
hardly a murmur of protest) was a graceful bow to the inevitable,
they should have known better. Tim Stoen, for one, should have
known precisely how humiliated Jones would feel; and from long
personal experience he knew better than anyone that Jim Jones had
never been a graceful loser. But, if Ryan and the others in the visiting party did not understand the effects of their visit, the committee's
strategy, or their presence on Jones's fragile psyche, there were many
inside the community who did. Dale Parks was scared stiff. It would
be especially bad, Dale thought to himself, if they brought television
cameras. He was sure Jones would burn at the prospect of a biased,
negative version of Jonestown appearing on national television.

Throughout the two weeks of negotiations for the visit the community had heard a good deal about Leo Ryan. "The general idea,"
Odell Rhodes remembers, "was that everything we were for, he was
against. I guess the word you heard most was 'troublemaker'—like
why didn't Ryan just mind his own damn business." On Wednes-
day, after the Ryan party landed in Georgetown and the Lamaha
Gardens staff reported by radio that he had brought Tim Stoen, other
members of the Committee of Concerned Relatives, and a platoon
of journalists with him, Jones let loose an angry I-knew-it-all-the-
time barrage. "He flat-out called him a liar," Odell Rhodes remembers. "He said Ryan promised him he wasn't bringing the rest of
them—so he was nothing but another liar. And I think that's the
way most people felt about it. Ryan was bad enough, but, if he had
to come, okay. But now he expected us to open up our doors to a
bunch of people we damn well knew were our enemies. Like why
the hell should we have to entertain a bunch of people we *know* are
out to get us?"

Nonetheless, as the Ryan party bounced up the muddy, rutted
Jonestown road, that was exactly what the community was preparing
to do—entertain them. "It was," Rhodes explains, "like, if they were
coming, we were supposed to treat them like guests. Show them the
best time we could."

The entire day, Friday, in fact, had been devoted to cleaning, cooking, and otherwise preparing for the visitors, especially for a dinner-dance scheduled for that evening—Jonestown's customary welcoming gesture for important guests. While the kitchen crew cooked a special dinner of barbecued pork sandwiches and the band rehearsed its program, those not involved with the preparations were treated to a welcome, if slightly anxious, day of leisure. Rhodes remembers spending most of his day off with his roommates, Marie Lawrence and Bob Rankin, discussing a long-cherished scheme to build a sleeping loft in a corner of the nursing-care cottage, a project that the three of them had been trying to shepherd through the Jonestown bureaucracy (Housing Committee, Building Committee, Finance Committee, et al.) for months. "I don't think any of us mentioned Ryan at all, but it was like there was something in the air. We are all uptight, and I remember Marie and I even kind of snapped at each other a few times, and we very rarely ever had any problems getting on with each other normally."

Later, perhaps an hour before the visitors arrived, Judy Houston ran up the steps to Rhodes's cottage eager to share the news that her aunt, Carol Boyd, would be one of the four Concerned Relatives in the visiting party. Flushed with excitement she launched into a discussion of the crucial question of what to wear for the occasion. "We had kind of a running joke between us. She was always telling me I wasn't much of a father because I never bought her any new dresses, and I was always telling her the next time I went into town—in two or three years—I'd buy her a whole new wardrobe." With a trip to town as far out of the question as it always was, the best Rhodes could offer was jewelry—a bead necklace and a ring he had fashioned from the handle of a silver spoon. "I think that's about what she had in mind all along, but I was such a soft touch she didn't even have to ask."

When the Ryan party arrived, shortly after dark, Judy Houston ran off to look for Carol Boyd, and Rhodes headed for the kitchen to pick up a dinner tray he could take back to the nursing-care cottage before his shift began at seven. The visitors, meanwhile, after introductions to Jones and his staff, immediately set down to business. Ryan and the Concerned Relatives began interviewing the first of the thirty-odd names on the Concerned Relatives list while the reporters questioned Jones briefly and members of his staff at greater length.

Dinner was served at eight and after dinner the band began its performance—by all accounts, a polished, high-energy spectacular. Rhodes, who never could resist a performance by the band, listened from the nursing-care cottage for a while, and then made his way down to the pavilion. "I guess by the time I got there they were just about closing the set. The minute I walked in I could see right away that it'd loosened everybody up. I mean, we always had a good time when the band played; but just looking at their faces you could see that Ryan and the rest of them were feeling pretty good too."

When the band finished playing, Marceline Jones introduced Ryan, who stood up and made a short speech. "He sounded like all the politicians who used to come to the Temple in San Francisco," Rhodes recalls. "He was real slick. He said how great the band was, and then he said something about how, from everything he'd seen, Jonestown looked like a pretty nice place to live—and the only thing wrong with it that he could see was that it wasn't in his district so we could all vote for him."

Surprised, and enormously relieved, Rhodes continued on about his work in a mood so buoyant "I started thinking to myself, 'Goddam', we did it—we changed his mind about us.' I guess at that point I pretty much stopped thinking about the whole deal. It just looked to me like everybody was getting along real good and I figured everything was going to be all right."

Whatever doubts remained in Leo Ryan's mind, the speech had been an act of pure political genius. When the community finally stopped applauding, the tension in the air was all but gone, and when the band picked up its instruments and let loose with a favorite Jonestown tune, the young people took to the dance floor while the older ones stood nearby clapping to the music.

Against a background of loud soul music, with the people of Jonestown obviously enjoying themselves, Ryan and the reporters pulled up their chairs and struck up a conversation with Jones and a few of his aides. Although Jones's manner was guarded and his replies often tinged with self-pitying references to his enemies and his health (he looked as terrible as ever and claimed he was dying of cancer), the conversation was civil, not friendly, but respectful on all sides. Despite the strain of swallowing the anger he felt toward people he was convinced were trying to destroy him, Jones kept his composure throughout; even when the conversation turned to potentially explosive questions about John-John Stoen, discipline in the community, and his own sex life, the tone of his answers showed more despair than hostility.

By the time the party broke up at about eleven, the consensus among the visitors was that, for the first five hours at least, Jonestown had been something of a surprise, considerably less sinister than anyone had expected. Although none of the visitors was quite prepared to vouch for the equilibrium of Jim Jones's mind, the achievement of carving Jonestown out of jungle spoke for itself, and, as many other visitors had discovered, it tended to dispose one to give Jones the benefit of the doubt. Moreover, the mood was hardly the mood of a concentration camp populated by inmates struggling to escape. As for Leo Ryan, first impressions aside, the hard evidence was that, of the nearly twenty names of the Concerned Relatives' list interviewed during the evening, none seemed to be brainwashed, terrorized, or otherwise obviously the worse for wear. And none of them had expressed any desire at all to leave Jonestown. Despite everything he had been led to believe, Leo Ryan was impressed.

As the pavilion emptied, the visitors milled around outside, bickering about sleeping arrangements. Only Ryan, his aide, Jackie Speier, Neville Anninbourne, and the two lawyers, Charles Garry and Mark Lane, had been invited to spend the night in Jonestown. The others were to stay in Port Kaituma, an arrangement that provoked some mild protests from some of the reporters. While they registered their complaints with one of Jones's staff, a young black woman darted out of the shadows, pressed a note into the hand of one of the reporters, Don Harris, and then disappeared. The woman was Monica Bagby, and the note asked Harris to arrange for her and a friend Vern Gosney, to leave Jonestown with the Ryan party the following day.

While Harris prudently stuffed the note in his boot and boarded the dump truck for the drive back to Port Kaituma, Jones and his staff gathered with Charles Garry and Mark Lane for a post-mortem of the first day of the visit. According to Mark Lane,[10] the conversation turned quickly to a report by Tim Carter, the double agent Jones had sent to infiltrate the Committee of Concerned Relatives in San Francisco. Carter described a Committee meeting in Berkeley in which Tim Stoen reported on the preparations for the Ryan investigation. According to Carter, Stoen made it clear he had helped plan the investigation from the outset and described how he had convinced Ryan that it was absolutely necessary to bring the press. Carter went on to outline Stoen's strategy, the strategy Jones had long since figured out on his own: If Ryan's group was turned away from Jonestown's gate, the media would film that; if Ryan was allowed to enter, Stoen predicted that at least ten members of the community would choose to defect with Ryan, and the media would report that. Either way, Jones would lose and the Committee would win. As Carter went on to report that the Ryan visit was intended to be only the first of a series of investigations, Jones, according to Mark Lane, turned to him and asked, "How can I be sure that one person won't leave and betray us:" When Lane attempted to reassure him, Jones reportedly shook his head in despair and told Lane, "Mark, while you were telling me that Ryan was not going to bring the press in here, Stoen was planning the whole thing. It's terrible."

As terrible as it was, from Jones's point of view, to imagine Tim Stoen sitting safely in Georgetown masterminding an embarrassing, potentially devastating coup against him, Jones did not yet know the half of it. While he slept—or tried to—nine other Jonestown residents, in addition to Monica Bagby and Vern Gosney, were lying nervously in their bunks waiting for the hour before dawn. The group (all were black), which included two men in their early thirties, Julius Evans and Richard Clark, Clark's girl friend, Diane Louie, Evans's wife, and three small daughters, and two younger men, Robert Paul and Johnnie Franklin, had been planning an escape through the jungle for several weeks, caching food and water for the long, difficult hike to the village of Matthew's Ridge, twenty miles to the southwest. Evans and Clark, the group's leaders, had finally decided to attempt their break on Saturday morning, in order to use the disruption of the community's normal routine the Ryan visit had caused to cover their disappearance.

Shortly before daybreak, at a clear, bright sunrise that would turn into a thick, oppressively humid overcast in a few hours, the group slipped into the jungle.

While Julius Evans, his youngest daughter strapped to his back, and his companions hurried towards Matthew's Ridge, the rest of Jonestown awoke to an unusually peaceful morning. Jim Jones remained in his cabin while Leo Ryan and Jackie Speier interviewed the remaining names on the Concerned Relatives' list. Once again, no one they spoke to expressed the slightest desire to leave the settlement. Shortly before ten the reporters and Concerned Relatives who had spent the night in Port Kaituma returned. While Don Harris showed Monica Bagby's note to Leo Ryan, the other reporters drank coffee and then set off for a tour of Jonestown—their first opportunity to see the community by daylight.[11] For a time they followed Marceline Jones through the school buildings and the medical facilities, but, then, evidently following the time-honored principle that what is not shown is what is worth seeing, several of the reporters broke away from the tour and began exploring the settlement by themselves. Whatever their intentions, the self-guided tour turned into a wildly disruptive farce which did a great deal to undo the comfortable feelings of the night before.

For some reason, one of the reporters decided that the secret story of Jonestown was hidden in a large, shuttered cabin, which turned out to be a dormitory full of frightened old ladies. After peeking through the shutters the reporters demanded to be allowed inside. An angry confrontation ensued, with several members of the community defending the old ladies' right to privacy, while Mark Lane and Mike Prokes, an aide to Jones who had himself once been a television news reporter, attempted to prevent a full-scale riot. Prokes and Lane finally managed to strike a compromise, allowing one of the reporters to stick his head inside the door, and then Mike Prokes ran back to the pavilion to report the incident to Jones.

Jones simply nodded sadly; he was not surprised. Of course the reporters had tried to provoke an incident: it was all part of Tim Stoen's plan, and the plan was working like a charm. Jones had just been told that the Evan's group was missing and presumed on their way to Kaituma or Matthrew's Ridge; he had also heard a rumor that several others intended to leave with Ryan. It was all going according to plan—Tim Stoen's plan.

In the meanwhile, while Jones brooded, Don Harris had begun setting up his cameras for a filmed interview with Jones. The other reporters returned from their tour and the interview began. Within a few minutes, under the pressure of persistent, hard questioning, Jones began to crack. He stopped answering the questions put to him and launched into a desperate, disjointed monologue: "The only thing I regret is that somebody hasn't shot me. We're a small community, we're powerless; we're no threat to anyone, but they won't rest until they destroy us. I wish they would just shoot me and get it over with, but I guess the media smear is what they use now—in the long run it's as good as assassination."

With the reporters finally treated to a glimpse of the Jim Jones they had come to see—the paranoid, delusional Jim Jones—the questions came even faster—and harder: questions about John-John, about weapons in Jonestown, about threats against those who wanted to leave.

"Lies," Jim Jones answered wearily, "it's all lies—we're defeated by lies . . . it's so very painful."

Suddenly, one of Jones's staff climbed up to the podium and whispered something in Jones's ear. His face sagged visibly and he threw up his arm to shield himself from the camera. The reporters strained to hear what was being said. It was another defection—an important one. Earlier that morning, Edith Parks, Dale Parks's seventy-year-old grandmother, had asked Leo Ryan to take the entire Parks family—seven of them—with him. The reporters pounced: If Jonestown was the perfect society, why were people leaving? Were they afraid? What were the guns for? How many others were afraid to leave?

Finally, Jones shook his head. "Let them go. Let them all go. Who cares if they go? The more that go, the less the burden. It's all lies, they all tell lies when they leave. Everyone is free to go. I thought they stayed . . . I thought they stayed because they were afraid of industrialized society, afraid of the ghetto. I must have failed. I must have failed." He stood up. "I just want to say goodbye . . . to hug them . . . to tell them I love them."

While Jones set off to find the Parkses, the Parkses were hurriedly conferring among themselves. Although everyone in the family did want to go home, Patti Parks, Dale's mother, was not at all sure now was the right time, and Dale Parks was frankly terrified. "I just couldn't see Jim letting anyone leave with television cameras and reporters all around. I just couldn't see how we were going to get out of there alive." Dale Parks did not know what to do, but he wished his grandmother had taken the time to tell the rest of the family what she was about to do.

When Jones finally found the Parkses, he realized immediately that there was doubt in their minds, and in a long, emotional con-

versation that migrated from the pavilion to the children's playground next to it, and then back to the pavilion, he pleaded with
Dale and Patti Parks not to desert him.

Moved by Jones's despair and confused about his chances of survival, Dale finally agreed: The family would stay, on the condition
that Jones's lawyers prepare a legal document guaranteeing their
right to leave whenever they chose. Jones accepted the bargain immediately. As soon as he did, Dale realized he had made a mistake.

"They were the same kind of promises he'd made to get me to
come to Jonestown in the first place. I finally decided that the other
people who stood up even before my family and said they wanted to
go home would probably be enough to make him believe he was
going to get a lot of bad publicity back in the States—and I knew he
wouldn't stand for any bad publicity. I started to realize that if we
stayed, we might well be involved in some kind of a murder-suicide
situation, so I felt our chances were probably better if we went, even
though, personally, I never expected to get out alive."

While Jones pleaded and the Parks family agonized over whether
to be hanged for lions or sheep, news of the Parkses' defection
reached another large, cohesive Jonestown family, the Bogues, the
family that included the community's master builder, Jim Bogue
and Juanita Bogue, the young woman Odell Rhodes had been courting. The Bogues were in much the same position as the Parkses,
eager to return to a normal life away from Jonestown but paralyzed
by their fear of Jones's reaction, and torn between themselves because an adopted daughter, Merilee, and Juanita's sister Tina's husband, Bruce Turner, did not want to leave. Finally, five of the
Bogues and Harold Cordell, who had been living with Jim Bogues's
wife, Edith, decided to go, leaving Merilee, Bruce Turner, and nine
members of Harold Cordell's family behind.

While the Parkses hurriedly packed their suitcases and the Bogues
ran frantically through the community saying their goodbyes, Mark
Lane and Leo Ryan attempted to reassure Jones that the departure of
some twenty-odd members of the community did not represent a
disaster. Ryan assured Jones that his impression of Jonestown would
not be colored by the fact that a handful of the population had decided to leave, and Lane assured him that both the Parkses and the
Bogues had promised they would not join the Committee of Con-

cerned Relatives' crusade. Jones was in no mood to be comforted. He stormed back to the pavilion and began giving orders to his aides.

While all hell was breaking loose around the pavilion, Odell Rhodes was just waking up from an unusually untroubled sleep, thoroughly—cheerfully—innocent of the events of the morning. He showered, dressed, and walked toward the medical tent for his morning dose of an antibiotic he was taking for a persistent infection in his bad leg. As he passed the pavilion, he saw Judy Houston talking quietly to her aunt. Judy jumped up when she saw him, dragged him over and introduced him, explaining proudly that Rhodes had made the necklace and ring she was wearing. Carol Boyd smiled and shook his hand.

"I guess I was still about half asleep," Rhodes remembers, "but I sure as hell wasn't picking up any bad vibrations from them. Hell, I doubt if they even knew what was going on."

Crossing in back of the pavilion toward the medical tent, Rhodes saw Jones and Dale Parks talking together in the children's playground. He thought nothing of it. He continued toward the medical tent, and then after taking the pills, as he started toward the kitchen for his breakfast, he literally bumped into Juanita Bogue, who was hurrying to board the dump truck for the ride out of Jonestown. Rhodes started to say something, but Juanita Bogue looked away and mumbled something about being late for guard duty at the front gate.

"I remember I told her I hoped maybe I'd see her later. She didn't say anything. If I didn't know, she sure as hell wasn't going to tell me."

Back at his cottage, still full of what seemed like a beautiful morning, Rhodes gave a cheery hello to one of his patients, an elderly, diabetic black woman. With a pained look on her face, she pulled Rhodes toward her and asked if it was true that everyone was leaving Jonestown. "She was afraid that everybody was going to leave and forget about her, I guess. I didn't know what she was talking about, but I think she must have heard somebody talking about something—the Evanses maybe—but she got it so backwards I couldn't figure out what she was trying to tell me."

A few minutes later, while Rhodes was straightening up around his bunk, Joe Wilson, one of Jones's bodyguards, walked into the cottage and asked Rhodes if he could lend a hand carrying a foot-locker stored in the cottage to a shed near Jones's cottage. "It was heavy," Rhodes remembers, "damned heavy, and I'd always kind of figured maybe there were weapons in it, but I still wasn't putting anything together. I kind of kicked myself about it later, because the message was there—I just wasn't picking up on it, I mean, the way that thing sounded when we were carrying it, I *knew* there was am-munition in it. After eight years in the service you *know* what am-munition sounds like, but I guess I must have figured something like maybe they were going to bring people through the cottage and they didn't want that sitting there right out in plain sight. I don't know—I guess the truth is I wasn't thinking very much at all, because, if I had been, I would have picked up on it. Like I remember Joe said something like how we better get a move on or they were going to be gone. But at that time that one flew right by me too. I just hadn't seen anything to get me thinking along these lines."

Back at the cottage again Rhodes finally heard a straightforward version of the Evanses' escape from Bob Christian, the nursing-care supervisor, who told him that the security people had turned the settlement upside down looking for Julius Evans and the others.

"It looks like they split into the jungle," Christian said.

"That," Rhodes remembers, "registered right away. But I still didn't have time to put it together with the other things because right while we were talking things started happening really fast—so fast you didn't have any time to stop and think."

While Rhodes and Christian talked a crowd had began to gather outside the cottage. Rumors about the Parkeses and the Bogues were now spreading through the community and fifty or sixty people were standing sullenly along the path between the pavilion and the resi-dential area behind the nursing-care cottage waiting to watch Mon-ica and Vern and the Parkses and Bogues pass by on their way to the dump truck that was parked on the far side of the pavilion.

Rhodes himself was still unaware that the others were leaving. "But as soon as I stuck my head out the door I knew something was wrong—something serious. There were all these people out there just standing around, not doing anything but talking to each other, and you very rarely saw a scene like that in Jonestown. Besides, just the way they were standing, everybody looking down the path, it was like there was so much tension in the air you could feel it in your bones."

Spotting a friend, Shirely Hicks, standing right below his porch, Rhodes leaned over and asked what was happening. "I don't think she even had time to say anything, because right at that point Harold Cordell came walking by with a knapsack on his back and a portable radio in his hand. It didn't take much to figure out where he was going, and besides, people were shouting things at him—all kinds of motherfuckers and asshole traitors. I remember one of them was his son Chris. Seemed like Chris was more pissed than anybody. He was screaming something about how his dad couldn't even leave the goddamn radio, he had to have that all for himself too."

As Tommy Borgue walked by, his adopted sister Merilee, who had refused to leave with the rest of the family, began shaking her fist and screaming that she was changing her name. "I mean people were mad. There was all kinds of talk about busting asses and that kind of thing, and it wouldn't have taken much to get it going right then. I was one of the few people who wasn't saying very much. I was standing there with Shirley, and I guess the two of us felt a little different than most people. I was kind of sad about the Bogues leaving because they were all good workers, and, of course, Juanita was kind of special to me, but the way I thought about it was, hell, if they want to go, we're going to be better off without them anyway."

The group in front of Rhodes's cottage could not see the area in back of the pavilion where the Jonestown dump truck was loading the defectors and the members of the visiting party. They could, however, see into the pavilion itself. When the last of the defectors had passed by, the crowd remained in sullen knots of threes and fours, watching—from a distance of about twenty yards—the scene inside the pavilion. There, Leo Ryan, Mark Lane, Richard Dwyer, Jones, and members of his staff were gathered around another family, the Simons, attempting to work out a Solomonic solution to an impossible problem. Just a few minutes before, while the other defectors were already boarding the truck, Al Simon had come running from his cottage, dragging his two children with him, ready to board the truck. By the time he reached the pavilion his wife, Bonnie, had caught up with him and was dragging the children in the opposite direction. Nobody—the Congressman, the lawyers, the diplomat, or Jones—could decide who would keep the children. Finally, Ryan announced the truck would go on without him so he could stay another day and attempt to mediate the Simons' dispute.

Suddenly, a husky young man in his late twenties, Don Sly, began walking toward Leo Ryan. Without a word, he grabbed Ryan from behind and drew a knife from his pocket. While Ryan managed to hold on to his wrist, Mark Lane and Richard Dwyer wrestled both of them to the ground and disarmed Sly, cutting his arm in the process.

From outside the pavilion, where Rhodes and the crowd stood, it was possible to see and hear the struggle but not to make out who had been attacked by whom. "I thought," Rhodes remembers, "it was all going to go down right then, because this woman started screaming that they were killing Jones. But, you could see Jones, so you knew it wasn't him, and then a couple of people hustled her inside, and Marceline Jones came over the loudspeaker and reassured everybody that everything was all right and we should all go back to our cottages and wait there."

Although badly shaken and covered with blood—Don Sly's blood from the cut he received while being disarmed—Leo Ryan was unhurt. While Sly was led away to the medical tent, Ryan caught his breath and allowed Dwyer and Lane to convince him to leave immediately, before there was further violence. Lane and Charles Garry would stay behind to sort out the Simons' problem and Dwyer would return in a few days to make sure Al Simon could leave if he still wanted to.

As Leo Ryan stood to leave the pavilion, Jim Jones looked directly in his eyes and said, "I guess this changes everything, doesn't it?"

"It doesn't change everything," Ryan answered, "but it does change something."

15

We Lay
Our Lives Down

While a shaken Leo Ryan, his shirt spattered with Don Sly's blood, walked slowly toward the waiting truck, the twenty-nine other passengers already aboard (including fourteen defectors) were joined by a last-minute addition. The new defector was Larry Layton, Debbie Blakey's brother, a slight, boyish thirty-two-year-old, who jumped on board claiming he was "pissed-off" with life in Jonestown. To the other defectors, who knew Layton as "Jim's robot," the claim not only rang false, it rang loud bells of alarm. Dale Parks, in fact, took one look at Layton and had the unnerving sensation he was—literally—staring death in the face.

While the truck inched slowly down the rutted Jonestown road, Parks circulated quietly through the Ryan party sharing his fears. Given the mood of the last few hours and, especially, the attack on Ryan, the warning was all too believable; but, with the truck still on Jonestown land, it was not clear to anyone what there was to do about Layton, at least until the truck reached neutral ground, and relatively safety, in Port Kaituma. The Ryan party had taken a stiff dose of Jim Jones and the jungle, and they were shaken, perhaps not as terrified as the defectors, but afraid nonetheless, and very nearly paralyzed by an acute attack of the same sense of helpless isolation that had gripped the community for so many months. They were concentrating on getting back to civilization—to law and order, television and telephones, and most of all airplanes—especially the two that were supposed to be waiting at the Kaituma airstrip. One of the stunned reporters, Charles Krause, the ringleader of the raid on the woman's dormitory, wrote later about the shock of realizing that "We were in the jungle where a press card was just another piece of paper." [12]

After a forty-five-minute ride the truck finally arrived at semicivilization, Port Kaituma, about 4:30—to a mixture of good and bad news. The good news was the reassuring sight of a patrol of three Guyanese soldiers, who gave the appearance, at least, of the presence of civil authority. The bad news was that the planes had not yet arrived. While the others waited at the airstrip, Richard Dwyer and Neville Anninbourne decided to walk to the local constabulary, telephone Georgetown, and report the attack on Ryan. When Dwyer and Anninbourne returned, they brought more bad news: Although the planes were on route, the only aircraft available—a twin-engined de Havilland Otter and a single-engined Cessna—had a combined seating capacity for only twenty-four of the refugees. With thirty-one bodies to transport, seven unfortunates would have to wait in Port Kaituma until one of the planes could make a return trip.

Leo Ryan immediately decided his first priority was to move the defectors as far away from Jonestown as quickly as possible. The logical candidates to leave behind were the reporters, and Ryan instructed Jackie Speier to assign their seats last. After a nerve-wracking thirty-minute wait, the first of the two planes, the smaller Cessna, landed, and Jackie Speier promptly assigned six defectors to board it. Larry Layton, who was not one of those assigned, immediately began to protest, for reasons that were not clear at the time but would become all too clear in a very few minutes: as soon as the plane landed Layton had somehow managed to sneak aboard and hide a handgun.

While Monica Bagby, Vern Gosney, and three members of the Parks family boarded the aircraft, Layton took his argument to Leo Ryan. With his mind on more important things, Ryan told Layton he could ride in whichever plane he wanted as long as he agreed to be searched for a weapon. With his weapon already on board, Layton let one of the reporters pat him down and then quickly boarded the Cessna.

Just as Layton boarded the larger plane, the Otter made its appearance; and at the same time another argument erupted. Over the noise of the approaching plane several of the reporters began lobbying frantically with Jackie Speier, trying to convince her to leave the Concerned Relatives behind so they could get back to Georgetown and file their stories. Speier told them to talk to Ryan. While they pressed their care with Ryan, the Otter finally landed, and as soon as the pilot threw down his ladder, the remaining defectors quickly began climbing aboard.

Neville Anninbourne and the Bogue family were the first to board; Patti Parks stood on the steps. Everyone else, including Ryan, Richard Dwyer, the reporters, and the three Guyanese guards stood below on the tarmac. The Cessna, meanwhile, was already warming its engines for take-off.

Suddenly, someone noticed a farm tractor pulling a flatbed cart loaded with a half-dozen men at the far end of the runway. The men were white, and the tractor and cart were obviously from Jonestown, but, although there was no doubt where it was from, its mission— for a few more seconds—was still not clear. While the smaller plane began to slowly start down the runway, all eyes—including the NBC film cameras—turned to watch the approaching cart.

With the cart still about seventy-five yards away, suddenly, inside the Cessna, Larry Layton opened fire, hitting Monica Bagby in the chest, before Vern Gosney and Dale Parks wrestled his weapon away. A moment later the men on the trailer, now at point-blank range, jumped off the cart and opened fire at the Otter with high-powered rifles, ignoring the Guyanese guards who, in turn, ignored the gunfire. (The Guyanese explained later that, since the fight was between Americans, all of whom were crazy anyway, they could see no reason to take sides.)

Standing on the steps, Patti Parks was hit in the leg and then, when she bent down to look at her wound, she was hit again, this time in the head, fatally. On board the Otter, Tina and Tommy Bogue were wounded as they struggled to push the entrance hatch shut. Below, on the runway, Leo Ryan and the NBC film crew were caught in the heaviest fusillade. Ryan and three others were killed within seconds. Eight others standing near the plane, including Jackie Speier, Richard Dwyer, two of the Concerned Relatives, and three other reporters were also wounded, three of them seriously. After perhaps a minute and a half, as suddenly as it started, the attack ended.

The Jonestown gunmen clamly climbed back aboard the tractor cart and drove slowly away. The wounded and frightened survivors—those still able to walk, including those aboard both planes—immediately scrambled for cover in the jungle. The dead, and several of the seriously wounded, lay in pools of blood on the runway. As a crowd of local Guyanese gathered at the scene, the Cessna, with only the pilots of both planes and Monica Bagby aboard, suddenly revved its engines and took off.

Despite the carnage, five dead and twelve wounded, the gruesome truth about the attack was that it could easily have been worse. With no resistance from the victims, although Bob Flick, the NBC producer, had tried unsuccessfully to beg a weapon from one of the Guyanese guards, the attackers could clearly have killed anyone—or everyone—they wanted to kill. They had made sure of finishing off only Ryan, Don Harris, Bob Brown, the NBC cameraman, and Greg Robinson, the *San Francisco Examiner* photographer. Those four had been shot repeatedly in the head while they lay wounded on the ground. The defectors had escaped relatively lightly. With the exception of Monica Bagby, who was shot by Larry Layton, and Patti Parks, who was shot in the head while bending down, all of the wounded defectors were shot below the waist, perhaps because, whatever their instructions, the Jonestown gunmen had not been able to bring themselves to cold-blooded murder of people who, until a few hours before, had been their comrades. Tina Bogue, in fact, remembers seeing one of the attackers aim at her head, then lower his rifle before pulling the trigger. Tom Kice, the leader of the attacking force, happened to be an old, close friend of the Parks family. Kice had even talked once or twice to Patti Parks, the woman who now lay dead on the stairs of the crippled airplane, about leaving Jonestown himself.

Although the attack had not gone precisely according to plan, it had, nonetheless, achieved the result Jones intended. That result was not wholesale slaughter; it was the murder of Leo Ryan. Jones's original plan had called for Larry Layton to board the first plane to leave on the assumption that Ryan would also board the same plane. Once the plane was airborne Layton was then to put a bullet in the pilot's head, sending the plane crashing into the jungle. Knowing, however, that Layton—his robot—was not capable of improvisation, Jones had sent the tractor squad as a back-up team. The back-up team had succeeded; Leo Ryan was dead.

Ryan's death was important to Jones for several reasons: as a matter of honor; as revenge; and as something more as well. For over a year Jones had prepared his followers for the destruction of their community. He had discussed it, predicted it, and rehearsed it time after time. Always the scenario was the same: with its enemies poised to destroy it Jonestown destroyed itself instead, thereby denying the enemies their triumph. In Jones's mind the time to destroy Jonestown had now arrived. He felt defeated and he was ready to die. All that was lacking were the enemies poised at the gate, ready to attack. By murdering Leo Ryan, Jones assured that the enemies would come. Ryan's death was Jones's way of validating his prophecy; the end he had promised the people of Jonestown was now imminent. This was the apocalypse Jones had expected all his life. Like so much that happened in Jonestown, the attack at the Port Kaituma airstrip had been theater, an act that conferred reality on an illusion.

Meanwhile, inside Jonestown, the vast majority of the community, who had been in their cabins since the Ryan party left, as yet knew nothing about Larry Layton, the back-up team, or the rest of Jones's plans. In his cottage Odell Rhodes was sitting on his bed, "trying to put it all together. I figured we were in for it. Not for what happened—I never thought it would come to that—but maybe for something like when Debbie Blakey left—or maybe a little worse." Whatever his conscious mind told him, however, Rhodes's subconscious was planning for the worst. "I didn't think about why I was doing it at the time, but one thing I did was change my clothes. I was wearing a pair of white pants and a light-colored shirt, and I changed into blue jeans and a black sweatshirt. Like I said, I didn't think about why I did it at the time, but I'd had jungle training in the army so I knew about wearing dark clothes in the jungle, so I guess a part of me was getting ready for something. I mean it sure as hell felt like something was going to happen, but what happened— I never would have believed that, I don't think anybody could have believed it was really going to happen."

Jim Jones, however, was already busy planning the unbelievable. As soon as the assassination squad left for Port Kaituma, Jones sent Mark Lane and Charles Garry back to the guesthouse where they had spent the previous night with an explicit, ominous warning to stay away from the pavilion area. (Lane and Garry later persuaded their two guards to point out a path through the jungles so they could "tell Jonestown's story to the world." Jones then called his medical and security staffs together and outlined their roles in the hours to come. The medical staff would prepare a mixture of potassium cyanide and Valium in half-gallon bottles. A fifty-five-gallon drum of imitation fruit juice would be prepared to mix with the poison. The security force would surround the Central Pavilion in two concentric rings, an inner ring armed with crossbows and sabres, and another beyond it armed with firearms.

Finally, he gave instructions to three important aides, Tim Carter, the San Francisco double agent; his brother, Mike; and Mike Prokes. The Carters and Prokeses were to carry a suitcase containing a half-million dollars in U.S. currency to the Soviet embassy in Georgetown.

As soon as the Carters and Prokeses left to arm themselves and to collect the suitcase, Jones picked up the public-address microphone and called the community together. Everyone, excepting only those few seniors who were too debilitated to be moved easily, was to come immediately to the pavilion. In a few minutes the pavilion was full and in another few minutes the apron around was also crowded with a hundred or so others who could not squeeze under the open-sided pavilion's roof. Most of the community was still dressed in the party clothes they had worn for Leo Ryan's visit.

At about five o'clock, almost exactly the same time as the attack at the airstrip, Jones began to speak. What he said was recorded on the tape recorder kept in the pavilion to record the community's meetings. The tape, forty-three minutes of the most graphic, lurid, and bizarre suicide note in history, begins with Jones, speaking in a calm, weary voice—for posterity as well as for his followers—reminding the community:

"I've tried to give you a good life, but in spite of all that I've tried, a handful of our people, with their lies, have made our lives impossible. There's no way to detach ourselves from what's happened today. We're sitting on a powder keg . . . and to sit here and wait for the catastrophe that's going to happen on that airplane . . . and it's going to be a catastrophe—it almost happened here. Almost happened, the Congressman was nearly killed here. . . . We've been so betrayed. . . . We've been so terribly betrayed. What's going to happen here in a matter of a few minutes is that one of the people on that plane is going to shoot the pilot. I know that; I didn't plan it, but

I know it's going to happen . . . and down comes that plane into the jungle and we had better not have any of our children left when its over because they'll parachute in here on us. I'm saying it just as plain as I know how to tell you. I've never lied to you. I never have lied to you—I know that's what's what's going to happen. That's what he intends to do, and he will do it. God can see, I'm so bewildered with many, many pressures on my brain, seeing these people behave so treasonous. It's just too much for me to put together, but I now know what He was telling me. . . . So my opinion is that we be kind to children, and be kind to seniors, and take the potion like they used to take in ancient Greece. Step over quietly because we are not committing suicide—it's a revolutionary act. We can't go back. They won't leave us alone; they're going back to tell more lies, which means more Congressmen, and there's no way—no way we can survive."

Odell Rhodes began to look nervously around. "I was beginning to get the message. I still didn't exactly believe he was really going to do it, but at that point I knew it was a possibility—I think maybe it was when he mentioned the children that I started worrying, because he always said that if it ever came down to it, he'd start with the children. So right then I started to think about moving away, but I was right up front just a few feet from him, and I knew I couldn't go anywhere without drawing a whole lot of attention to myself."

Making himself conspicuous was the last thing Rhodes wanted to do. One quick look around the pavilion was enough to convince him that the community was ready to do whatever Jim Jones asked. It also revealed the security force, standing tight-lipped and serious, weapons in hand. Rhodes had never seen the security force deployed around the pavilion during a meeting before, and the sight chilled him. He slumped down in his seat and began to do some very serious thinking.

He was only half listening to the meeting itself; with variations, Rhodes had heard most of it before. First someone suggested fighting back, as someone always did; and, as he had so many times before, Jones explained that the community could not fight the black, socialist soldiers of the Guyanese Defense Force.

"We can do it," Jones admitted, "but if our children are left we are going to have them butchered. We can make a strike, but we'll be striking against people we don't want to strike against. What we'd like to do is get the people who caused this stuff. And some people are prepared—and know how to do it, to go into town and get Timothy Stoen. But there's no plane; you can't catch a plane in time. He's responsible for it; he brought these people to us—he and Deanna Mertle; but, people in San Francisco will not be idle over this; they'll not take our lives in vain!"

The prospect of revenge on Tim Stoen brought cheers, and, listening to the crowd, Odell Rhodes began to suspect he might be the only person in the pavilion having his doubts. He was wrong. When the cheering subsided, a near-sighted, heavy-set black woman in her mid-fifties, Christine Miller, stood up to speak her mind. She asked a simple question about the possibility of escaping to Russia, an alternative Jones had raised several times during discussions of what the community would do at the end. He had told the community that the Russians had provided him with a secret radio code to be used to inform the Soviet embassy in the event Jonestown came under attack.

"Is it too late for Russia?" Christine Miller asked, her voice cracking from the strain of speaking in front of a thousand excited comrades.

"Here's why it's too late for Russia," Jones answered quickly. "They're out there. They've gone with guns and its's too late. I didn't want them to kill anybody . . . but they said deliver up Udjara [the Jonestown nickname for Don Sly, the man who attacked Leo Ryan at the pavilion earlier that afternoon]. Do you think I'm going to deliver them Udjara? Not on your life."

After Don Sly offered to give himself up (even though he knew, he said, he would be killed on sight), Jones countered: "No, you're not going. You're not going. I can't live that way. I've lived for all, and I'll die for all."

"Well," Christine Miller suggested, "I say let's make an airlift to Russia. That's what I say. I don't think nothing's impossible."

Patiently, Jones explained that the emergency radio code was only to be used in case of a CIA coup that toppled the Guyanese government. But, with Christine Miller pressing him, he agreed to put the call in anyway: "Well, we can check on that, check with the Russians to see if they'll take us in immediately. Otherwise we die."

Once again, as they did everytime Jones mentioned death, the community exploded with applause, and when the noise subsided

Jones continued: "You know, to me death is not the fearful thing. It's living that's treacherous. I have never, never, never, never seen anything like this before in my life. I'm telling you, it's not *worth* living like this. *It is not worth living like this!*"

Christine Miller, however, was not yet quite convinced. "I think," she said simply, "that there were too few who left for twelve hundred people to give up their lives for those people who left."

Once again Jones tried to explain the seriousness of the situation. Larry Layton and the others had gone to kill Leo Ryan and the defectors. He was powerless to stop them. And, once Ryan was dead, the enemies would have the excuse they were waiting for; they would attack.

Christine Miller insisted that she understood what Jones was saying, but she could not understand why the community could not flee to Russia.

"To Russia?" Jones shook his head with exasperation. "You think the Russians are going to want us with all this stigma? Maybe we had some value before, but now we don't have any value."

"Well," Christine Miller shook her own head right back at him, "I don't see it like that. I mean, I feel like that as long as there's life there's hope. That's my faith."

"Then how come everybody's dying?" Jones shot back. With annoyance creeping into his voice, perhaps at Christine Miller's stubborn insistence on throwing the move to Russia—a fantasy Jones had never taken seriously—back in his face, he told her: "Some place that hope runs out. Because everybody dies. I haven't yet seen anybody that didn't die. And I'd like to chose my own kind of death for a change. I'm tired of being tormented to hell—that's what I'm tired of. Tired of it!"

Responding to the anger and despair in his voice, the crowd now began to shout at Christine Miller, urging her to sit down and let them get on with it. Jones then pointed his finger at her: "I'm going to tell you, Christine. Without me, life has no meaning. I'm the best friend you'll ever have. I've always taken your troubles right on my shoulders. And I'm not going to change that now. It's too late! I've been running too long—I'm not going to change now."

Jones waited while the crowd cheered, then continued in a softer voice: "Maybe next time you'll get Russia. The next time around. What I'm talking about now is the dispensation of justice. This is a

revolutionary suicide council. I'm not talking about self-destruction—I'm talking about that we have no other road . . ."

"It's not that I'm afraid to die," Christine Miller interrupted
quickly.

"I don't think you are."

"But, I look at all the babies and I think *they* deserve to live. You
know?"

"I agree. But they also deserve much more. They deserve peace."

"We all came here for peace."

"But have we had it?"

Before Christine Miller had a chance to answer the crowd gave
Jones the answer he wanted to hear, a ringing chorus of a single
word, "No." Jones shrugged and looked back at Christine Miller:

"I tried to give it to you. I laid down my life practically. I practically died every day to give you peace. And you're still not having
any peace. You look better than I've seen you in a long while, but
it's still not the kind of peace I wanted to give you. A person's a fool
to say you're winning when you're losing."

Again, Jones went back over the same ground: Tim Stoen, betrayal, his enemies, the pain of defeat, the agony of living. But
Christine Miller was still not ready to concede:

"When we destroy ourselves . . . we've let them, the enemies,
defeat us."

"No, We win. We win when we go down. Tim Stoen won't have
anybody else to hate; and then he'll destroy himself. I'm speaking
here not as the administrator. I'm speaking as a prophet today."

With a thousand people screaming at her to accept the word of
the prophet, Christine Miller made her last stand:

"What I think, what I feel and I think is that we all have our right
to our own destiny as individuals. And I think I have a right to
choose mine—and everybody else has a right to choose theirs."

"I'm not taking it from you," Jones insisted, and as the crowd
rushed to support him, one of his aides, Jim McIlvane, picked up
the argument: "Christine, you're only standing here because *he* is
here! So I don't know what you're talking about, having an individual life. Your life has been extended to the day you're standing
here—because of *him!*"

Straining to be heard above the cheers that followed, Christine

Miller tried an appeal to Jones's omnipotence: "Can't you save so many people?"

"I have saved them," Jones replied wearily. "I *have* saved them. I made my expression, I made my manifestation—and the world was not ready for me. Paul says there are men born out of due season. *I've* been born out of due season. I've been born out of due season—just like we all are. And the best testimony we can make," he went on, his voice rising with excitement, "the best testimony we can make is to leave this goddamned world!"

The crowd, which up until now had waited patiently, taking its cues from Jones, expecting him to give them a sign for action, can wait no longer. People are screaming, shouting, some of them struggling to reach Christine Miller and pull her away from the microphone. One elderly woman Odell Rhodes remembers, in particular, clawing frantically at the air, as someone held her around the waist, trying to scratch out Christine Miller's eyes.

"You *is* too afraid to die!"

"You won't do no fucking good in Russia, that's for sure."

"Will you let me—will you make her sit down and let me talk while I'm on the floor?" Christine Miller asks Jones.

"I am listening to you," Jones sighs. "You ask me about Russia. I'm right now making a call to Russia. What more do you suggest?"

The crowd responds with suggestions of its own. They are ready to get on with it, ready to die. Finally, Jones's son, Johnny, calms them down, and a shaken Christine Miller makes her last, desperate appeal:

"Do you want to see John-John die?" She asks, daring Jones's most sensitive nerve.

"What's that?" He is stunned.

"You mean you want to see John-John, the little one. . . ."

"Are you saying," someone asks from the back of the pavilion, "that he thinks more of John-John than the other children here?"

Again, the pavilion erupts with cries of protest. Christine Miller has challenged Jones at the very core of his commitment; she has questioned the community's faith in its leader; she has questioned the family.

Now, Jones himself calls for quiet, then he turns to Christine

Miller. Should he, he demands, sacrifice Udjara in order to save John-John? "He's no different to me than any of my children. I can't separate myself from the actions of *any* of my people. If you'd done something wrong, I'd stand with you. If they wanted to come and get you, they'd have to take me first."

A voice rises above the crowd: "Dad," a young woman cries, "we're all ready to go. If you tell us we have to give our lives now, we're ready. All the children and the brothers are with me."

Jones looks Christine Miller directly in the eye: "For a month," he says, his voice thick with emotion, "I've tried to keep this thing from happening, but I now see it's the will of the sovereign being that this happened to us. Now we lay our lives down in protest against what's been done . . . the criminality of the people, the cruelty of people. . . . And I don't think we should sit here and take any more time for our children to be endangered. . . ."

His words are lost in the roar of the crowd; and, by the time the cheering stops, Christine Miller has sat down.

Graciously, Jones praises her, for speaking her mind, for not running with the other defectors, for staying with her brothers and sisters. "I like you, I personally like you very much. You had to be honest. But you stayed. If you'd wanted to run, you'd have run with them, because anybody could have run today. I know you're not a runner . . . and your life is as precious as John-John's. . . ."

"That's all I've got to say," Christine Miller mumbles, finally ready to rejoin her brothers and sisters.

"What comes now folks? What comes now?" Jones asks the community, but before there is an answer Tom Kice and the squad of assassins return from the airstrip. The crowd's attention turns; rumors begin to spread through the pavilion.

"Stay peace, stay peace," Jones orders, while Johnny Jones leaps off the stage to receive Tom Kice's report.

There is a moment of confusion in which Jones fears that Richard Dwyer, the embassy official, has come back with the attackers. After a minute of chaos, with Jones shouting, "Get Dwyer out of here before something happens to him!" the confusion is cleared when it turns out someone has said something about Udjara, not Dwyer, and Jones has confused their names.

Finally, Johnny Jones breaks in to relay the report from the assassins:

"Pop, the Congressman is dead."

"It's all over," Jones sighs. "It's all over, all over. What a legacy, what a legacy. . . . They invaded our privacy, they came into our homes. They followed us six thousand miles away. . . . Well, the Red Brigade showed them justice. The Congressman's dead." He turns to the medical staff: *"Please,* get us the medication. It's simple, it's simple. There's no convulsions with it—it's simple. Just, please, get it before it's too late. The GDF will be here soon. I tell you—get moving, get moving, get moving. . . . Don't be afraid to die. You'll see, if these people land out there, they'll torture some of our children here. They'll torture some of our people—they'll torture our seniors. . . . Now, please, please, can we hasten? Can we hasten our medication? You don't know what you've done. . . . Are you gonna get that medication here? You got to move. Marceline, we got forty minutes."

Two nurses, Judy Ijames and Annie Moore, now bring the mixture of powdered fruit juice, cyanide and Valium to the stage. They place it on a low folding table. This time there is no demonstration. Without being asked a young mother, Ruletta Paul, sitting in the front row with her infant child, stands up and walks up to the table. From a few feet away, Odell Rhodes watches in disbelief as Ruletta Paul takes a cup of poison from the table:

"She just poured it down the baby's throat. And then she took the rest herself. It didn't take them right away. She had time to walk down outside. I watched her go, and then the next woman, Michelle Wilson, she came up with her baby and did the same thing."

Over the public-address system Judy Ijames is giving instructions to the crowd:

"The people that are standing there in the aisle go stand in regular lines. Everybody get back behind the table and back this way, okay? There's nothing to worry about. Everybody keep calm and try to keep your children calm. Older children can help lead the little children and reassure them. They're not crying from pain. It's just a little bitter tasting, but they're not crying out of any pain."

16

Escape

"Right about then," Odell Rhodes remembers, "that's when I got up. Everybody's starting to line up, so they're all moving around and nobody's going to think anything about me moving too. But I'm going in the other direction. I mean, I'm just sitting there maybe ten feet away, and I can just see somebody handing me a cup and saying, 'Here's yours.' Well, I'm not about to do it. I mean, I would have fought for Jonestown, no questions asked, but to kill myself—what good's that going to do? The truth is, if you get right down to it, as much as I loved Jones for taking me off the streets, at that moment, right then, I went right back to the streets. Like, if Jones wants to go around killing Congressmen, that's his problem. I got my own problems to worry about. I didn't kill the Congressman, I didn't want to kill the Congressman, and I sure as hell didn't want to kill Juanita or any of the rest of them—so why should I pay for it?"

While Rhodes made his way out of the pavilion, the first group to die, mothers and their small children, were moving through the line. While the mothers took a paper cup of poison for themselves, a nurse squirted a dose of poison in the babies' mouths with the barrel of a hypodermic syringe.

"There was a lot of noise," Rhodes remembers. "It was organized, but it wasn't organized the way most things in Jonestown were organized. There was a lot of confusion, people screaming, people running around trying to find their families, people hugging each other goodbye—that kind of thing."

In the pavilion, Jim McIlvane had taken the microphone from

Jim Jones. McIlvane, who considered himself an expert on "after-life experiences," reassured the community they would meet "on the other side." Death, McIlvane told them, was nothing but "a little rest. A little rest—it feels good, it never felt so good, family. I'll tell you, you've never felt so good as how that feels."

Many of them dying, however, were finding that death from cyanide poisoning was not quite so easy as advertised. Despite the admixture of Valium, which was intended to forestall the severe convulsions cyanide causes, most of the dying were convulsing violently. It was a grotesque sight, and as more people died, there were more and more screams of horror. Eventually, an elderly black woman, Irene Edwards, took the microphone to give her comrades a grandmotherly scolding: "I just want to say something to everybody that I see is standing around crying. This is nothing to cry about. This is something we should rejoice about. You should be happy about this. They always told us that we should cry when we're coming into the world. But when we're leaving it, and we're leaving it peaceful, I think we should be, you should be, happy about this. I was just thinking about Jim Jones. He has just suffered and suffered and suffered.

"I've been here about one year and nine months and I never felt better in my life, not in San Francisco but in a town called Jonestown. I don't want this life—I had a beautiful life—and I don't see nothing I should be crying about. We should be *happy!*"

Despite Irene Edwards the screams grew louder and the confusion more numbing until, finally, Jones returned to the microphone: "Please, for God's sake, let's get on with it. We've lived—we've lived as no other people have lived—and loved. We've had as much of this world as you're going to get. Let's just be done with it—let's be done with the agony of it. It's far, far harder to have to watch you every day, die slowly . . . and this, this is a revolutionary suicide, because none of us self-destructed . . . so they'll pay for this. . . . They brought this on us, and they'll pay for that. I leave that destiny to them."

Odell Rhodes, meanwhile, had made his way out of the pavilion. "I was thinking about the house I lived in, because they stored mattresses up in the rafters there and I thought if I could get there, I could climb up with the mattresses. But right between me and it was a guard with a crossbow. So I just kind of leaned on this fence, trying to think, and, while I was there, somebody asked me to help carry this little boy, Derek Walker—he was eight or nine, I guess—to the field in front of the pavilion where they were laying the children down.

"The moment I touched him he started going into convulsions, and I couldn't even hold him, they were so strong. His eyes were rolled back in his head and all you could see of them was bright red—and there was foam coming out of his mouth, this awful pink foam, like you were watching his lungs come out of his mouth. I couldn't believe people could look at that and still want to go through with it; but the thing was, unless you thought about it that way, seeing all those kids dying like that, it made you feel weak. It made you want to give up and die yourself."

Rhodes carried the boy to the field and held his head as he shook and gasped for air, "like he was trying to cry but he couldn't, because he couldn't get enough air. I guess I looked around right about then and a couple of bodies away there was Niki, Niki Mitchell. I really loved Niki. She'd come over on the plane with me, she was in my class, and she was just the brightest, sweetest kid you ever saw. I don't know how else to say it—she was just full of life. She was just growing up, just about to be a woman, and there she was. She was dead. I hate to say it, but I left the boy I was with and went over to her, even though she was already dead. And then I just sat there like I was in a trance or something, until her brother came over to where we were. Well, he took one look at her, and then he went right up to the pavilion, got himself a cup, and came back to where we were. And then I watched him drink it.

"So I did what I could for him, and then, by this time there were, I don't know, maybe a hundred people out there in the field, so I just started going around doing what I could do for the rest of them. I was still thinking about getting away, but it was only just in the back of my mind then. There was too much going on; you couldn't ignore all those kids; you couldn't walk out on them while they were dying like that."

Meanwhile, over the public-address system person after person— all ages, all races—rises to add another vote for death. The theme is the same: his followers want to thank Jim Jones, thank him for bringing them to "this land of freedom," thank him for this "chance to die with our brothers and sisters."

In between the testimonials Jones returns to the microphone and urges them to die: "We tried to find a new beginning," he says, "but it's too late now. . . . You can't separate yourself from your brothers and sisters. I don't know who fired the shot. I don't know who killed the Congressman, but, as far as I'm concerned, I killed him. He had no business coming. I told him not to come. Now I would expect us to die with a degree of dignity. Don't lay down with tears and agony. . . . Don't be this way. Stop this hysterics. This is not the way for people who are socialistic-communists to die. No way for us to die. We *must* die with some dignity."

Whenever Jones is away from the microphone for more than a few minutes, the noise increases—the confusion grows. But each time, just as it seems something must happen, some explosion in the crowd, some resistance, Jones takes the microphone back and the sound of his voice soothes the crying.

"Oh God," he says at one point, "Mother, mother, mother, mother—please, please, please don't do this. Don't do this. Lay down your life with your child, but don't do this. . . . Free. . . . Free at last. Free at last. . . . You say it's never been done before? It's been done by every tribe in history, every tribe facing annihilation. All of the Indians of the Amazon are doing it right now. They refuse to bring any babies into the world—they kill every baby that comes into the world. They don't want to live in this kind of world. So be patient, be patient . . . I don't care how many screams I hear, I don't care how many anguished cries, death is a million times preferable to ten more days of this life.

"Adults, Adults, Adults, I call on you to stop this nonsense. I call on you to stop exciting your children when all they're doing is going to a quiet rest. Are we black and socialist, or what are we? Now stop this nonsense. It's all over and it's good. . . . Hurry, hurry, hurry, my children. All I say, let's not fall into the hands of the enemy . . . quickly, quickly, quickly. . . . No more pain now. No more pain, I said. No more pain. We're not letting them take our lives. We're laying down our lives."

Still Odell Rhodes continued to walk among the dead and dying in the grassy field in front of the pavilion. As he cradled a dying child, he felt a hand on his shoulder.

"It was Marceline Jones. She saw me, I guess, so she came over and hugged me and told me she appreciated what I was doing. I kind of think, maybe, she felt the same way I felt about it. There was something in her eyes, like, what a fucking waste.

"I don't know why, but somehow that snapped me out of wherever I was. I looked around at all those bodies, so damn many bodies, and all of a sudden something happened to me. It was like my mind split in half, like half of me was watching the other half in a movie or something. I got very calm, and I started thinking clear—real clear. Once in Detroit when I thought this cop was going to blow me away I felt like that. It's not like you feel brave or anything; it's just calm, calm and clear.

"I got up and walked over toward the school tent. That's where they were mixing the poison, and I could see that they had another fifty-five-gallon drum ready to go."

Rhodes watched two staff members carrying the drum toward the pavilion, and then he heard Jones say: "Lay it here—the vat with the green C thing, so the adults can begin."

"I figured," Rhodes remembers, "that it's getting to be now or never, but while I'm looking around trying to see what my chances are, people are coming up and hugging me, saying goodbye. But I'm not saying goodbye like everybody else; I'm looking around all the time. I remember seeing Marie Lawrence over by the playground with a crossbow and Bob Rankin someplace else with a gun. They were my friends; I lived with them, but I knew they'd kill me if they had to."

Rhodes edged away from the school tent fighting back a small voice in his mind that was beginning to tell him there was no place to run. "I just wanted to keep moving. I knew I had to look like I was doing something, or somebody'd want to know why, so I'm just trying to keep moving, while all the time I'm looking around, looking for a way out."

He heard someone call his name. "It was Brenda Mitchell, Niki Mitchell's mother. She wanted to know if I'd seen her children." Rhodes walked with Brenda Mitchell through the rows of bodies and pointed out Brenda Mitchell's dead children. "She leaned on me for a minute, and then she started crying real softly, and after a while she kind of pulled herself together and said she guessed she might as well go through the line herself."

Rhodes moved back in the other direction, back toward the school tent. A hundred feet away he walked past a group of teenagers, many of them his students. "They were all crying, but it wasn't like they

were afraid. They were talking about how they were going to see
each other on the other side. It wasn't like they were going to die at
all. It was more like moving day—when somebody moves out of the
neighborhood and everybody's crying, not because where they're
going to is so bad, but more because they're sad to be leaving one
another.

"I was watching them, and thinking about what to do, and I guess
that's when Judy Houston saw me. Those kids were all her friends
and she was going to go through the line with them. But, when she
saw me, she ran right over and gave me a big hug. She said I'd
always be her dad—and we'd be together on the other side. I didn't
know what to say, because I didn't plan on being on the other side.
And when she left I turned away, because I didn't want to see anymore. Seeing Niki was bad enough. I didn't want to see Judy too; I
didn't know if I could stand it."

In the pavilion, a young woman had begun to play a funeral
march on an electric organ. It was uncertain playing, and from
where Rhodes heard it, over the public-address speakers, it sounded
thin and distant, as if it came from beyond the grave. He stopped
and listened to Jim Jones speak over the music: "We've stepped over,
one thousand people who said we don't like the way the world is.
Nobody takes our lives from us. We laid it down. We got tired. We
didn't commit suicide; we committed an act of revolutionary suicide
protesting the conditions of an inhumane world."

Rhodes shook his head and tried to block out Jones's voice: "When
you listened to him, you felt like you were already dead. And I knew
I had to keep my mind on what I was doing. I was just trying to keep
moving, and keep track of all the people I didn't want to see, the
ones who might ask me how come I wasn't in line."

He moved back toward the school tent, stopping once again to say
goodbye to a friend. Then, standing once again near the fence in
front of the tent, "All of a sudden—I don't even know why I heard
it, but I did—I heard the doctor, Larry Schact, saying he needed a
stethoscope. He was inside the school tent and I was outside, so I
don't even know who he was talking to, but when I heard him say it,
it clicked. I said to myself, this is it—this is the best damn chance
I'm going to get, and right away I started walking up toward the
medical tent."

A few feet away a nurse, Phyllis Chaikin, walked back from the pavilion toward the school tent. Rhodes intercepted her. "Phyllis, Larry says he needs a stethoscope," he said, hoping she would assume he had been sent to find one. "She didn't even say anything; she was kind of an all-business type of person and she just turned right around and started for the medical tent, and I went right along with her."

As they passed the guard positioned between the pavilion and the medical complex, Rhodes held his breath. "He hardly even looked at us. Phyllis was one of those people who basically had authority to do anything she wanted, and I guess he just figured I was with her."

Now beyond the line of guards, thanks to Phyllis Chaikin, Phyllis Chaikin became the enemy. "I didn't know what I was going to do. I knew it was my best chance—probably my only chance—so I was thinking, well if I have to hit her, or something worse, I guess I'll just have to do it. But I was going to wait until we were inside, and I was hoping like hell there was nobody else in there." As Rhodes steeled himself to assault Phyllis Chaikin—a woman he knew well, and liked—Phyllis Chaikin pointed to the next building, the nursing office: "You look in there," she told Rhodes, "I'll look in Larry's office."

Rhodes walked calmly up the steps into the building and kept right on walking. In the back room, a day room for seniors, a half-dozen invalids sat in wheelchairs waiting to be taken down to the pavilion. "Did you come to help us?" a woman asked. "It's not time yet," Rhodes answered. As calmly as he could, he walked through the day room and out the back door. He took one quick look around for guards, then scrambled under the stairs and crawled under the building. When he turned around he saw a woman in an orange dress staring out the window in his direction from the next cottage. "I didn't think she'd seen me, but even if she had, it was too late to do anything about it. I just plastered myself up against the wall. And then I waited."

While Rhodes hid, Stanley Clayton was still looking for his own way out. Clayton had been in the kitchen preparing dinner when the summons to the pavilion came over the loudspeaker. Since the kitchen crew was normally exempted from meetings, Clayton and the rest of the crew ignored the announcement until Jimmy Jones ran into the kitchen and told them to forget about dinner. "Well," says Clayton, "right then I knew it was bad because that never happened before, somebody telling us to forget dinner."

When Clayton reached the pavilion, children were already dying. "I took one look at that and I built up my determination so strong. I said, 'Stan, they might shoot your ass but you ain't drinking no poison.' Didn't make no damn bit of sense for me to die because twelve people left, or twenty-two, or however many it was. I said good for them—I wish it was me. And I built up my determination so strong—no matter what they did to me, I wasn't drinking no poison."

Clayton quickly canvassed the others in the kitchen crew who had talked about leaving Jonestown before. "Everybody had some other type of reason. Like Karen said she's going to wait on Ed, see what he does, and I know Ed ain't going because he's got a wife and a baby, but Larisse says just wait until I find my children and I'll go with you. So I go look for my companion, Janice, but I know I can't talk to her about going because she already turned me in once, so I just tell her, shit, I don't like this and I'm waiting for her to feed me something I can respond to, but she doesn't, so I just hug her goodbye. And then one of Larisse's children comes up and she tells her, 'Moma, Richard's gone.' Richard was her other baby, and when Larisse hears that her eyes just roll over and she faints dead away. So right then I figure if I'm going, I'm going by myself."

Clayton, like Rhodes, realized the importance of moving around, as if he had been assigned some task. "I was just truckin', and lookin', when I saw these two teenagers, this boy Danny, a Guyanese who'd come to live with us, and another boy named Frankie—and they didn't want to do it. Frankie's eyes were all bugged out, I mean he was scared something awful, and Jim McIlvane, he's a real big dude, and he's standing right over them. To me it was like McIlvane, he was the baddest ass bully in Jonestown, and I'm thinking if I don't get out of here, I'm gonna have McIlvane in my face too, and I know I'm gonna take a swing at him, and we're gonna be fighting, so I figure I best get my ass out there."

Clayton walked around the pavilion toward the radio room. He was stopped by a guard, Armando Griffin. "I told him I was looking for my buddy Ed, 'cause me and Ed were gonna do it together; but he says, 'Ed's dead.' So I told him he's wrong, Ed's waiting for me over by the radio room, so he walks over there with me and we don't find Ed, so I just said I guessed he was right and then I walked back the other way and tried going over toward the playground."

At the playground he was stopped by Marie Lawrence. Clayton told her he had been assigned to scout the area behind the playground for stragglers, and she passed him through. "There was more guards back there, but one of them was a pretty good buddy so I said, 'Hey man, I'm getting ready to go now,' and I gave him a big hug like I was saying goodbye, and then I pointed over toward the school tent where there was a whole bunch of people just about getting in the line, and I said, 'I guess I'll walk over there and say goodbye to my people.' Now, those people over by the school tent, they were all inside the guards, but from where I was, the shortest way over there was to cut straight across in back of where all the other guards were. So he just said, 'Okay, man,' and I took off and and as soon as he turned his back I went under this one building, came out the other side, and just started truckin'." As he ran toward the jungle, Clayton fully expected a bullet in the back of his head. "But, I didn't care about that because, see, I'd made up my mind if I was going, that was the way I wanted it.

"And then I was in the jungle, and my heart's going crazy, and right then it hits me, 'Stanley, you're so goddamned stupid, you ran the wrong damn way.' "

Clayton had escaped into the jungle on the north-west side, with nothing but jungle for two thousand miles in front of him.

"It was like I din't know if I should be crying or laughing, and right then it gets kind of comical, because I sit down on this log to rest and the damn log's full of ants—and when they start crawling up my neck, I jump like hell and roll around on the ground trying to get them ants off me. I almost died right there, and all the time I'm laughing like it's the funniest damn thing I ever saw."

Underneath the cottage where he was hiding, Odell Rhodes waited for night to fall. "It could have been five minutes, or it could have been five years," Rhodes admits. Eventually, night fell. "Then it started getting real quiet, so I figured most everybody must be gone, and I was trying to decide if I should make a break for the jungle. I was kind of worried they might send somebody out to look under buildings and the other places you could hide, so I was thinking about my chances, and then I heard an announcement over the

P.A. for everybody with weapons to report to the radio room. I counted out a minute to let them get there, and then I took off."

The jungle was several hundred yards away across plowed fields, and Rhodes, trying to run on his bad leg, fell several times before he reached the first stand of foliage bordering the fields. Carefully, he edged his way around the perimeter of the settlement and a half-hour later reached the road to Port Kaituma.

"First I tried to find this house where these Guyanese I knew lived, but I couldn't find it in the dark, so I just stayed on the road and walked on into town. I wasn't scared exactly, and I wasn't happy exactly either. I guess I wasn't much of anything. I wasn't really thinking about anything. I remember I kept singing songs to myself in my head, kind of like whistling in the dark, I guess, except I wasn't about to make any noise.

Trapped in the jungle on the far side of Jonestown, two miles from the road to Port Kaituma, Stanley Clayton felt he had only two choices: either spend the night in the jungle or risk going back through Jonestown to the Port Kaituma road.

"I was hungry and cold, and my clothes were all wet from sweat and rolling around on the ground, and I got this thing on about having my passport. So I kind of scouted it out real good, and then I just kind of trucked back in there."

After a stop in the kitchen for a sandwich he made but did not eat ("I took one look at it and it hit me they might have put something in the food"), he helped himself to a beer from Jim Jones's private stock and started toward the office to look for his passport—and anything else useful that might have been left lying about.

"I was just going through the door and I heard this shot—bam. Holy shit, my heart just about stopped." Clayton froze, waiting for the sounds of an approaching search party to decide which way to run. He heard nothing. Although he could not have know it at the time, he had heard Jonestown's last suicide, Annie Moore, one of Jim Jones's nurses, who shot herself in the head with the same gun Jim Jones had taken his own life with minutes before.

When Clayton finally calmed down he found his passport, changed clothes, and started off toward the front gate. "There were dead dogs all over the road—they even shot them. But it just didn't feel like there was anyone left, so I'm truckin' down the road feeling pretty good, when I hear this noise which sounds to me like a tractor coming up the road toward me."

Clayton immediately turned off the road and waited by the edge of the jungle for the tractor to approach. "I said to myself, they seen you and they're just waiting down there for me to walk right up on them. So I waited some more, but then I just couldn't handle waiting like that anymore, so I started kind of creeping up keeping real close to the jungle." As he approached the area where the noise came from, Clayton realized what he had heard was the sound of one of the electric generators. "So the only thing I got to worry about now is the front gate, and when I get there I start tossing rocks at it, so if there's someone inside, he's going to come out where I can see him."

The gatehouse was empty. Clayton walked past the front gate unchallenged and headed toward the house of his Guyanese friend Kelly Foran (the same house Rhodes had failed to find earlier). "They were all asleep, but they opened up the door and took me in, and I started telling them, 'You all ain't going to believe what's going on down in Jonestown.' I was right too. They didn't believe a damn word of it. They thought I was crazy."

17

After the End

Terrified, pumped full of adrenalin, and still half-expecting the long arm of Jim Jones to reach out from beyond the grave, both Odell Rhodes and Stanley Clayton spent uncomfortable, sleepless nights. Although neither had any way of knowing it at the time, Rhodes and Clayton had been the only two members of the community to escape. Two others, Grover Davis, the seventy-four-year-old with poor hearing and a dislike for rock and roll music, and Hyacinth Thrush, an eighty-year-old semi-invalid, had survived inside Jonestown. Everyone else was dead.

Stanley Clayton spent Saturday night in Kelly Foran's house. After eating and drinking everything in sight, Clayton spent the rest of the night vainly trying to convince Foran and his wife and sons that everyone in Jonestown was dead. Finally, with dawn breaking, Clayton finally managed to persuade Foran to look for himself by pointing out that if what he said was true there would be no reason for the Forans not to help themselves to Jonestown's tools and supplies. Foran and his sons left when the sun rose, and, when they returned a few hours later with their arms full of contraband and their eyes glazed with horror, Clayton set out down the road to Port Kaituma.

Odell Rhodes had reached Port Kaituma shortly before midnight the night before. He went directly to the local constabulary and told his story to a sceptical group of volunteer deputies whose credibility had already been stretched beyond the breaking point by the attack at the airstrip. Eventually, Rhodes was put on the telephone to a police inspector in Georgetown. "I think he believed me. He said he'd be down in the morning with the army, and he told me not to worry. I was still pretty damned scared. Every time I heard a noise outside I figured that's them. The constable and the deputies were ready to protect me, but it would have been a couple of single-shot shotguns against everything they had in Jonestown, so I wasn't feeling very safe at all."

For his own protection Rhodes was shut up in a bathroom, the only room in the constabulary without an open exposure to the outside, and given a bottle of rum for his nerves. "I hadn't had a sip in six months, so I got good and drunk right away. But, I didn't go to sleep. About the last thing I wanted to do was shut my eyes. I mean, there was no telling what I was going to see if I shut my eyes."

When Stanley Clayton finally made it into town shortly before noon the next morning, he was immediately arrested and thrown into a cell with the Carter brothers and Mike Prokes, who had been arrested the night before on their way to Georgetown with the suitcase full of money for the Soviet embassy. In everybody's mind, especially the police, was the fear, stirred by rapidly spreading rumors, that Jones had sent a squad of assassins out from Jonestown with instructions to finish off the defectors and any other survivors who appeared in Port Kaituma. To the police, the Carters, Prokes, and Clayton all seemed like excellent prospects. None of them had any intention of assassinating anyone but neither the Carters and Prokes nor Clayton were sure about one another.

"I tried telling them guards," Clayton remembers, "that those dudes was on one side, and I was on the other, but they just tossed me in with them anyway. I didn't like being locked up with them nohow."

Prokes and the Carters felt much the same way about Clayton—unsure, as one had always been in Jonestown, who might be acting under secret orders from Jim Jones.

"We were all," Odell Rhodes says, "scared silly of one another. First thing in the morning they took me down to the rum shop to see the Bogues. Juanita took one look at me and started to give me a hug, and then all of a sudden I guess she remembered she didn't know what the hell I was doing there, so she turned right back around. I couldn't blame her. When they told me about Stanley, they asked if I wanted to go over and talk to him. I said, 'No way,' I mean, when we finally got together, Stanley and me, it took us about two minutes to figure out we were both coming from the same place. But the thing of it was, after being in Jonestown for so long, and especially after what we'd all just been through, the last person you felt like trusting was somebody else from Jonestown."

Rhodes spent most of the day, Sunday, telling and retelling his story to officers of the Guyanese army and the deputy national police commissioner, Cecil (Skip) Roberts. Roberts, the official with whom Rhodes had spoken by telephone on Saturday night, wanted Rhodes to help guide the army troops into Jonestown. "I told them they could lock me up and throw away the key, but I wasn't going back there unless they gave me a weapon."

After Roberts explained that the first approach would be by helicopter from a thousand feet in the air, Rhodes relented. "From the air," he remembers, "it looked real peaceful. In fact, from up there, they didn't even look like bodies. It looked like lots of scraps of bright paper on the ground, like the morning after the circus leaves town."

The main force of Guyanese soldiers finally entered Jonestown early Sunday evening. In addition to corpses, they found the two remaining survivors. Because of his bad hearing, Grover Davis had missed the initial summons to the pavilion. When he finally wandered down to see where everybody else was, the children were just beginning to die. Fortunately for him, Davis had approached the pavilion by a shortcut through the kitchen. He took one good look at what was happening, and turned right around and slipped out the same way he had come. Unchallenged by any of the guards, he then climbed into a dry well where he hid until Sunday morning. Finally, frightened and exhausted, Davis crawled out of the well Sunday morning and immediately went back to his cottage to sleep. He was very nearly shot by the soldiers searching the settlement Sunday night who took the frightened old man struggling awake from a deep sleep for a ghost returning from the dead.

Davis later explained why he had not so much as considered joining the suicide: "I went down there to die in peace and that's what I meant to do, but I didn't mean to go one minute before I was called. I wasn't surprised though, wasn't surprised it happened; I knew something bad was gonna to happen there. The thing was, Jim Jones had the power. He wasn't the onliest God who ever was, but he had the power; and then when we got to the Promised Land he turned his back on it. He gave up, and a man who has the power, he can't never turn his back on it, or else God's gonna punish him for it sure as He made little green apples."

The other survivor, Hyacinth Thrush, avoided the suicide by pure, random luck. A semi-invalid, unable to walk more than a few steps on her own power, Hyacinth Thrush was simply overlooked. Asleep in her cabin when the suicide began, she slept peacefully through the night, completely unaware of what was happening a few hundred yards away. Not until her breakfast failed to appear on schedule Sunday morning did she hobble outside and smell—literally smell—what had happened. She later told Odell Rhodes how sorry she was to have missed the opportunity to die with her brothers and sisters.

Monday morning Stanley Clayton, Mike Prokes, the survivors from the Ryan party, and the group led by Julius Evans, which had arrived safely in Matthews Ridge Saturday night, were all flown to Georgetown. In Georgetown forty-six members of the Jonestown community in the Lamaha Gardens headquarters had already been placed under house arrest. The Lamaha House was unusually crowded at the time of the suicide largely because the Jonestown basketball team, which included Jim Jones's son Stephan, happened to be preparing to play a series of games the following week.

During the suicide Jones radioed the Lamaha staff and instructed them to join the suicide. Sharon Amos, the staff's public-relations officer, immediately took her three small children to a bathroom, killed them, and then slit her own wrists. The rest of the staff and the members of the basketball team did not follow. All, however, were placed under arrest as possible accomplices in the murder of Sharon Amos's children. There was a widespread fear, both among the survivors and the Guyanese authorities, that the basketball team's presence in Georgetown had been no accident. Many believed they had been sent to Georgetown as an assassination squad to settle accounts with the Stoens, the Concerned Relatives, the defectors, and whatever other stragglers appeared in Georgetown.

After Monday Odell Rhodes and the Carter brothers were the only surivors who remained in Port Kaituma. Rhodes and the Carters, with a little help from Skip Roberts, had volunteered to go back to Jonestown with the army and identify the bodies. "There was no way they could do it by themselves from pictures or something," Rhodes remembers. "It wasn't easy even when you knew all the faces. Everybody was bloated up pretty bad. A few of them, when you rolled them over, they just split right open. And, when you found someone lying face down, their faces just kind of took the shape of the ground.

"It wasn't easy at all. It's so hot there, and the smell and the heat together was just awful; and, knowing what it came from, there was no way in hell you could get used to it. I could only do it for maybe an hour at a time, and then I'd have to get away from it. And when we got to the field where all the children were, I didn't want to go down there at all; but I knew there was something wrong there because you could hardly even see the children. There were adults all piled up over them. I told them the children were all underneath there, but I guess nobody really wanted to go down and start pulling bodies off to take a look. I know I didn't."

Because of the way the bodies had been piled on top of one another, the Guyanese army's preliminary estimate of the number of dead never rose above 600. Eventually, ten days later after a U.S. army mortuary team arrived and began removing the bodies, the children were finally counted and the actual total reached 914.

Exactly 912 had died of cyanide poisoning. Two had died from gunshot wounds. Surrounded by his wife and most of the security force, Jim Jones lay dead in his chair at the front of the pavilion, a single bullet hole in his head. In Jones's cabin, Annie Moore, his personal nurse, also lay dead from a bullet wound surrounded by most of the Jonestown administrative staff, including Jones's mistresses Carolyn Layton and Maria Katsaris and the two children Jones claimed to have fathered, Carolyn Layton's son, Kimo, and John-John Stoen.

"Jones," Odell Rhodes remembers, "was kind of a shock. Everybody else—not just the black people, but everybody else too—had turned completely black. The coroner there told me it had something to do with the poison. But Jones was different. I guess it was because he shot himself. He turned into what he hated most. He was white. To me, he looked like about the whitest thing I ever saw."

Rhodes spent the next two days inside Jonestown identifying bodies and guiding the Guyanese investigators through the settlement. For much of the time he worked with the Guyanese coroner, Dr. Leslie Mootoo. One of the tasks Rhodes performed under Dr. Mootoo's supervision was to inspect the bodies he had identified for blisters on the upper arm, evidence that the cyanide had been administered—presumably to the unwilling—by hypodermic injection. With the exception of a very few of the more feeble seniors, Rhodes saw no signs of blisters. Although no one—Dr. Mootoo, the press, or Odell Rhodes himself—wanted to believe it, the evidence was that the vast majority of the 912 who died had taken their own lives.

In the days following the tragedy television, newspapers, and magazines told the outlines of a bizarre story: a Congressman murdered in a remote jungle; nearly a thousand men, women, and children led to their deaths by an insane fanatic. The story was so bizarre, so lurid, so unbelievable that—inevitably—it attracted reporters from all over the world. Georgetown was inundated by the working press, several hundred men and women who moved with speed, purpose, and expense accounts never before glimpsed in the leisurely city of Georgetown. Georgetown's taxis, communications facilities, and hotels were overwhelmed, especially the two first-class hotels, the Pegasus and the Park. In the Park Hotel, the survivors from the Ryan party, the Evans group, Odell Rhodes, Stanley Clayton, Hyacinth Thrush, Grover Davis, Mike Prokes, and the Carter brothers were jammed together with hordes of reporters, many of whom were sleeping six to a room, two to a couch.

The next two weeks turned into an enormous wake, financed largely by the press. Nobody who had any connection with Jonestown whatsoever was in any danger of having to buy himself a drink. And, despite (or perhaps because of) a year of abstinence in Jonestown, most of the survivors were more than ready to make up for lost drinking time. Shell-shocked, depressed, many of them unable to sleep, they had little incentive to stay sober.

Odell Rhodes spent many of his days and most of his nights in the Park Hotel bar brooding about his inability to cry. "It bothered the hell out of me. After what I'd seen, all those kids and practically everybody in the world I cared about—they were all dead; and I couldn't even cry. I felt terrible and I was having nightmares all the time, but I just couldn't cry. I started thinking, if only I could cry, I'd feel better. But I couldn't do it. And it made me feel like some kind of freak, like there was something wrong with me."

Rhodes and many of the other survivors began to confide their problems to a psychiatrist from New Jersey, Dr. Hardat Sukhdeo, who was also staying in the Park Hotel. Dr. Sukhdeo, a medical school professor with a research interest in movements like the People's Temple, happened to have been born in Guyana. When the Jonestown story broke, he suspected that the survivors might need psychiatric counseling the Guyanese health-care system would be hard-pressed to provide. He hurried to Georgetown and began offering his help. Amidst the pressure and confusion from endless questioning by the police and the press, most of the survivors were more than ready for a sympathetic ear and a supportive presence, especially one who was more interested in what they were feeling than what they had seen.

As he listened to the descriptions of their feelings, Sukhdeo found something that surprised him: "What they were feeling wasn't grief; the grief hadn't even hit them yet. At first I didn't understand what was going on, but, then it hit me. It was guilt. They felt guilty—they felt guilty they were still alive, and a few of them even felt as if they were responsible for what happened. Jim Jones had such a guilt machine in Jonestown. He made them feel guilty for everything—personally responsible for every bad thing that happened. They felt responsible for Jonestown's failure; they felt responsible because Jim Jones was so depressed he wanted to kill himself. The guilt was a way of life there—and the truth was, the survivors were feeling the same guilt that killed the others."

"When he told me that," Odell Rhodes remembers, "I didn't believe him. I mean, what the hell did I have to feel guilty about? I worked my ass off for Jonestown. But, then we started talking about my dreams. There was this one dream I was having all the time where I was digging graves for everybody who died. All of a sudden I got to this one grave, and it was for Monica—and Monica was still alive, so I didn't know what I supposed to do. I'd start to go on to the next one, and then I'd wake up.

"Dr. Sukhdeo told me that maybe that next grave was for me, so that's why I woke up. He told me I wasn't maybe all the way certain I deserved to live. After that it started to make some sense to me. I mean Jones was always talking about guilt, about how you had to use your guilt to make your commitment stronger, so I guess—somehow—it got to me."

When Hardat Sukhdeo asked Juanita Bogue, the intelligent and perceptive young woman who left with the Ryan party, what she was feeling as she left Jonestown that afternoon, she answered immediately: "I was scared, but more than anything else I felt guilty. But I knew that even if I stayed, I would have felt guilty too; even just thinking about leaving made you feel guilty."

Juanita Bogue remembered the angry taunts of the crowd as she walked toward the pavilion with her suitcase: "If it had been somebody else leaving and me standing there, I would have done the same thing. Because even if I'd only thought about leaving for a second, I would have felt so guilty about that I'd want to take it out on the people who left."

Odell Rhodes, who stood with the crowd, agreed: "I think most people there were so mad because we'd been taught that being a defector was about the worst thing a person could do. So it was like, if anybody defected, it was everybody's fault. I guess it's like in a family. If a child runs away or gets into some kind of bad trouble, you start feeling like it must be your fault, like you didn't do everything you could."

"I know," said Juanita Bogue, "if I'd stayed that day, and the rest of my family had left, I would have felt so guilty that the first thing I'd have wanted to do was kill myself."

Stanley Clayton agreed: "If I had to make my decision to get away right then, I never could have done it. I was watching my friends trying to decide, and they couldn't do it. Because the way we were taught, the worse you felt about something, the more you wanted to be doing what everybody else was doing. The thing about me was, I'd decided a long time ago I was leaving. I just didn't know when."

Despite his fears and the sense of failure that had led him to conclude that life was not worth living, the ironic and incredible truth was that in a perverse and horrible way Jim Jones had actually succeeded; he had managed the most improbable—and perhaps the rarest—feat a leader of human beings can attempt: he had fused an entire community into a single organism. Whatever one felt, all felt; whatever happened to one, happened to all. He had convinced nearly a thousand human beings that they lived only for each other. And, whatever the morality of the enterprise, that was exactly what he had set out to do.

Except for the way it ended November 18 had been very much

like any other day in Jonestown. And Jim Jones's call to death had been very much like the appeals that had rallied the community so many times in the past. As he asked his followers to die with him, Jones had used the same words he had used so many times to promise a better life: community, solidarity, family, peace, freedom. The words were the same. Only their meaning had changed. They had come to mean death.

18

Survivors

During one of his conversations with Dr. Hardat Sukhdeo in the Park Hotel in Georgetown Odell Rhodes asked the psychiatrist what he thought about Rhodes's chances of forgetting about the People's Temple and leading a normal life.

"He told me flat-out," Rhodes remembers, "that going back might be kind of rough. He said that all the reasons I joined up with the Temple in the first place were still going to be there. And then he told me he thought there was a good chance I'd go back to drugs. I believed the other stuff, but I told him there was no way I was ever going back to drugs—no way in hell."

Rhodes returned to the United States on December 30, the day before New Year's Eve. He flew directly from Miami to Detroit eager to be with his family even though he was not at all sure how his often unpredictable uncle, Jay Aiken, might receive him. "I guess I shouldn't even have worried about it, but, at the time, I just wasn't thinking real straight. Anyway, it turned out real good. The only thing my uncle was pissed off about was the way all the reporters had bothered him. But, he said he was real proud of me. He said that the first time he heard about it on TV he went around telling people that any son of his would have enough sense to get his damn butt right out of there. And, when he read about two guys escaping, he said he knew I was one of them."

New Year's Eve at the Aikens' was an especially happy celebration—one that lasted for a day and a half. "It was so good being back there I got up to going maybe an hour or an hour and a half without thinking about Jonestown." But the following day, when his cousins and friends returned to work, and Rhodes found himself with nothing to do, the memories came back. He decided to take a long walk.

"It was a real nice day—I mean a real nice day for Detroit in January—so I just figured I'd get some air. I didn't have anything in mind and I wasn't going anyplace in particular. I just wanted to have a look around."

Three hours later, before the winter sun set, Rhodes was sitting on the same park bench in Grand Circus Park where he had first seen the People's Temple bus caravan in 1976. And, for the first time since 1976, his veins were full of heroin.

Within a few days heroin was once again the center of Rhodes's life. "It was the strangest damn thing. It happened so fast I didn't even realize what I was doing. I kept thinking I just needed to let it all hang out for a while, and then I'd be all right. By the time I realized I wasn't all right, I was already in trouble. I started thinking about how I should call Dr. Sukhdeo, because he told me to get in touch with him if anything like that started happening. But it was just like the old days. The worse I got, the less I wanted anybody to help me. I didn't even want anybody to know I was still alive."

Rhodes moved out of the Aikens' house and into a small residence hotel near Grand Circus Park. It was the same sort of place he had lived during his eight years on the streets, the sort of place where the night desk clerk patrols the halls with a baseball bat painted Day-Glo pink in his hand. "Anything you think might happen there," Rhodes admits, "probably does."

Meanwhile, in California, where the vast majority of Jonestown's other survivors returned, there were other problems. In general, the survivors broke into two groups: those who had left Jonestown the day of the tragedy, and those who happened to have been in Georgetown. The second group, which included Jones's son Stephan and the other members of the Jonestown basketball team, was much larger, and the members of the smaller group—the Parkses, the Bogues, Monica Bagby, Vern Gosney and the Evanses—were openly afraid that those who had survived in Georgetown considered them traitors and held them responsible for the tragedy.

The truth was that all of the survivors, in both groups, were depressed, confused, and—almost without exception—desperately unhappy. What had happened on November 18 haunted everyone, and, if some were more inclined to blame Jim Jones and others more inclined to blame his enemies, all of them shared the same problems: nightmares, severe depression, insomnia, and an unshakable. compusive desire to hide from the outside world. Few were able to work steadily, or even to summon enough energy to look for a decent place to live. With some exceptions the majority huddled together in cramped quarters reliving the experience of Jonestown.

Of all the survivors Stanley Clayton had managed perhaps the most accurate assessment of the problems of readjusting to life back home. Clayton, the last of the survivors to leave Guyana, decided early in January that he was never going home. "I figured I could make out pretty good in Guyana, and I just didn't want to go back no-how. I figured, if I went back, sooner or later I was just gonna get my ass in trouble again, just like always did." During his stay at the Park Hotel Clayton met and fell in love with a Guyanese woman, and late in December Stanley and Donna Clayton were married. A few weeks later Clayton decided to make a brief trip home to visit his family before settling down permanently in Georgetown. He arrived in Oakland and promptly spent the next two months hiding in his grandfather's house. "I don't rightly know what happened to me, but it seemed like, soon as I got there, it was like I couldn't do nothing for myself anymore."

After two trips to California, during which he interviewed and counseled as many of the survivors as he could locate, Hardat Sukdheo began to worry about the potential for further suicides among the survivors. In March, in a Modesto, California, motel, during a news conference he had called to defend the People's Temple, Mike Prokes, one of the three aides who had carried the suitcase of money for the Soviet embassy, locked himself in a bathroom and put a bullet in his head. In the statement Prokes had distributed to the press moments before taking his life, he argued that responsibility for the mass suicide belonged to those who had waged the war to destroy Jonestown. When he spoke of his despair at ever readjusting to life in a country whose values seemed so alien to him, he spoke for many of the other survivors as well.

Throughout the early months of 1979 Jim Jones, Jonestown, and the People's Temple became the subject of two growth industries:

media analysis and lawsuits. Magazines, newspapers, television programs, classrooms and cocktail parties echoed with discussions of suicide, mind control, cults, moral responsibility, and California madness. Lawsuits totaling some twenty times the total of all known People's Temple assets were filed and cross-filed in California and federal courts. The federal government decided to dun the survivors for hotel bills and airline ticket expenses incurred in the days after the tragedy; relatives of many of the dead, including Leo Ryan's family, sued the Temple for damages; in turn, other relatives sued Leo Ryan's estate. The court-appointed executor of the Temple's affairs watched the law suits accumulate and announced that, in his opinion, any suits finally adjudicated and found to have merit would pay off, if at all, with pennies to the dollar.

During most of the spring a gruesome dispute over the burial of the victims raged between the federal government, a number of state governments, relatives of the dead, and several private cemeteries. No one seemed to know who should pay the expense of burying the victims, especially the several hundred who remained unidentified. In addition, financial arrangements aside, government officials and private lawyers were having a difficult time finding a cemetery willing to open its ground to such controversial corpses.

Amidst the confusion a few enterprising capitalists found ways to turn disaster into cash. Fulfilling his pledge to tell Jonestown's story to the world, Mark Lane embarked on a national lecture tour. One feature film and one film for television lept into production, and in San Francisco a group of entertainment promoters made plans to turn the Geary Street Temple into a punk-rock night club.

In Washington a staff investigative team from the House Foreign Affairs Committee labored to uncover the facts surrounding Leo Ryan's death. Charges of CIA involvement in the tragedy flew back and forth between Mark Lane, who believed the agency might have been implicated in Ryan's death, and members of Leo Ryan's former staff, who believed Jones himself might have been a CIA agent. When it finally appeared, the House Committee's report answered few questions, at least in the edition released to the public, which omitted numerous sections of classified material.

Meanwhile, Tim Stoen, the man who knew more than anyone else about the fight to bring Jim Jones down told his side of the story to the Congressional staff investigators, granted a few interviews to the press, then slipped out of public view to begin building a private law practice in southern California. In San Francisco his estranged wife, Grace, began once again to start her life over. Debbie Blakey was also trying to put the People's Temple behind her, but her situation was complicated by the fact that her brother Larry remained one of Jonestown's most troublesome loose ends. Layton and Charles Beikman remained throughout 1979 in a Guyanese jail awaiting trial, Layton charged with conspiring to murder Leo Ryan, and Beikman with helping Sharon Amos murder her children at the Lamaha Gardens on the night of the mass suicide.

By late spring 1979 many of the Jonestown survivors were beginning to emerge from the shock of the tragedy. Jim Bogue was building a house for his family in northern California; Dale Parks and Julius Evans were both working as paramedics in San Francisco hospitals; and Monica Bagby was finishing high school and making plans to enter college. In May, Stanley Clayton, finally emerged from his grandfather's house. With some help from Hardat Sukhdeo, who by now was shuttling across the country trying to provide counseling and support services, Clayton found a job and began saving money to bring his wife and her son to California.

Meanwhile, in Detroit, in early June, while injecting heroin into a vein in his neck, Odell Rhodes stuck the needle into his larynx. For several weeks he was in enormous pain. He could hardly breathe; he could not talk above a hoarse whisper; and he could not eat solid food. He lost thirty pounds in three weeks and he was told that, were he to catch cold, he might very well choke to death on his own mucus. Frightened and angry with himself, Rhodes finally summoned up the will to do something to save himself. The first step, he decided, was to leave Detroit.

San Francisco had worked once before and the people he felt closest to were all in the Bay area, so, with the help of his family and the psychiatrist from New Jersey, Rhodes moved to San Francisco. After a month of recuperation Rhodes found a job driving a delivery van for a messenger service and began to think about his future. He registered for night classes at the City College of San Francisco with the eventual aim of a career as a youth counselor. "I figured I liked working with kids more than just about anything, and whatever mistakes they might make—well, I probably already made them."

Finally, by the beginning of the new year, 1980, most of the Jonestown survivors had begun to feel at least the possibility of leading normal lives. None would have claimed to have forgotten Jonestown or the People's Temple, but most felt that the future had become as real as the past, and most preferred to talk about anything except the People's Temple.

Then, in mid-February, Al and Jeannie Mills, who had been operating a nursing home in Berkeley, California, as well as an institution called the Human Freedom Center—a kind of halfway house for ex-members of religious cults—were murdered, along with their teenage daughter, Daphne, in their home near the University of California in Berkeley.

Rumors of a People's Temple assassination squad spread through the media; Grace Stoen, Debbie Blakey, and Tim Stoen were reported to be unavailable for comment; and most of the survivors wondered if the past would ever leave them alone. The police questioned the Millses' teenage son, Eddie, who had been in the house at the time of the murders, and then announced that they had no reason to believe that the Millses' deaths were connected with the People's Temple—and no reason to believe that they were not. A few days later an associate of the Millses at the Human Freedom Center publicly accused another ex-associate, a psychologist, of the murders. He denied the charge; and the police continued to insist they had no suspects and no active leads in the case.

Most of the survivors preferred not to think about the Millses at all. "I guess," said Odell Rhodes, "I've spent enough time thinking about death. Too much time. It's like, if I let myself, I could think about it all the time. For one thing there's hardly a day that goes by that I don't see somebody on the street who reminds me of somebody from Jonestown. One day I even saw somebody who looked like Jim Jones's twin, and I wasn't the same for a week.

"It's not like I'm going to forget about Jonestown. I'm never going to forget about Jonestown. To me Jonestown's about the best thing I ever did in my life, and I still don't think of it as a bad place. It's a place where something terrible happened, but to me, anyway, that's not the same as saying it was a bad place. I loved it there, and up to the minute I left I never wanted anything in my life as much as I wanted Jonestown to succeed.

"I could easily have died for Jonestown. And I guess I'm pretty lucky to still be here. I mean, maybe the army had something to do with me getting out, and maybe the streets had a lot to do with it, but luck had a lot to do with it too. Because I loved Jonestown.

People might not understand that, but it's true—I loved it. I guess the point is that I'm still alive. And now I figure I owe it to myself to do the best I can with my life. I mean, when I think about it, the fact that I'm still alive, it's a pretty amazing thing, because when you get right down to it there was really only one thing I wasn't willing to do for Jonestown."

Notes

1. This account is taken from private conversations and from Jeannie Mills, *Six Years With God* (A&W Publishers, 1979.)
2. Ibid., p. 120.
3. Ibid., p. 121.
4. Ibid., pp. 121–122.
5. Ibid., p. 131.
6. The affidavit was entered in several slightly different versions. This version is taken from Mark Lane, *The Strongest Poison* (Hawthorn Books, 1980), p. 244.
7. Both of these incidents are recounted by Jeannie Mills in *Six Years With God*, pp. 253 and 284.
8. *The Assasination of Representative Leo J. Ryan and the Jonestown, Guyana Tragedy*, Report of a Staff Investigative Group to Commitee on Foreign Affairs, U.S. House of Representatives, 1979, p. 99.
9. This account depends in part on the account of Mark Lane in *The Strongest Poison*, pp. 106–113.
10. Some of this material is from Lane, *The Strongest Poison*, pp. 140–141.
11. Various accounts of this incident have appeared in Lane, *The Strongest Poison*, pp. 142–149; Charles Krause, *Guyana Massacre* (Berkeley Publishing Company, 1978), pp. 65–68; and Ron Javers and Marshall Kilduff, *The Suicide Cult* (Bantam Books, 1978), p. 158.
12. Krause, *Guyana Massacre*, p. 85.